Pathways through Crisis

Pathways through Crisis

Urban Risk and Public Culture

Carl A. Maida

ALTAMIRA
PRESS

A Division of
ROWMAN & LITTLEFIELD PUBLISHERS, INC.
Lanham • New York • Toronto • Plymouth, UK

ALTAMIRA PRESS
A division of Rowman & Littlefield Publishers, Inc.
A wholly owned subsidiary of The Rowman & Littlefield Publishing Group, Inc.
4501 Forbes Boulevard, Suite 200
Lanham, MD 20706
www.altamirapress.com

Estover Road
Plymouth PL6 7PY
United Kingdom

British Library Cataloguing in Publication Information Available

Library of Congress Cataloguing-in-Publication Data

Maida, Carl A.
 Pathways through crisis : urban risk and public culture / Carl A. Maida.
  p. cm.
 Includes bibliographical references and index.
 ISBN-13: 978-0-7591-1132-5 (cloth : alk. paper)
 ISBN-10: 0-7591-1132-4 (cloth : alk. paper)
 ISBN-13: 978-0-7591-1245-2 (electronic : alk. paper)
 ISBN-10: 0-7591-1245-2 (electronic : alk. paper)
 1. Cities and towns—Psychological aspects. 2. Community life. 3. Social problems.
I. Title.

 HT153.M316 2008
 307.76—dc22   2008028356

Printed in the United States of America

∞™ The paper used in this publication meets the minimum requirements of American
National Standard for Information Sciences—Permanence of Paper for Printed Library
Materials, ANSI/NISO Z39.48-1992.

To the memory of
Florence Carina Rondinelli

They enter the new world naked,
cold, uncertain of all
save that they enter. All about them
the cold familiar wind—

William Carlos Williams, *Spring and All*

Contents

Acknowledgments   ix

Introduction   xiii

1   A World of Strangers   1

2   Global Economy and Local Dilemma   33

3   Campaign against Stigma   65

4   Facing Crises through Culture   95

5   Strangers in the City   129

6   Worlds Turned Upside Down   161

7   The City Is the Frontier   187

8   Common Worlds   233

Index   249

About the Author   261

Acknowledgments

The National Institutes of Health, National Institute of Mental Health, National Science Foundation, Ford Foundation, Robert Wood Johnson Foundation, Joan B. Kroc Foundation, John D. and Catherine T. MacArthur Foundation, Natural Hazards Center, Helena Rubinstein Foundation, Spencer Foundation, State of California Departments of Health Services and Industrial Relations, and the U.S. Environmental Protection Agency have generously supported my research efforts over the years. The research studies described in the book have been previously reported in technical sessions at annual meetings of the American Anthropological Association and the American Association for the Advancement of Science.

I have benefited from the resources of the Louise M. Darling Biomedical Library at UCLA and the Oviatt Library at California State University, Northridge and from exhibitions documenting the interplay of the arts and ideas of the modern period at the Los Angeles County Museum of Art, the Metropolitan Museum of Art, the Brooklyn Museum, the Oakland Museum, the Smithsonian Institution, The Phillips Collection, and the Corcoran Gallery of Art in Washington, D.C.

The content and organization of the book were inspired by the curricular goals and framework of the New Liberal Arts (NLA) Program of the Alfred P. Sloan Foundation, which seeks to improve scientific and technological knowledge within liberal education. Since the 1990s, I have used the NLA model to develop interdisciplinary curricula for undergraduate and graduate students in the liberal arts and professional studies, with core concepts derived from the humanities; social sciences; and science, technology, and society studies. Individual chapters and earlier manuscripts of this book have benefited from the support and comments of many people. I have appreciated the critical advice of Richard Adler, Sam Beck, Roberto Belloso, Steven Biel,

Gayle Byock, Robert Chianese, Ian Coulter, Ruth Chlebowski, Tim Dagodag, Robert Edgerton, Robert Emerson, Norman Farberow, Marlene Grossman, David Hakken, Krista Harper, Bettyann Kevles, Marvin Marcus, Fred Massarik, Ken Mazey, Ken Meter, Claudia Mitchell-Kernan, Torin Monahan, Hector Myers, Joseph Partansky, Karen Reeds, Dick Roberts, Liseth Romero-Martinez, Susan Scrimshaw, Jerome Seliger, Alan Steinberg, and Chuck Thegze.

I would also like to thank Daniel Kevles and Marianne de Laet for inviting me to present earlier versions of chapters 3 and 7 at the Seminar on Science, Ethics, and Public Policy, and at the Seminar on Anthropology of Science, Technology, and Medicine, both sponsored by the Division of Humanities and Social Sciences at the California Institute of Technology. I am grateful to Jack Meinhardt, acquisitions editor at AltaMira Press, for his encouragement and support throughout this book project. I would also like to thank Marissa Marro Parks, editorial assistant at AltaMira Press, and Karen Ackermann, production editor at Rowman & Littlefield, for their guidance on editorial matters. Thanks also to Barbara Yablon Maida, who has provided both sound editorial advice and creative support throughout this project.

All previously published materials have been substantially rewritten and reorganized for the purposes of this book.

The selection from the poem, *Spring and All*, 1923, appears on page 183 of *The Collected Poems of William Carlos Williams, Volume 1, 1909–1939*, edited by A. Walton Litz and Christopher MacGowan (New York: New Directions Publishing Corporation, 1986). Reprinted by permission of New Directions Publishing Corp.

Earlier versions of some sections of chapters 1 and 8 were published in the Introduction, *Sustainability and Communities of Place*, edited by Carl A. Maida (New York: Berghahn Books, 2007).

Earlier versions of some sections of chapter 2 were published in Carl A. Maida, Norma S. Gordon, and Norman Farberow, *The Crisis of Competence: Transitional Stress and the Displaced Worker* (New York: Routledge, 1990).

An earlier version of chapter 3 was published under the title "Campaign Against Stigma: Patients and the Ongoing Therapeutic Revolution," *International Journal of Self-Help and Self Care* 2:1 (2003–2004): 57–83.

Earlier versions of some sections in chapter 3 were published in Carl A. Maida, Alfred H. Katz, Deane L. Wolcott, John Landsverk, Gayle Strauss, and Allen R. Nissenson, "Psychological and Social Adaptation to CAPD and Center Hemodialysis Patients," *Loss, Grief and Care* 5:1 (1991): 47–68; and Carl A. Maida, Alfred H. Katz, Gayle Strauss and Cecilia Kwa, "Self-Help, Social Networks and Adaptation in Lupus," *Self-Help: Concepts and Applications*, edited by Alfred H. Katz, Hannah L. Hedrick, Daryl H. Isenberg, Leslie M. Thompson, Therese Goodrich, and Austin H. Kutscher (Philadelphia: Charles Press, 1991). Used with permission of The Charles Press, Publishers, Inc.

An earlier version of some sections of chapter 4 was published under the title "Social Support and Learning in Preventive Health Care," *Social Science and Medicine* 21:3 (1985): 335–339.

Earlier versions of some sections of chapter 6 were published in Norma S. Gordon, Norman Farberow and Carl A. Maida, *Children and Disasters* (Philadelphia: Routledge, 1999); and Carl A. Maida, Norma S. Gordon, Alan Steinberg and Gail Gordon, "Psychosocial Impact of Disasters: Victims of the Baldwin Hills Fire," *Journal of Traumatic Stress* 2:1 (1989): 37–48.

Earlier versions of some sections of chapter 7 were published in "Science, Schooling, and Experiential Learning In Pacoima," *Anthropology of Work Review* 26:2 (2005): 16–20; and "Disaster, Civic Engagement, and Community-Building in Pacoima," *Proteus: A Journal of Ideas*, 18:2 (2001): 21–28.

Earlier versions of some sections of chapter 8 were published in "Virtual Arenas: Computer-Mediated Communication in an AIDS Research Program," *Anthropology of Work Review* 19:1 (1998): 10–17.

Introduction

Pathways through Crisis examines the formation and activities of emergent organizations by means of which urban Americans frequently respond to crises in metropolitan life. The crises considered here range from natural disasters and epidemics to events not usually recognized as a community crisis, such as widespread layoffs or massive arrivals of immigrants, both of which may create strains within a locale. When such crises occur, city dwellers often discover that for a variety of reasons established mechanisms cannot respond adequately to the community's needs. Consequently, various social formations—informal networks; mutual aid groups; and associations based on ethnic, civic, and voluntary ties—move into the vacuum to act as pathways through crisis. Case examples of such social formations drawn from over two decades of ethnographic fieldwork, including participant observation, survey research, and clinical studies, make up the main portion of this book. These case studies are approached primarily in terms of two questions: How do these organizations come into existence and how successful are they in achieving their goals?

To answer the first question, I discuss the conditions that led to the formation of a number of specific organizations. To answer the second question, I describe a number of emergent social formations in terms of their efforts to provide benefits for the community that is in need—benefits that include raising individual problems to a level of common concern, objectifying an event through shared conceptual categories, destigmatizing the survivors' condition through rational discussion and reframing, and empowering survivors by providing common negotiation and advocacy mechanisms that are far more effective than the efforts of individuals acting alone. Most of the case studies presented here originate in the greater Los Angeles area, a metropolis that may be seen as a "social laboratory" in the way that social scientists of the Chicago School in the 1920s saw their city. However, to establish that these examples are not atypical, findings about crisis-driven social formations in Los Angeles are compared to reports about community responses to crises in other urban areas, both in the United States and in other parts of the world. Additionally, contacts with established and emergent organizations that help urban communities return to normal after a crisis made it clear that such organizations cannot be fully understood if one focuses solely on the way they operate today. Complex service organizations—hospitals, labor unions, schools, and voluntary agencies—often have a long history that illuminates their present structures, goals, assumptions, and methods. For the most part, these organizations were established between the 1890s and the 1920s— decades that witnessed the transformation of the country from a largely agrarian, Victorian world to modern society. These organizations, together with the political party, were vehicles used by generations of newcomers to the city to establish their identities and to enhance their lives.

Therefore, following the lead of anthropologist Eric Wolf and others who have been rediscovering history in the social sciences, this work attempts to place recent examples of crisis-driven urban social formations into a larger context.[1] Such formations engender "cultures of solidarity," which are based upon collective action and cultural expressions that typically arise from the lived experience of workers—but also other constituencies within modern and late-modern societies—as they move toward creating and sustaining solidarity.[2] What characterizes these social formations is a style of cultural expression that emerges from within the wider culture yet embodies oppositional practices and meanings specific to the local experience.[3] The approach here is to show that such community responses have been an emergent form of modern local self-government in America dating back at least to the Progressive Era. The period may be seen as a time when informal social formations became especially popular and Americans used powerful tools to deal with various crises that, in the view of many, were being either ignored or mishandled by established social mechanisms. This phenomenon, of course, has an even longer historical precedent in Western democracies—a recurring pattern in which citizens assume vital tasks and responsibilities by means of ad hoc organizations. Such lay initiatives represent what is perhaps the most fundamental and least appreciated form of civic engagement: the direct and highly active participation of citizens in public affairs by means of such nongovernmental and voluntary organizations.

Seen in a historical light, the case studies presented in *Pathways through Crisis* reveal a largely unrecognized ongoing pattern of social formation and social action that is as much a part of American civic life as municipal elections. Unlike the latter, however, many of the crisis-driven formations examined here have no formal status and receive little notice from social scientists or historians. They come into existence sparked by the need to solve some local crisis. In some cases, they cooperate with established institutions, which then "extend" their services to the community in need; in other cases, they may be at odds with these formal organizations. In most instances, they disappear when the fallout from the crisis is under control. On rare occasions, however, they manage to spread geographically and extend themselves historically, overcoming the resistance they typically meet from the forces occupying the center of American political and social discourse. These essentially lay, or vernacular, social formations then create a new public culture distinguished by innovative communicative practices and political styles.

The local formation that achieves wider and longer-lasting success does so because its agenda addresses a crisis that is recognized to exist beyond the boundaries of the original locale. The initial local community thus becomes a large, national constituency and the local organization simultaneously expands into a national advocacy organization with the power to move specific issues from the margins to the center of American discourse and to redefine the way these issues are perceived. A typical example of such metamorphosis is Mothers Against Drunk Driving (MADD), the organization that grew out of community response to a local incident into a widespread and powerful organization that has brought about significant changes in laws and attitudes concerning drinking and driving.[4] On a broader scale, instances of emergent social formations that have moved from the margins into the center of American life and fostered major changes in culture and social policy include the women's, environmental, civil rights, disability rights, and AIDS advocacy movements.

Because this book provides a synthesis of historical, comparative, and field-based social dynamics of both formal organizations and emergent groups, it draws from the work of historians who have found novel insights in the archives of science, medicine, industry, urban life, and mass culture; in social scientific and documentary accounts; and in the visual arts. I have especially valued the work of Carl Schorske and other social historians, and historically informed social scientists interested in the structural aspects of urban social formations, particularly how these dynamics reflect changes in knowledge and public culture.[5] Robert Putnam investigated civic traditions in modern Italian politics and emphasized the primacy of civic engagement as a central form of civic virtue.[6] Thomas Bender studies the extent to which the sense of civic obligation depends upon the character of "urban knowledges."[7] Both seek to document the ways in which civic community is represented in what Pierre Bourdieu would call the *habitus* of modern citizens, namely the bundle of conventions and habitual ways and perceptions that order lives in particular times and places.[8]

Finally, a note about the book's focus on greater Los Angeles: I see this city as a representative "late-modern" American metropolitan area that has faced a number of well-publicized crises in recent decades.[9] These include the 1992 civil disturbances, the 1993 wildfires, and the 1994 Northridge Earthquake. The Los Angeles area has also been affected by crises that received mostly local attention yet were just as devastating to the people involved: the massive layoffs in Southern California's aerospace and defense industries at the end of the Cold War, and the severe cuts in the public sector brought about by a shrinking state and municipal revenue base. The aftermath of these disasters forced Los Angeles to rebuild its municipal infrastructure and to help thousands of survivors recover from the economic and emotional traumas of a series of devastating urban catastrophes.[10] Established organizations mediated the formal crisis response, but at the same time this sequence of disasters led to the emergence of various lay-initiated efforts to serve needs that were not receiving sufficient attention elsewhere.

Los Angeles has become the nation's busiest trade center as it reconstructed after a decade of economic recession, civil disorder, floods, wildfires, and the devastating earthquake. In 1994, as the city was recovering from the nation's most destructive natural disaster at the time, the flow of electronic goods, aircraft products, and computers through harbors and airports in the Los Angeles Customs District surpassed New York as the nation's busiest customs district. Los Angeles stands today as the nation's trading hub on the Pacific Rim, having conducted $329.4 billion in "two-way trade" in 2007. The San Pedro Bay port complex on the Pacific Ocean is the largest container-shipping facility in the nation, and the fifth-largest port complex in the world. With such trading partners as Japan, China, Taiwan, and South Korea eager for the commodities and services produced by California's high-technology, multimedia, and entertainment industries, and as the principal North American distribution hub for these nations' own export goods, the city's future is dependent upon its economic reorientation to the Asian-Pacific region.[11] Los Angeles is developing a society based upon the mass movement of economic refugees and migrants from countries of the impoverished Southern Hemisphere.[12] With over 16,000 manufacturing enterprises, it is the nation's largest manufacturing center, with over 450,000 jobs. Los Angeles is a core region for the production and distribution of innovations in microchip-based technologies and biotechnology, and of health care, financial, and telecommunications services—industries that have come to define the regional economy of Southern California, the national economy, and the emerging pattern of global economic relations. The recent history of Los

Angeles and its metropolitan region, therefore, has made it an especially active arena for innovative social formations. By looking closely at how these originated and how well they were able to accomplish their objectives, we may learn much about how both formal and informal organizations that were created to mediate the various risks accompanying metropolitan life could be redesigned or otherwise adapted to best serve the special needs of contemporary urban environments.

NOTES

1. Eric R. Wolf, *Europe and the People without History* (Berkeley: University of California Press, 1982); Eric R. Wolf, *Pathways of Power: Building an Anthropology of the Modern World* (Berkeley: University of California Press, 2001).

2. Rick Fantasia, *Cultures of Solidarity: Consciousness, Action, and Contemporary American Worker*s (Berkeley: University of California Press, 1988), 17.

3. Raymond Williams, *The Sociology of Culture* (New York: Schocken, 1981).

4. John D. McCarthy, "Activists, Authorities, and Media Framing of Drunk Driving," in *New Social Movements: From Ideology to Identity*, edited by Enrique Laraña, Hank Johnston, and Joseph R. Gusfield (Philadelphia: Temple University Press, 1994), 133–67.

5. Carl E. Schorske, *Fin de Siècle Vienna: Politics and Culture* (New York: Random House, 1981); Carl E. Schorske, *Thinking with History: Explorations in the Passage to Modernism* (Princeton, NJ: Princeton University Press, 1998); Péter Hanák, *The Garden and the City: Essays on the Cultural History of Vienna and Budapest* (Princeton, NJ: Princeton University Press, 1998).

6. Robert D. Putnam, *Making Democracy Work: Civic Traditions in Modern Italy* (Princeton, NJ: Princeton University Press, 1993).

7. Thomas Bender, *The Unfinished City: New York and the Metropolitan Idea* (New York: The New Press, 2002).

8. Pierre Bourdieu, *Outline of a Theory of Practice*, trans. Richard Nice (Cambridge, UK: Cambridge University Press, 1977).

9. Mike Davis, *City of Quartz: Excavating the Future in Los Angeles* (New York: Random House, 1992); Raphael J. Sonenshein, *Politics in Black and White: Race and Power in Los Angeles* (Princeton, NJ: Princeton University Press, 1993); Mike Davis, *Ecology of Fear: Los Angeles and the Imagination of Disaster* (New York: Metropolitan Books, 1998); Kevin Starr, *Coast of Dreams: California on the Edge, 1990–2003* (New York: Knopf, 2004).

10. Michael J. Dear, ed., *From Chicago to L.A.: Making Sense of Urban Theory* (Thousand Oaks, CA: Sage Publications, 2002); Robert Gottlieb, Mark Vallianatos, Regina M. Freer, and Peter Drier, *The Next Los Angeles: The Struggle for a Livable City* (Berkeley: University of California Press, 2006); Robert Gottlieb, *Reinventing Los Angeles: Nature and Community in the Global City* (Cambridge, MA: MIT Press, 2007).

11. Paul M. Kennedy, *The Rise and Fall of the Great Powers: Economic Change and Military Conflict from 1500 to 2000* (New York: Random House, 1987), 441–42.

12. Roger Waldinger and Mehdi Bozorgmehr, eds., *Ethnic Los Angeles* (New York: Russell Sage Foundation, 1996); James P. Allen and Eugene Turner, *The Ethnic Quilt: Population Diversity in Southern California* (Northridge, CA: The Center for Geographic Studies, California State University, Northridge); William A. V. Clark, *The California Cauldron: Immigration and the Fortunes of Local Communities* (New York: Guilford, 1998).

Chapter One

A World of Strangers

Metropolitan life, with its risks, opportunities, and uncertainties, has sustained a turbulent landscape for over a century in the United States.[1] Modern American cities are places of physical and temperamental restlessness, whose skyscrapers contribute to a sense of place that is vertical, fragmentary, and horizonless. These structures continue to dominate and define our cityscapes today, although many original skyscrapers—New York's Ritz Tower, Flatiron, and Woolworth buildings, and Chicago's Monadnock and Rookery buildings—have been overshadowed by larger ones; the tallest ones remain landmarks that identify their respective cities, such as the Empire State Building and Rockefeller Center in New York, and the Chicago Tribune Building. From above, the flow of people through the vertical city appears to be anonymous, random, and unstructured.

An "extended city" developed in Southern California as an escape from the industrial metropolis that had defined urban form at the turn of the century. Unlike Eastern and Midwestern cities modeled on European urbanism, Los Angeles was designed as a "new American city" of suburban villages linked by a network of trolleys. The freeways continued this fragmented and insular structure, and high-speed automobile travel intensified the experience of the city as "an extended repetitive fabric."[2] In Los Angeles, one encounters "natural" realms—beaches, mountains, and deserts—that promote private experience.[3] These contrast with the "civic" or public realms of plazas, town squares, and boulevards that organize public life in older European and American cities. The pattern of the extended city reinforces the privatization of life, fragmented governance, and change subject to the less personal forces of markets, consumer behavior, mass advertising, and the decisions of industrial entrepreneurs and corporate boards. In both the vertical and the extended city, the seemingly endless movement of people and commodities within the urban landscape suggests that energy is created and dissipated quickly. Urban dwellers routinely experience countless interactions and reactions that partly account for the general sense of nervousness that pervades city life. The pace of living is intense and temporal relations are more precisely patterned. These distinctly urban conditions overstimulate the senses and generate stress disorders. Ways to mediate the stresses of modernity developed in the late nineteenth century, such as the forms of therapeutic practices and systems of mutual aid that help people cope in a world of strangers. This chapter considers the diverse perspectives through which modern cities can been viewed, from those of architects and city planners who design them, to those of social scientists who study how residents cope with the routine and the unpredictable in urban life.

THE NETWORKED CITY

Two types of networks—one technological and the other organizational—sustain life in modern cities. Since the middle of the nineteenth century, an urban infrastructure of vast technological networks has evolved in industrial cities as the wellspring of metropolitan life that continues to shape and reshape the urban environment in ways often invisible to city dwellers.[4] Interlocking networks of roads, bridges, and mass transit guide people along urban pathways toward "destinations" within a region. Municipal water systems connecting the neighborhoods of the rich and the poor provide a substance critical to both personal and industrial life. The need to remove wastes from the urban environment has led to new technologies and networks to handle municipal sewage, wastewater, and garbage. Electrical and natural gas networks of wires and pipes supply the energy to control household and industrial environments. A telecommunications infrastructure of overhead and underground wires connects people in a "deep community" of messages along what is now called the "information highway." Urban infrastructure developed with the rapid growth of city populations in the late nineteenth century, along with the introduction of new building methods and mass-produced materials, such as glass and steel. This pattern took shape on the North American continent when Chicago was forced to reconstruct in the wake of an enormous disaster. Chicago's Great Fire of 1871 killed almost three hundred people and destroyed over $200 million in property. The fire burned down about a third of Chicago's 61,000 buildings and left 100,000 homeless. In a single night, the city's entire downtown was destroyed. Daniel Burnham and fellow architects Louis Sullivan and John Root were instrumental in rebuilding Chicago out of the "wasteland created by the Great Fire."[5] In the 1880s, the Chicago School of Architecture invented a new building type, the skyscraper, to reconstruct the burned-over district. This concrete and steel highrise office building, with elevators, self-supporting metal frames and fireproofing, arose like the phoenix from the ashes of the Great Fire. Modern technologies and the need to revive a ruined city moved architects to design a modern cityscape that made Chicago the Midwestern metropolis. Chicago's architects experimented with new materials that enabled them to develop "foundations capable of supporting great loads on the unstable subsoil" along the Lake Michigan shoreline.[6] Thanks to innovative, daring approaches to rebuilding Chicago's commercial infrastructure in the 1880s, Burnham & Root became the city's premier architectural firm, as Chicago became the nation's most dynamic city of the late nineteenth century—one that transformed both the American natural and cultural landscapes. The scale and intensity of American industrial development was most evident in the Middle West, which, over three generations, moved from a wilderness to an agrarian culture and then on to become the nation's industrial center. After the fire, Chicago emerged as the nation's prototypical modern city. Its resurrection was spearheaded by Progressive architects, engineers, and entrepreneurs intent on exploiting the commercial advantages of its "Great Western" hinterland. At the edge of a vast countryside of prairies, forests, and rangelands, Chicago positioned itself as a market center capable of expanding along with the sweeping economic and ecological changes that defined American life between 1890 and 1930.[7]

Cities were able to expand more economically, and thus decentralize, as a result of declining energy costs.[8] The cost factor motivated decision makers in both private industry and the public sector to invest in infrastructure, chiefly by expanding railways, roadways, and utilities into the commuter suburbs. As the new middle classes grew dissatisfied with urban blight, they campaigned for increased services to reform the built environment. However, with this popular mandate came an expansion of governmental responsibilities. To meet demands for higher standards of city living, including gas and electricity, elevators, and boilers, local governments were required to provide an array of costly services.[9] They undertook municipal projects, such as street plans to regulate the network of pipes and wires needed to deliver utility services. Cities adopted bureaucratic procedures and more centralized decision making; enlisted experts to develop safety standards, public health, and housing codes; and hired inspectors to enforce them.[10] This regulatory framework and its bureaucratic style continue to organize most city-building decisions and to influence design criteria regarding physical infrastructure. Ordinary citizens have little say in matters relating to property, land use, and construction

of infrastructure systems, as most issues are settled politically, or at best bu-
reaucratically through government intervention.[11] The continuous process of
city building is influenced by a diverse set of professional groups—federal
government, labor, builders, developers, materials suppliers, bankers, insur-
ers, administrators, architects, and engineers—that operate from a narrow
band of interests. The reorganization of urban space requires a fragmented
political decision-making process since most projects are so technically complex that they require expert knowledge of the law, finance, and design to initiate and carry out. Professional groups remain the principle stakeholders in
this process, having learned how to influence and manipulate the opinions and
the behavior of the political, technical, legal, and financial decision-making
bodies that control access to a city's space.[12] The experience of city building
in the late nineteenth century transformed professional culture from a *civic*
professionalism, associated with the civic humanism of commercial cities in
Renaissance Italy, to a *disciplinary* professionalism.[13] During the colonial era
and in the new republic, a few educated and powerful individuals who shared
a sensibility and adhered to common rules of discourse maintained civic culture. The educated classes cultivated a civic role through self-improvement
and the nurturance of an urban cultural legacy, chiefly through libraries,
philosophical and historical societies, mechanical and agricultural associations, and informal discussion groups.[14] In frontier cities, intellectual life was
organized around the "principle of mutual instruction" that inspired these discussion groups.[15]

    After the Civil War, civic culture in America was eroded by an emerging
urban order based on cultural diversity and egalitarianism, and a spatial and
institutional configuration that was both socially and culturally segregated.[16]
Nineteenth-century New York, like London and Paris, was "a city of class-
homogenous, disconnected spaces" designed to promote individualism, and
even "civic solitude," so as to maintain public order.[17] Within the urbanized
society, individuals appeared to be moving together as a crowd, but were actually, in Richard Sennett's words, "detached from the space in which they
moved, and from the people the space contained."[18] By promoting discon-
nection among people, urban individualism fostered mutual indifference, and
eventually led to the loss of any sense of a shared fate among city dwellers,
thereby eroding civic humanism. Urban space was reconfigured through residential segregation and specialized land-use to create sharper boundaries,
just as many social categories familiar to antebellum Americans became
blurred. This penchant for setting racial and class boundaries extended to cultural life, as intellectual communities grew more specialized and exclusive.[19]
With fragmentation of the elites and the waning of public culture, a new professional system arose that was both "multicentered and nonlocal" and em-

phasized individual membership in an intellectual community.[20] In contrast to the disorder and fragmentation of late nineteenth-century city life, the specialized professional disciplines provided a conceptual focus and reference group for the urban intellectual. Situated within an "epistemic community," professionals now turned to their disciplinary peers for collegiality and critical guidance rather than to the broader urban public.[21] They sought positions on the faculties of the newer urban research universities, such as Johns Hopkins and the University of Chicago, and thereafter turned away from general city culture.[22] The new industrial city brought about the "society of organizations."[23] Its laboratories, corporations, hospitals, and markets helped pave the way for modernity. Technical and scientific innovations, but also social and cultural movements, emerged in modern organizations. With their emphasis on specialized knowledge and tasks, these milieus were largely responsible for the massive pull away from traditional forms of communal solidarity. The rapid pace of innovation within modern organizations destabilized local economies. These technical and social advances leveled entire craft traditions and ways of livelihood. As de-skilled artisans and others sought work outside their local areas, they abandoned the communal bonds that had sustained traditional societies for centuries. The techniques, products, and values of modern organizations thus challenged local cultures. These advances produced crises that have shaken traditional societies as nation-states incorporated tribal and communally held lands into their jurisdictions. Cities encroached upon agricultural settlements, dislocating many from the countryside. Ecological crises, such as the ravages of strip mining and deforestation, resulted in forced displacement and resettlement. Although these transformations and discontinuities have defined modernity since the late nineteenth century, they continue to have an unsettling presence today.[24]

STRANGERS TO THE CITY

In the half century between 1870 and 1920, the percentage of the nation's population that lived in urban areas increased from 28 percent to 52 percent. The new American city was the abode of strangers: uprooted preindustrial people from Eastern Europe and the Mediterranean, African American migrants from the rural South, and young middle-class men and women who had grown up in small towns and on farms. All were drawn into this vortex of enterprise and labor. Settling in ethnically or racially distinct neighborhoods, or "urban villages," each group attempted to preserve its culture and language. These communities provided considerable stability of cultural pattern and informal support, particularly for first-generation families. They fostered local pride through successful enterprises, such as restaurants, bakeries, and construction firms, which became widely recognized and patronized by those from outside the community. However, a chief purpose of the immigrant ghetto was to bind people to their own neighborhoods and limit their participation in a wider set of social, economic, and political roles.[25] The local neighborhood therefore served to institutionalize immigrant families' estrangement from the surrounding metropolis by restricting their housing and occupational choices, often beyond the first and second generations.

During this period, Western European cities grew to absorb uprooted peasants who had abandoned the countryside to live and work in urban industrial areas. While many were displaced by famines, pogroms, land clearings, and depressions, others exited the agrarian sector voluntarily.[26] Georg Simmel aptly describes the stranger in late nineteenth-century European cities *not* as "the wanderer who comes today and goes tomorrow, but rather as the man who comes today and stays tomorrow."[27] Strangers, according to Simmel, were transitional types who would eventually find a permanent, albeit marginal, place in the modern industrial city. They were frequently journeymen, artisans, and traders who intermittently resided in the city to sell goods or services, and then returned to their small towns in the countryside. As brokers or middlemen, they understood city ways well enough to participate in an urban labor market.

These competent newcomers transferred their skills in bargaining and persuasion to secure a niche for themselves in the city's commercial sector. Through this transition, they formed ego defenses capable of protecting their nascent urban identities. By contrast, underemployed rural workers migrating to the city, including the technologically displaced, experienced more difficulties than members of these relatively higher-skilled groups. Most lower-skilled and low-paid workers were forced to accept casual, insecure, and less desirable jobs, such as street vendors, servants, and day laborers. As representatives of antiquated rural cultures, these people were especially marginal to fast-paced city life. Paradoxically, they became strangers to life in the countryside because of their incipient urbanity. Many settled permanently in the city to resolve the dissonance of living between two worlds. However, they were met with ambivalence and even antagonism by those who had established themselves, economically and socially, within the industrial order.[28] The new middle classes of Europe and the United States idealized the "good life" and folk traditions of the peasant, and cherished the crafts and other commodities of the countryside. The heirs to a culture of competitive individualism, they were nostalgic for the communal bonds and forms of association still prevalent in agrarian life. While they frequently ridiculed the newcomers' displays of unfamiliar speech, clothing, and customs in the city's public spaces, middle-class individuals profited from new careers built upon professional custodianship over the needs of the uprooted.[29] Modern social welfare, medical care, public law, and criminology grew out of a concern for the needs of strangers, but also out of a fear of social disorder in crowded American and European cities. The manner in which health and social services continue to be organized and delivered, through "a degree of social distance between the helped and the helper,"[30] attests to the awkwardness and apprehension common to each party to the encounter. There are good reasons for this stance, as helping transactions carry the possibility of emotional or physical danger to both giver and receiver. The helping professional develops a persona of detached objectivity as a defense in the face of danger, contagion, and threat. This clinical mentality, motivated by a sense of altruism and responsibility in caring for the sick, deviant, or disadvantaged client, is frequently characterized by an arrogance derived from expert knowledge and control over certain goods or entitlements. Professional altruists serve as moral arbiters of human needs, or the basic goods requisite for personal survival and human dignity, such as food, shelter, clothing, income, and health care. This ethos is embedded in the structures, goals, assumptions, and methods of complex service organizations, such as welfare agencies, public schools, prisons, hospitals, and clinics.

Few early twentieth-century observers of industrial cities held a more optimistic view of urbanization than the Victorian moralists who comprised the first generation of professional "uplifters." Stressing the city's emancipative possibilities, rather than its dissipative influences, Robert Park observed in the American Midwest many of the same dynamics that an earlier generation feared and sought to control, but from a different perspective. Park even claimed in a 1915 essay that the city is "the natural environment of the free man," presumably because it permitted many individuals to shed their rural conservatism in the face of cultural and technological innovations associated with urban living.[31] Viewing Chicago as a social "laboratory," rather than a seething cauldron of mass disorder and violence, Park and his colleagues at the University of Chicago used survey research, team observations, and ecological investigations to understand the city's modernization.

Ernest Burgess and Roderick McKenzie mapped the spatial dimensions of the expanding metropolis. Based upon the distribution of activities according to land values, their model depicted the city as a series of concentric circles. It distinguished the activities carried out within each circle or ecological zone. The first circle contained "the Loop," Chicago's affluent central business district. The second circle was the "zone of transition" with its slums and immigrant enclaves. Beyond were working men's homes, residential and "commuter" zones. These rings of residential settlement designated a new pattern of urban segregation—through housing—in the industrial city. The electric streetcar lines connecting the central city to the suburbs reinforced this residential pattern, making it easier for the middle classes to settle in districts beyond the city limits, and then commute in and out to work and to shop.[32] During the time when Chicago sociologists were considering metropolitan dynamics in the light of suburban development, French novelist Jules Romains characterized the daily movement of Parisian commuters from the suburb to the city and back again, as a form of a pulsation marked by

> the way in which the suburbs, the circumference, shot more than a million people in practically converging directions at it, . . . But in the evening this spongy mass disgorged the million people who had saturated it. It expelled them back to the circumference, to the inner and outer suburbs, in myriads whose movements were all uniform. It was a pulsation which in no way resembled that of a human organism. It involved no dilation, no contraction. The city palpitated like a focus of radiation that turns back upon itself. . . . It was rather in the imperious fashion of those physical organisms, apparently immobile and inert, which, by their mere presence, modify a whole sphere of the world around them, letting loose, and at the same time controlling forces, tendencies, radiations in it.[33]

The Chicago School sociologists believed a moral order underlay the city's spatial arrangements and patterns of movement. To them, the rationality of urban structure was expressed in the city's physical arrangements. They saw cities as analogous to biotic communities of plants and animals in a natural economy. Competition for space was embedded in urban ecology as much as in any forest or meadow. The physical and functional features of the urban landscape were living expressions of winners and losers in this competition. The urban division of labor was analogous to the competition, dominance, and succession found in nature. Park and his colleagues viewed the dissatisfaction of new immigrants and industrial workers with their conditions as a reflection of their moral and social instability. As theirs was an equilibrium model, Chicago sociologists prescribed system maintenance through philanthropy and social reform to steer unstable groups away from labor unrest and crowd violence.

Louis Wirth further explored the effects of urban fragmentation on Chicago neighborhood life. He found that the variety of neighborhoods, districts, and sections of the industrial city segmented the population into functional units, which were the artifacts of modernity. The city's structural features, such as size, density, and heterogeneity, shaped social relations. Its division of labor influenced land use, labor, and other features of the political economy. City life was thus organized around the ties and interactions of individuals within each urban zone. For Wirth, social disorganization, marginality, and deviance ensued from the fragmented and territorial nature of the metropolis, and not from innate characteristics of intelligence or temperament.

Robert Redfield first tested the Chicago School's model of urbanism in 1920s Mexico.[34] In the village of Tepoztlan, sixty miles from Mexico City, Redfield sought out ethnographic evidence for the integration of folk communities into urban society. Adopting Park's ecological approach, he mapped concentric zones around Tepoztlan. The village's central plaza was to be the "periphery of change." Redfield speculated that from within this zone change agents, perhaps inspired by Mexico City's civic reform agenda, would diffuse urban traits to peasants in the countryside. However, Tepoztlan was already too large and complex a town to be classified as a folk society gradually transforming itself in the image of the metropole. In fact, during Redfield's visit, rival religious and "Bolshevik" factions in the village and rebels in the countryside were embroiled in a violent struggle for political control.

Redfield next studied four communities—a tribe, a peasant village, a town, and a city—on the Yucatan peninsula to understand how they underwent disorganization, secularization, and reorganization in the process of more frequent contact with urban society. His developmental model of urbanism compares characteristics of the folk community with those of civilization along a "folk-urban continuum." Folk communities, such as peasant villages, are "intermediate between the primitive tribe and the modern city." These communities are transitional for they mediate competing technical and moral spheres. Like the "strangers" observed by Simmel, many of the peasants marginalized by the modernization of folk communities migrated to urban centers.

CITY OF NETS

Strangers still preside on the current metropolitan scene. In the late-modern city, these transients either chose to leave or were forced to abandon the familiar landscapes of their home communities to create new lives. Michael Ignatieff underscores a similar paradoxical relationship of homelessness and belonging today that Simmel observed almost a century ago:

> We think of belonging as permanence, yet all our homes are transient. Who still lives in the house of their childhood? Who still lives in the neighborhood where they grew up? Home is the place we have to leave in order to grow up, to become ourselves. We think of belonging as rootedness in a small familiar place, yet home for most of us is the convulsive arteries of a great city. Our belonging

is no longer to something fixed, known and familiar, but to an electric and heart-less creature eternally in motion.[35]

Like their turn-of-the-century counterparts, contemporary strangers en-counter an urban world structured by the division of labor and market rela-tions and the fragmentation of social roles. This latter condition is particularly traumatic because it compels individuals to reorient their inner lives. Com-plex urban cultures require one to forge an identity capable of taking on mul-tiple social roles. City people have a well-developed repertoire of behavioral styles that they use to manage their identities. They receive messages on the basis of superficial impressions and stereotyped behavioral cues. The urban-ite learns to act according to these fragmented impersonal encounters and to define a situation with minimal information. City life consists of the count-less efforts by people to maintain status and identity through situationally de-fined behavior. City dwellers develop a variety of ways to cope with the hy-perstimulation of body and psyche that comes from living in a world of strangers.[36] Many embrace the occupations, forms of life, and mass leisure that characterize the urban milieu. Others are estranged from the institutions of mass culture, opting to participate in deviant, often destructive subcultures. Still others recreate a network of close-knit social bonds similar to those found in smaller-scale communities.

As people move to the city, they leave behind a set of personal attachments. These bonds of kinship and friendship are central to a person's identity and sense of place. Upon resettlement, newcomers have to reconstruct their ties for support at work and for mutual aid in their neighborhoods. These are fre-quently unfamiliar worlds that require caution in entering and establishing oneself. Adaptation to city life compels newcomers to redefine interpersonal relations in an impersonal milieu. They will often develop bonds of urban eth-nicity through efforts to retain their language and culture in mutual assistance associations, churches, and fraternal organizations. Through their new attach-ments, essentially rural people and other strangers to the city reorient their lives. These networks of kin and close friends provide them with support as they undergo crises, adapt to city ways, and face modernity.

After World War II, anthropologists began to closely observe the lifeways of city people. The methods of situational analysis and social-network analy-sis were developed to interpret the process of individual adjustment to urban-ization. Ethnographers from England's Manchester School looked to Max Gluckman's principle of situational selection in their studies of urbaniza-tion.[37] Gluckman contended that rural and urban life were two distinct social systems. How they differed had to be analyzed from the standpoint of patterns of adult social behavior within each system. Manchester School anthropologists described one such pattern, namely the urban web of kin and close friends, in spatial terms as a social network.[38] In African industrial towns, migrants had created social networks after resettlement that differed considerably from their rural ties. In East London, a town in South Africa, Philip Mayer studied the cultural styles of two groups of Xhosa peasants from the rural hinterland who had migrated to work in the town's factories.[39] "Red" Xhosa were traditionalists who steadfastly refused to adopt Western values, choosing to remain animist and illiterate. They earned their title by their habit of smearing ochre on their bodies and continuing to wear the customary red blanket. "School" Xhosa were trained in Christian mission schools in their homelands. They had developed the literacy and Western values necessary to fully participate in the town's leisure activities.

"Red" Xhosa retained their tribal values by frequent visits to their homelands. When at home, they would visit conservative village elders who reinforced their decision to retain traditional ways. The visiting relationship was sustained in town through a conscious restriction of leisure activities to home friends who also retained "Red" traditions. These tightly knit networks of like-minded countrymen perpetuated rural ways in the urban setting. The "Red" Xhosa were like many migrant groups in towns and cities with a high density of people from a common homeland or ethnic heritage. They principally associated with their countrymen and constructed a network based upon premigration ties. The success of this strategy depends strongly on numbers. When fewer people with a common background reside in an area, newcomers are obliged to engage in town life more actively. "School" Xhosa embraced the town's culture by participating in its leisure activities. These situations compelled them to associate with members of different social classes and ethnic groups. The activities afforded them a window on town life through which they could view progressive values, beliefs, and social roles. They were the paths to modern life for rural migrants choosing to become "town rooted." Through their engagement with the culture of the town, "School" Xhosa created loosely knit networks that oriented them toward modernity.

Regional associations, like those formed by Xhosa migrants in East London, are cultural milieus that help to mediate the rural-to-urban transition. Migrants who share a common local tradition comprise the membership of these voluntary organizations. Members develop ties of urban ethnicity through their efforts to retain rural traditions, ritual, and beliefs. The association provides a milieu that blends traditional sentiments with modern situations. It serves the interests of elites such as professionals and politicians within the migrant community. These urban "big men," who serve as leaders, use their positions to establish a power base. The "chief" will often establish ties of patronage between himself and the newcomers that may later sustain a loose coalition for support in a political campaign or labor action. This coalition will usually break up after the campaign or strike ends, freeing individuals to return to their routine activities. Regional associations thus instill a modern sensibility in essentially conservative people accustomed to the security of their traditional lifeways. These milieus facilitate a gradual transition to the less certain conditions of modernity by socializing progressive roles, building coalitions, and developing political interests among their members.

Robert Merton found similar dynamics at work in postwar American civic culture where a leader's style of social influence was frequently an expression of a personal orientation to the community. Merton offers a functional analysis of local and cosmopolitan types as contrasting world orientations.[40] While the "local" is fully enmeshed in local problems, to the exclusion of national and global ones, the "cosmopolitan" is principally oriented to the world outside the locality. Local types are parochial and town rooted, having lived in the community for a long time, and are likely to be more involved in local politics than ecumenical cosmopolitans who tend to be relative newcomers. While local influentials are apt to take a "quantitativist" approach to sociality and maintain dense town-based social networks, cosmopolitans advance their careers through ties to members of other communities and are more selective, hence "qualitativist," in their social ties within the town.

This dichotomy plays out in the kinds of organizations each is likely to join: locals choose fraternal and service organizations where they can extend their circle of personal relationship; cosmopolitans associate with others who share a particular set of skills or knowledge, and thus participate in professional societies and hobby groups. While the cosmopolitan influential establishes a leadership role as a result of specialized knowledge or experience, the local influential derives a following because of a sympathetic understanding or intimate appreciation of the community and its residents. Therefore, the cosmopolitan exerts interpersonal influence as an expert, a role requiring some degree of social distance between the person seeking advice and the knower, and the local influences community life through lay knowledge requiring close attention to and intimate familiarity with personal relationships.

Apart from these more pragmatic uses of social networks in public life, a personal network—the close-knit set of relationships based on kinship, friendship, and neighborliness—is frequently called upon for help during life crises.[41] Individuals will mobilize their personal networks for advice and counsel during these periods of increased stress. Families depend upon their wider networks for support and guidance. For example, couples in postwar London found their marriages were deeply affected by the world outside the home. The couples organized their activities through either segregated or joint conjugal roles. A segregated pattern suggests a clear division of labor and interests between husband and wife. A joint pattern indicates that husband and wife engage in activities together, with little task differentiation. How a couple constructed a family world was influenced by their network of relationships outside the household. Networks varied with the degree of connectedness, which was how the couple's associates were linked to one another. In close-knit networks, the couple's kin and friends maintained frequent contacts with one another. Loose-knit networks indicated the relative paucity of such contacts.

Working-class families in postwar London maintained close-knit social networks since they had limited social and physical mobility. Because working-class people lived and worked in the same community, they engaged one another in a variety of situations, affording more opportunities for relatives and friends to offer help and advice. Each partner was bound by relationships established before the marriage. These ties inhibited a fuller involvement between spouses and reinforced the segregation of domestic activities within the working-class household. Middle-class families had characteristically loose-knit social networks because of pressures toward social mobility, and professionals frequently worked in a different community than the one in which they resided. Spouses depended more upon each other for support and direction than in working-class marriages. Their ability to work together on domestic tasks was an expression of a fuller involvement between spouses. Family life in postwar Britain underwent extensive changes as many young couples relocated from urban, working-class communities to the new public-housing estates in the suburbs. Newcomers in one such estate had grown up in the East London borough of Bethnal Green. The sense of community in Bethnal Green emerged from the ties that people maintained over time. Michael Young and Peter Willmott point out how affiliations in the borough were based on extended networks of family members and close friends:

> People do not, after marriage, throw off the past which contains their former family and friends. They combine past and present. They continue to belong to the same community, and since the sense of belonging which comes from knowing and being known by so many of their fellow residents is something that most Bethnal Greeners prize, this alone goes some way to explain their attachment. But their sense of belonging cannot be explained simply by long residence. It is so deep because it is rooted in a lasting attachment to their families.[42]

This people-centered world was lost after relocation. In the housing estate, young couples lived amid strangers, their new lives centered around their houses and jobs. A nuclear family replaced East London's wider world of intimacy. These families dwelled in a house-centered world characterized by the pursuit of status and material acquisition. The move away from Bethnal

Green interposed a barrier of distance between their extended families and themselves. The newcomers lost the close-knit networks that supported families across generations. Gone were the reference groups of kin and close friends providing access to jobs, as well as objective norms to evaluate their lives. In their place, suburban families devised subjective norms and ascribed status based on acquiring and displaying personal possessions. Their strong ties to extended community networks gave way to emotional attachments to their homes and objects in the domestic environment.

Late twentieth-century urbanites have also constructed networks around themselves to serve as personal communities. Barry Wellman discovered that residents in East York, a densely settled working-class community in central Toronto, Canada, had few ties within their neighborhoods.[43] They sought neither solidarity on street corners nor sociality in public squares. Instead, East Yorkers maintained a network of ties to friends, kin, and coworkers that stretched throughout metropolitan Toronto and beyond. The urbanites sustained relationships by frequent visits, phone conversations, and gatherings, which depended upon Toronto's municipal amenities. The city's infrastructure, especially its transportation and communications systems, became the context for their personal communities. In this way, East Yorkers maintained a number of social worlds, in the home, at work, among kin, and in leisure activities. Members of each domain were linked only to the person at the center of the network for a specialized purpose. These were loosely knit networks, as members seldom associated with one another apart from that individual. East Yorkers' personal communities provided the everyday companionship and emotional support, but also direction during life crises to survive in the metropolis. Through interpersonal skill and resourcefulness, these social artisans had crafted smaller worlds from the manifold of city life.

CRISIS, TRAUMA, AND EMBODIMENT

Social phenomenology, attachment theory, and traumatic stress studies can help explain how crises in the physical and social environments influence both the individual and community life. Each provides a framework for understanding how individuals construct and maintain coherent lives amid dislocation. Social phenomenology, or field theory, is grounded in perceptual experience, bodily expression, and institutional life.[44] The body is a community of senses that organizes an individual's experience and gives meaning to the world. A sense of community, or the social life-world, develops when the individuals in the community share sets of commonly shaped experiences and a coherent worldview. A person becomes conscious of his own identity and of his social world and gains a sense of perceptual coherence as he learns sets of skilled actions in the family, at play, in school, and at work. The emergent network of relationships situates an individual in a social field of institutional and community life. Individuals develop a mazeway, or cognitive image of their culture, by understanding how material conditions and events in the social field guide their actions. This perceptual framework, based upon a sense of the consistency of the environment, guides individual adaptation in crises.

Attachment theory proposes that personal identity and self-concept develop through bonding with significant persons within the social field—at home, at work, and in the community.[45] This constellation of attachments provides a secure base to anchor a person in his social world. The sense of security may be severely affected after a major crisis that uproots one's home or disrupts one's community. Traumatized individuals will often experience a social void accompanied by feelings of intense loss of these anchors in the physical and social environment. In the wake of urban dislocation in Boston, for example, residents of the West End, a close-knit, working-class community, found themselves "grieving for a lost home." Their personal identities and sense of orientation had been forged and maintained in the familiar spatial and physical arrangements of West End residences and neighborhoods. Upon relocation, they had lost the secure base of their homes, but also of the city blocks where they had felt at home with neighbors and close friends. After observing firsthand the human costs of Boston's urban renewal efforts, Marc Fried reflected upon the primacy of the spatial dimension to a person's self-image and sense of well-being:

[A] sense of spatial identity is fundamental to human functioning. It represents a phenomenal or ideational integration of important experiences concerning environmental arrangements and contacts in relation to the individual's conception of his own body in space. It is based on spatial memories, spatial imagery, the spatial frame-work of current activity, and the implicitly spatial components of ideals and aspirations.[46]

A sense of loss is common among those who have experienced residential displacement due to urban renewal, community relocation and forced migration, or relocation after destruction caused by natural or technological disasters. The destruction of a community and the displacement of its residents is an acknowledged stressor, because of the shared perception of loss. The displaced worker, the chronically ill or disabled person, the refugee, and others who migrate from their homelands, however, also experience these feelings of loss. Individuals undergoing these life crises report a sense of alienation, disorientation, pessimism about the future, depression, and other posttraumatic symptoms that are associated with community crises. The phenomenon of posttraumatic stress is a cogent framework for understanding the effects on emotional functioning of sudden, life-threatening events, such as disasters, wars, and civil disorders. Individuals suffering traumatic stress manifest such persistent symptoms of heightened emotional arousal as difficulty falling or staying asleep, irritability, and difficulty concentrating, along with some physiologic reactivity. They frequently report generalized anxiety reactions such as tiring easily, feeling on edge, having excessive worry, and experiencing an increase or recurrence of such physical symptoms as headaches, weight loss or gain, heart palpitations, and insomnia. Those experiencing such event-related reactions have been diagnosed as having some form of posttraumatic stress disorder, or PTSD. The disorder is now a medically recognized impairment that results from one or a series of traumatic events.[47]

Studies of emotion and behavior suggest that certain psychological attributes may contribute to competence and resilience when coping with extreme situations. These traits are likely to influence personal coping styles and other psychological resources that mediate between traumatic stress and psychopathology. Three such cognitive attributes are internal locus of control, the sense of coherence, and self-efficacy.[48] Locus of control refers to the degree to which an individual perceives that consequences arise from his own actions, efforts, or characteristics as opposed to forces beyond his control, for example fate, luck, chance, powerful others, or the unpredictable. Persons with a strong sense of external control tend to see little if any relationship between their own actions and subsequent events. By contrast, "internals" believe that some control lies within themselves. The sense of coherence refers to an individual's perception of the internal and the external environments as predictable. Persons with a strong sense of coherence view the world as comprehensible, manageable, and meaningful. They believe in working through challenging situations and that things will work out as well as can reasonably be expected. A related trait, namely self-efficacy, refers to an individual's sense of personal ability to perform tasks or to cope with new or challenging situations. Together, internal control and a strong sense of coherence and self-efficacy strengthen the coping response by steering an individual toward behaviors that reinstate balance, or homeostasis, in cognitive and emotional functioning.

Those traumatized by extreme circumstances perceive the immediate environment in a confused way: the familiar appears less familiar and their sense of personal security is challenged. As neighborhoods and pathways vanish, their spatial perception becomes distorted: the loss of the security provided by familiar settings is translated into a loss of the ability to gauge depth, distance, and orientation. Common to survivors of involuntary resettlement, disaster, and other dislocations is a paradoxical reaction: denial that the event, such as the aftershock of an earthquake or the prospect of further displacement, will recur, even when presented with evidence of its likelihood. The resulting anxiety produces a form of cognitive dissonance in which persons find themselves doing things that do not fit with what they know to be the case.[49] Those who have experienced repeated critical events, for example, appear to be less able to risk attachment to a place or locale—home, workplace, or community. They tend to be less willing to develop cohesive personal relationships, and less able to formulate a clear, purposive view of the future.

ADAPTIVE LEARNING AND HUMAN SURVIVAL

Cultural processes, such as norms, values, and expectations, operate as precedents to guide human adaptation, notably the crisis response. Culture forms part of a milieu, or adaptive nexus, in which humans learn to cope by taking these precedents into account.[50] It acts as a collective memory for human groups to store and retrieve knowledge to model future events.[51] Adaptive behavior, or strategic coping, requires the anticipation of outcomes, using foresight and intentionality as cognitive potentials. In this sense, culture is a form of anticipatory behavior specific to humans, for much of our time is spent reorganizing the world to resist randomness or entropy.[52] Humans are goal directed and self-organizing systems that adapt new and old information to anticipate outcomes.[53] The capacity for *internal* adaptation is seen in coping, a short-term process of stress reduction through which individual organisms respond to fluctuations in the environment.[54] We also have the capacity to relate with the environment through image making. This form of *external* adaptation rests on the ability to symbolically represent the physical world as a cognitive map.[55] A cultural worldview reflects the shared cognitive categories of people who experience, and work within, a *local* set of spatial and temporal arrangements. Culture unifies the cognitive maps of different individuals within a locale by imposing "consistency among meanings" as a paradigm for working with the energetic world. By unifying the mental and the energetic in a symbolic system, a local society provides the means to reproduce its own self-organization.[56]

Living systems theory posits an articulation between humans and the global environment.[57] This model assumes that human technical and social spheres are mediated by individual and collective behavior, which is influenced at the biosocial level by physiological and metabolic processes. A living system depends upon subsystem components for its survival, such as information channels, memory, decision centers, motor outputs, and reproductive elements. All living systems, from cells to Earth, rely on matter, energy, and information flows. Anthropological holism and living systems theory regard purposive behavior, or culture, as an open system interacting with the environment through positive feedback. The holistic approach views culture as developing in relation with the environmental niche, and social practices as adaptive responses to particular ecological pressures. Historical ecology regards landscape as a manifestation of this dialectical relationship between human action and natural systems over time.[58] Living systems theory similarly uses cognitive potentials to explain adaptation in crisis. The systems view holds that organizations and communities, like individuals, will need to draw upon competencies derived from adapting to past crises as sources of feedback. Moreover, how each system experiences a critical event and the emergent pattern of responses will influence the direction of change through later stages of its development.[59]

Using this framework, one may characterize three main evolutionary transitions in human history. Agriculture marked the achievement of long-range predictive control over the food supply through intensive land-use techniques. The Industrial Revolution liberated people from this direct symbiotic relationship to the land, but severed their local dependence upon the land itself. The second industrial revolution constituted the emergence of human systems capable of large-scale intervention into natural systems, exemplified by human population growth and greater control over the earth's resources. This includes subterranean exploitation of energy and metals; vertical expansion into the atmosphere and oceans for nitrogen, minerals, and food; and control over areas of the electromagnetic spectrum. This last transition brought with it the power to transform the planet into a "whole system."[60] The processes of control in the global system, that is, extraction, production, distribution, transportation, and communication, are regulated by diverse ideologies. Global pressures have required local communities to reinvent the symbolic and organizational elements of their cultures in the face of new technologies and ways of life.

At a different scale, local community, or locality, denotes both a physical space and a distinct sensory order where concentrations of people engage in complex networks of social relations.[61] Primary relationships of kinship, friendship, and neighborliness, based upon face-to-face interaction, are the most immediate forms of association. Less personal relationships, based upon transaction, are the secondary modes of activity. A loose social organization derives from this multiplicity of contexts, events, and situations. Localities retain their flexible and somewhat amorphous structure because they can accommodate diverse social relationships within their boundaries and control the outcomes of most external intrusions. As highly organized segments of a population, localities support a social structure where individuals take on multiple roles within many cross-cutting networks. Within this configuration, social resources are viewed as potentials and as rights accrued by virtue of a person's status and role within each network. A locality maintains internal control through everyday routines and rituals, and through the networks that govern interpersonal behavior. Local power resides in the internal control of both human and material resources, and tends to limit the encroachment of external institutions, such as state or corporate bureaucracies.

The concept of sustainable development links the transfer of capital, labor, and natural resources within the global economic system.[62] Through a comparative framework that situates the historical role of the environment within capitalist development, resource exploitation and structural underdevelopment in the Southern Hemisphere can be seen as a consequence of environmental change in the industrialized Northern Hemisphere. With global change, localities throughout the world have undergone ecological crises, such as resource depletion, changes in land use, and biodiversity loss. These conditions are frequently accompanied by anthropogenic hazards, such as climate change, greenhouse warming, and emerging epidemic diseases, as well as chaotic environmental episodes such as drought, flooding, and violent storms. Despite efforts to maintain internal control of their economies, many localities become enmeshed in global markets and, as a result, experience increased pressures to change their styles of work and land tenure practices, and to specialize in order to remain competitive. Local communities not only become dependent upon external market forces, but are also bound by the policies of development programs designed to introduce technological change. In the past, localities would call upon culture to guide decisions about resource use, as in the case of sustained yield resource management. Locally determined strategies were directed to sustaining an internal equilibrium and were not motivated by demands from outside the local system.[63] Delocalization results when people become less affected with local concerns, especially in decisions about the management of common resources, and in their stance toward their neighbors who have been marginalized by consequences of global change. Through its encounter with these displacements, the new ecological anthropology has come to view the community as embedded within larger systems at the regional, national, and international levels, and to study the impact of a multitiered and globalizing world on the locality.[64] Within political ecology, environmental justice research has addressed the ways poor communities organize to confront disproportionate, high, and adverse environmental exposure.[65] The global economy has led to the transformation of cities such as New York, London, Tokyo, Sydney, Toronto, Miami, and Los Angeles as "transnational market spaces," more oriented to world markets than to their national economies.[66] Global cities are strategic places in the world

economy where the centralized control and management operations required
to direct a geographically dispersed array of economic activities are located.
As the hubs of global financial markets, these cities are places where there is
considerable foreign direct investment and where the broader social structure
has grown more international. Their workforces deliver highly specialized
services, including finance, telecommunications, and advertising, to diverse
linguistic and cultural communities worldwide. The emergence of globally
oriented service industries within these cities, together with the decline of
mass production, has created new inequalities and economic polarization.
There is a growing earnings disparity between those within the city linked to
the international economy and those who remain marginal to it. There is also
a disparity in consumption patterns between those employed in the major
growth sectors that have high-paying jobs and low-wage workers employed
by small, low-cost service operations. Economic globalization has contributed to a "new geography of centrality and marginality" that elevates certain localities as central to the international economy, while rendering others
marginal to the production and distribution of global capital. The turn from
the local toward the global resulted in the population movements and dislocations that characterize a crisis, referred to as "late capitalism" or "post-
Fordism," first in the developed Northern Hemisphere, and more recently in
the rapidly developing Southern Hemisphere.

An explanatory model for how local societies use positive feedback when
the system goes out of control is the revitalization movement.[67] In its attempt
to maintain equilibrium, a locality spends considerable energy in socializing
its members for roles in community networks. One product of social learning
is an individual's mazeway—the set of cognitive maps containing images of
self and world, as well as the adaptive strategies for satisfying personal goals.
The mazeway functions to alleviate and reduce stress because constituents
possess a practical knowledge of the cultural regularities within their total perceptual field. When this self-image fails to conform to the real system, perhaps
because of some external pressure, such as an ecological, socioeconomic, or
political crisis, many will experience a form of cognitive dissonance. Mazeway disintegration, or the perception of disorganization and one's displacement from the familiar environment, occurs during periods of collective
stress when the social fabric is disrupted.[68] To cope with this phenomenon,
some groups may attempt to take control of a locality in the name of tradition.
Others may join together in a progressive revitalization movement with the
goal of finding a solution to maintain a steady state, often by uniting all factions around an ideal holding the promise of a new social equilibrium. Should
the movement succeed, and a reframed mazeway emerge to accommodate
both traditional and progressive elements of the locality, most constituents

would then begin to reorganize their lives within the changed environment. However, without a successful crisis response to facilitate social reorganization, a locality faces extinction through breakdown from within, rendering it vulnerable to external control.[69]

Anthropology, ethology, and neuroscience view ritualization, embedded in a revitalization movement, as adaptive behavior in its ability to encode cultural knowledge.[70] Ritual symbols prompt social action because their referents call up polarities between physiological phenomena and normative values, such as reciprocity, respect, generosity, and kindness.[71] Social dramas, or "dramas of living" in Kenneth Burke's words, are recurrent forms of social experience that include both life crises (marriage, puberty, death) and political crises.[72] Attendant with these crises is the experience of liminality—a gestation process or transitional state analogous to the "subjunctive mood" of culture, such as fantasy, hypothesis, and conjecture. Individuals will engage in performance behavior, such as singing, chanting, playing music, dancing, dressing up, feasting, drinking alcohol, and using hallucinogens, to "live through" this passage from a structural past to a structural future. Ritual—as a performance—uses these multiple sensory domains to dramatize the liminal state in order to provoke an exchange between the physiological and cultural poles, and to restore a sense of *communitas* among participants, especially in the wake of urban transformation, socioeconomic dislocation, and cultural reorientation.

NETWORKS AND REORIENTATION

The dislocations caused by the extreme situations of our time have spawned a new pattern of psychological survival, which Robert Jay Lifton calls "the protean self."[73] Like Proteus in Greek mythology, this persona is capable of taking on multiple roles to survive the restless flux of late modernity. Those who construct a protean self achieve a sense of coherence despite the fragmentation and chaos of modern life. Paradoxically, the protean self maintains a coherent core in a fragmentary, or piecemeal, fashion. Ideas and actions are pragmatically selected and discarded to meet specific challenges. Any sense of coherence and self-authenticity that emerges from this struggle is fragile and impermanent. Individuals often mobilize their personal networks to reorient their lives after a major crisis. Their networks become pathways to care and offer support, stress reduction, and even resistance to disease. Personal communities of kin, close friends, and others can bolster an individual's morale or reestablish a sense of coherence that is significantly undermined by a crisis. It often requires a person to reinstate trust in the consistency of the environment. As the structures that mediate the individual and the outside world, personal networks are central to this task. They provide an individual with incentives for initiating social action. Emotional aid and material resources often flow through the networks of those dislocated from their familiar environments. Informal social resources, such as mutual aid organizations, cooperatives, and other forms of voluntary association, promote strategies for survival amid the fragmentation that accompanies dislocation.[74] Through them, individuals become cognizant of alternative forms of problem solving, help seeking, and negotiating after crises. Those who embrace these resources gain support and mutual aid, but also realize an expressive dimension through their participation. The forms of association mobilized during a crisis affect survivors' lives since their sense of belonging reduces the isolation that results from dislocation, and the emergent ties help survivors to restore their psychological and social equilibrium. Through facing a crisis and coping with peers in voluntary efforts, they learn pragmatic strategies of self-construction. These social milieus, often as mutable or protean as their constituencies, cultivate a collective strength and a personal identity capable of surviving the multiple crises of late modernity. This form of engagement, called "life politics," concerns issues such as environmental risks, nuclear power, food security, and reproductive technologies, where self-identity is influenced by globalizing processes.[75]

Networks of civil engagement—mutual aid organizations and other small-scale voluntary associations—were essential to community life in the face of myriad dislocations that marked the onset of modernity in the United States and elsewhere.[76] Robert Putnam and his associates have demonstrated, through extensive study of the role of civic traditions in the development of contemporary Italian regional governments, that "the denser such networks in a community, the more likely that its citizens will be able to cooperate for mutual benefit."[77] Since the medieval period, civic legacies in the towns of northern and central Italy were built upon institutions that supported social solidarity, such as voluntary associations and mutual aid societies. These networks of civic engagement were crucial to the management of collective life in Italian communal republics. The roots of civic community were thus embedded in a pattern of associational life that traced its ancestry to earlier periods of civic inventiveness. This was the situation in nineteenth-century Italy, where local communities, governed for centuries by civic republicanism, were obliged to develop new forms of collective action for mutual benefit to confront the risks of a rapidly changing social order. In facing the dislocations associated with modernity, localities throughout Italy relied on their civic traditions to guide them in forging a new sense of civic commitment. The emergent "modern" form of civic community, built upon cooperative organizations, cultural associations, and other vehicles for civic mobilization created amid the turmoil of nineteenth-century life, was largely responsible for the success of the regional governments established in northern and central Italy during the 1970s.

As they did when their cultural fabrics were rapidly transformed by technological and social advances associated with nation building and industrialization a century ago, contemporary Italian localities called upon their civic traditions to direct them in the task of reshaping civic culture in the face of regionalization. In these regional governance efforts, cities and their surrounding rural areas framed joint strategies that both stabilized urban fresh food supplies and created clusters of rural industries that extended from the factory to cottage levels. Similar strategies have been adopted in France and Holland, as well as by the European Union. By comparison, in the United States, massive transformations of civic life during the 1960s and 1970s have brought about considerably different outcomes. For one thing, there has been a tendency to polarize urban areas from rural areas, strengthening transnational market spaces at the expense of sustainable communities and local food networks. Further, the American civic universe has since been characterized by national advocacy organizations that are professionally dominated and far less dependent upon voluntary participation than were the local membership organizations of previous eras.[78] As a result, the public sphere where people actively engage in politics and policy making has changed.[79] In the United States and elsewhere in the North, the move away from local associations to global advocacy organizations has had an impact on local communities worldwide. Until recently, these localities have used cultural dynamics similar to the ones Putnam describes to survive the transition to urban, industrial life in the nineteenth and twentieth centuries, and to confront the turbulence of globalization in our own times. The historical and contemporary cases that comprise the rest of the book explore the ways residents of local communities have reinvented their civic cultures, blending traditional sentiments with fully modern sensibilities, to sustain both local networks and the sense of civic identity amid large-scale dislocations that have led many to characterize the twentieth century, and perhaps also the twenty-first, as the "century of permanent crisis."[80]

NOTES

1. Andrew Kirby, ed., *Nothing to Fear: Risks and Hazards in American Society* (Tucson: University of Arizona Press, 1990); Ulrich Beck, *Risk Society: Towards a New Modernity* (Thousand Oaks, CA: Sage Publications, 1992); Scott Lash, Bronislaw

Szerszynski, and Brian Wynne, eds., *Risk, Environment, Modernity: Towards a New Ecology* (Thousand Oaks, CA: Sage Publications, 1996).

2. Richard S. Weinstein, "The First American City," in *The City: Los Angeles and Urban Theory at the End of the Twentieth Century*, edited by Allen J. Scott and Edward W. Soja, 22–46 (Berkeley: University of California Press, 1997), 30–31.

3. Reyner Banham, *Los Angeles: The Architecture of the Four Ecologies* (New York: Penguin, 1971).

4. Joel A. Tarr and Gabriel Dupuy, eds., *Technology and the Rise of the Networked City in Europe and America* (Philadelphia: Temple University Press, 1988), xiii–xvi.

5. Ross Miller, *American Apocalypse: The Great Fire and the Myth of Chicago* (Chicago: University of Chicago Press, 1990), 136.

6. William Cronon, *Nature's Metropolis: Chicago and the Great West* (New York: Norton, 1991); Carl Smith, *Urban Disorder and the Shape of Belief: The Great Chicago Fire, the Haymarket Bomb, and the Model Town of Pullman* (Chicago: University of Chicago Press, 1994); Donald L. Miller, *City of the Future: The Epic of Chicago and the Making of America* (New York: Simon & Schuster, 1996).

7. Miller, *American Apocalypse*, 136; William H. Jordy, *American Buildings and their Architects: Progressive and Academic Ideals at the Turn of the Twentieth Century* (Garden City, NY: Doubleday, 1976), 8; William H. Wilson, *The City Beautiful Movement* (Baltimore: Johns Hopkins University Press, 1989).

8. Josef W. Konvitz, *The Urban Millennium: The City-Building Process from the Early Middle Ages to the Present* (Carbondale: Southern Illinois University Press, 1985), 133–34.

9. Eric H. Monkkonen, *America Becomes Urban: The Development of Cities and Towns, 1780–1980* (Berkeley: University of California Press, 1988), 218.

10. Michael H. Ebner and Eugene M. Tobin, eds., *The Age of Urban Reform: New Perspectives on the Progressive Era* (Port Washington, NY: Kennikat Press, 1977), 8.

11. Konvitz, *The Urban Millennium*, 133.

12. Konvitz, *The Urban Millennium*, 144–45.

13. Thomas Bender, "The Cultures of Intellectual Life: The City and the Professions," in *Intellect and Public Life: Essays on the Social History of Academic Intellectuals in the United States*, 3–15 (Baltimore: Johns Hopkins University Press, 1993), 6.

14. Thomas Bender, "The Erosion of Public Culture: Cities, Discourses, and Professional Disciplines," in *Intellect and Public Life: Essays on the Social History of Academic Intellectuals in the United States*, 30–46 (Baltimore: Johns Hopkins University Press, 1993), 33.

15. Bender, "The Cultures of Intellectual Life," 8.

16. Bender, "The Erosion of Public Culture," 33–34.

17. Richard Sennett, *Flesh and Stone: The Body and the City in Western Civilization* (New York: W.W. Norton, 1994), 322–23.

18. Sennett, *Flesh and Stone*, 323.

19. Bender, "The Erosion of Public Culture," 43.

20. Bender, "The Cultures of Intellectual Life," 9.

21. Bender,"The Cultures of Intellectual Life," 10.

22. C. Wright Mills, "Graduate Schools and Professionalization," in *Sociology and Pragmatism: The Higher Learning in America*, edited by Irving Louis Horowitz (New York: Oxford University Press, 1964), 67–83; for early twentieth-century intellectuals seeking community outside of academia, see Steven Biel, *Independent Intellectuals in the United States: 1910–1945* (New York: New York University Press, 1992).

23. Peter F. Drucker, *Post-Capitalist Society* (New York: Harper Collins, 1993).

24. Lewis Mumford, *The Brown Decades* (New York: Dover, 1971); Richard D. Brown, "Modernization: A Victorian Climax," in *Victorian America*, edited by Daniel Walker Howe (Philadelphia: University of Pennsylvania Press, 1976), 29–44; Alan Trachtenberg, *The Incorporation of America: Culture and Society in the Gilded Age* (New York: Hill and Wang, 1982); Nell Irwin Painter, *Standing at Armageddon: The United States, 1877–1919* (New York: Norton, 1987); Thomas J. Schlereth, *Victorian America: Transformations in Everyday Life, 1876–1915* (New York: Harper Collins, 1991); Samuel P. Hays, *The Response to Industrialism, 1885–1914*, 2nd ed. (Chicago: University of Chicago Press, 1994); Walter Licht, *Industrializing America: The Nineteenth Century* (Baltimore: Johns Hopkins University Press, 1995); Rebecca Edwards, *New Spirits: Americans in the Gilded Age, 1865–1905* (New York: Oxford University Press, 2006).

25. John R. Logan and Harvey L. Moloch, *Urban Fortunes: The Political Economy of Space* (Berkeley: University of California Press, 1987), 124–25.

26. "Intermittent catastrophes forced individuals and households to relocate. During famines, pogroms, land clearings, and depressions, people left their homes en masse. . . . Yet despite the gigantic scale and pathos of these forced movements, they are dwarfed by the steady flow into the city of short-distance migrants who chose both the time and place of their re-settlement. This undramatic relocation also fluctuated with the business cycle. Highest during times of depression and in periods of peak economic growth, levels of migration decreased with the return of better times and again with sagging levels of opportunity." Paul J. Hohenberg and Lynn Hollen Lees, *The Making of Urban Europe, 1000–1994* (Cambridge, MA: Harvard University Press, 1995), 252.

27. Georg Simmel, "The Stranger" (1908), in *Georg Simmel: On Individuality and Social Forms*, edited by Donald N. Levine (Chicago: University of Chicago Press, 1971), 143; Alfred Schutz, "The Stranger: An Essay in Social Psychology," *American Journal of Sociology* 49 (1944): 499–507; Donald N. Levine, "Simmel at a Distance: On the History and Systematics of the Sociology of the Stranger," in *Strangers in African Societies*, edited by William Shack and Elliott Skinner (Berkeley: University of California Press, 1979), 21–36; Lyn H. Lofland, *A World of Strangers: Order and Action in Urban Public Space* (Prospect Heights, IL: Waveland Press, 1983); Zygmunt Bauman, "Making and Unmaking of Strangers," *Thesis Eleven* 43 (1995): 1–16; Simonetta Tabboni, "The Stranger and Modernity: From Equality of Rights to Recognition of Difference," *Thesis Eleven* 43 (1995): 17–27.

28. "[T]he technologically displaced were hardly ever taken back into their former occupations. They shifted, first, from the originally dominant agrarian sector to the expanding sector of mining, manufacture, and construction, and within this sector

form the standard consumption and investment industries—textile and steel—to chemical and electro-technical production. The process culminated in the mass movement of workers into the labor-intensive part of the service sector, in particular into trade, finance, and professional and administrative services, both public and private." Adolph Lowe, *Has Freedom a Future?* (New York: Praeger, 1987), 97.

29. C. Wright Mills, *White Collar: The American Middle Classes* (New York: Oxford University Press, 1951); Richard Sennett, *Families against the City: Middle Class Homes of Industrial Chicago, 1872–1890* (Cambridge, MA: Harvard University Press, 1970).

30. Quoted in Harold. L Wilensky and Charles N. Lebeaux, *Industrial Society and Social Welfare: The Impact of Industrialization on the Supply and Organization of Social Welfare Services in the United States* (New York: Russell Sage Foundation, 1958), 141, in Richard M. Titmuss, *The Gift Relationship: From Human Blood to Social Policy* (New York: Pantheon, 1971), 216.

31. Robert Park, "The City: Suggestions for the Investigation of Human Behavior in the City Environment," *The American Journal of Sociology* 20 (1915): 584. Quoted in Paul Boyer, *Urban Masses and Moral Order in America, 1820–1920* (Cambridge, MA: Harvard University Press), 286; see also Maurice R. Stein, "Robert Park and Urbanization in Chicago," in *The Eclipse of Community: An Interpretation of American Studies*, 13–46 (Princeton, NJ: Princeton University Press, 1960).

32. Sam Bass Warner Jr., *The Urban Wilderness: A History of the American City*, 2nd ed. (Berkeley: University of California Press, 1995), 108–9.

33. Jules Romains, *The Sixth of October*, trans. Warre B. Wells, vol. 1, *Men of Good Will* (New York: Alfred A. Knopf, 1933), 161–62; quoted in Konvitz, *The Urban Millennium*, 141–42.

34. George W. Stocking, "The Ethnographic Sensibility of the 1920s and the Dualism of the Anthropological Tradition," in *Romantic Motives: Essays on Anthropological Sensibility*, edited by George W. Stocking (Madison: University of Wisconsin Press, 1989), 229–335; for other analyses of ethnographic "modernism," see: Susan Hegeman, *Patterns for Americans: Modernism and the Concept of Culture* (Princeton, NJ: Princeton University Press, 1999); Marc Manganaro, *Culture, 1922: The Emergence of a Concept* (Princeton, NJ: Princeton University Press, 2002).

35. Michael Ignatieff, *The Needs of Strangers* (New York: Viking, 1985), 141.

36. Georg Simmel, "The Metropolis and Mental Life," (1903), in *Georg Simmel: On Individuality and Social Forms*, edited by Donald N. Levine (Chicago: University of Chicago Press, 1971), 324–39.

37. Max Gluckman, "Anthropological Problems Arising from the African Industrial Revolution," in *Social Change in Modern Africa*, edited by Aidan Southall (London: Oxford University Press, 1961), 67–82; J. Clyde Mitchell, *Cities, Society, and Social Perception: A Central African Perspective* (Oxford: Oxford University Press, 1987); T. M. S. Evans and Don Handelman, *The Manchester School: Practice and Ethnographic Praxis in Anthropology* (New York: Berghahn Books, 2006).

38. Ulf Hannerz, "Thinking with Networks," in *Exploring the City: Inquiries Toward an Urban Anthropology*, (New York: Columbia University Press, 1980), 163–201.

39. Philip Mayer, *Townsmen or Tribesmen* (London: Oxford University Press, 1971).

40. Robert K. Merton, "Patterns of Influence: A Study of Interpersonal Influence and of Communications Behavior in a Local Community," in *Communications Research 1948–1949*, edited by Paul F. Lazersfeld and Frank N. Stanton (New York: Harper and Row, 1949), reprinted in *New Perspectives on the American Community*, 3rd ed., edited by Roland L. Warren (Chicago: Rand McNally, 1977), 277–90.

41. Elizabeth Bott, *Family and Social Network: Roles, Norms, and External Relationships in Ordinary Urban Families*, 2nd ed. (New York: Free Press, 1971).

42. Michael Young and Peter Willmott, *Family and Kinship in East London* (Harmondsworth, UK: Penguin, 1957), 187.

43. Barry Wellman, Peter J. Carrington, and Alan Hall, "Networks as Personal Communities," in *Social Structures: A Network Approach*, edited by Barry Wellman and S. D. Berkowitz (Cambridge: Cambridge University Press, 1988), 130–84.

44. Yi-Fu Tuan, *Space and Place* (Minneapolis: University of Minnesota Press, 1977); Bryan S. Turner, *The Body and Society: Explorations in Social Theory*, 3rd ed. (London: Sage, 2008); John O'Neill, *The Communicative Body* (Evanston, IL: Northwestern University Press, 1989); David Seamon and Robert Mugerauer, eds., *Dwelling, Place and Environment* (New York: Columbia University Press, 1989); Chris Shilling, *The Body and Social Theory*, 2nd ed. (London: Sage, 2003).

45. John Bowlby, *A Secure Base* (New York: Basic Books, 1988); Peter Marris, *Loss and Change* (London: Routledge, 1974); Colin M. Parkes and Joan Stevenson-Hinde, eds., *The Place of Attachment in Human Behavior* (New York: Basic Books, 1982).

46. Marc Fried, "Grieving for a Lost Home," in *The Urban Condition: People and Policy in the Metropolis*, edited by Leonard J. Duhl (New York: Basic Books, 1963), 156.

47. Charles R. Figley, ed., *Trauma and Its Wake*, vol. 1, *The Study and Treatment of Post-Traumatic Stress Disorder* (New York: Routledge, 1985); Bessel A. van der Kolk, "The Body Keeps the Score: Memory and the Evolving Psychobiology of Post-traumatic Stress," *Harvard Review of Psychiatry* 1 (1994): 253–65; John Briere, *Psychological Assessment of Adult Posttraumatic Stress States: Phenomenology, Diagnosis, and Measurement*, 2nd ed. (Washington, DC: American Psychological Association, 2004).

48. Aaron Antonovsky, *Health, Stress and Coping* (San Francisco: Jossey-Bass, 1979); Aaron Antonovsky, "The Sense of Coherence as a Determinant of Health," in *Behavioral Health*, edited by Joseph D. Matarazzo, Sharlene M. Weiss, J. Alan Herd, Neal E. Miller, and Stephen M. Weiss (New York: Wiley, 1984), 114–29; Albert Bandura, "Self-Efficacy Mechanism in Human Agency," *American Psychologist* 37 (1982): 122–47; Albert Bandura, *Social Foundations of Thought and Action* (Englewood Cliffs, NJ: Prentice-Hall, 1986); Richard R. Lau, "Beliefs about Control and Health Behavior," in *Health Behavior: Emerging Research Perspectives*, edited by David S. Gochman (New York, Plenum, 1988).

49. Leon Festinger, *A Theory of Cognitive Dissonance* (Stanford, CA: Stanford University Press, 1957).

50. John W. Bennett, *Human Ecology as Human Behavior* (New Brunswick, NJ: Transaction Books, 1995), 36.

51. Richard Newbold Adams, *The Eighth Day: Social Evolution as the Self-Organization of Society* (Austin: University of Texas Press, 1988), 71.

52. Bennett, *Human Ecology as Human Behavior*, 25–26.

53. Emilio F. Moran, *Human Adaptability: An Introduction to Ecological Anthropology* (Boulder, CO: Westview Press, 1982), 98.

54. Alexander Alland, *Adaptation in Cultural Evolution: An Approach to Medical Anthropology* (New York: Columbia University Press, 1970), 40–41.

55. Bennett, *Human Ecology as Human Behavior*, 32.

56. Adams, *The Eighth Day*, 81–82, 90.

57. James Grier Miller, *Living Systems* (New York: McGraw-Hill, 1978).

58. Carole L. Crumley, "Historical Ecology: A Multidimensional Ecological Orientation," in *Historical Ecology: Cultural Knowledge and Changing Landscapes*, edited by Carole L. Crumley (Santa Fe, NM: School of American Research Press, 1994), 1–16.

59. Alf Hornborg and Carole L. Crumley, eds., *The World System and the Earth System: Global Socioenvironmental Change and Sustainability Since the Neolithic* (Walnut Creek, CA: Left Coast Press, 2007).

60. John W. Bennett, *The Ecological Transition: Cultural Anthropology and Human Adaptation* (New York: Pergamon, 1976), 10.

61. Anthony Leeds, "Locality Power in Relation to Supralocal Power Institutions," in *Urban Anthropology: Cross-Cultural Studies of Urbanization*, edited by Aidan Southall (New York: Oxford University Press, 1973), 15–41.

62. Michael Redclift, *Sustainable Development: Exploring the Contradictions* (London and New York: Routledge, 1987).

63. Bennett, *The Ecological Transition*.

64. George Marcus, "Ethnography in/of the World System: The Emergence of Multi-Sited Ethnography," *Annual Review of Anthropology* 24 (1995): 95–117; Akhil Gupta and James Ferguson, eds., *Anthropological Locations: Boundaries and Grounds of a Field Science* (Berkeley: University of California Press, 1997); Conrad P. Kottak, "The New Ecological Anthropology," *American Anthropologist* 101 (1999): 22–35; Michael Burawoy, Joseph A. Blum, Sheba George, Zsuzsa Gille, Teresa Gowan, Lynne Haney, Maren Klawiter, Steven H. Lopez, Seán Ó Riain, and Millie Thayer, *Global Ethnography: Forces, Connections, and Imaginations in a Postmodern World* (Berkeley: University of California Press, 2000).

65. Manuel Pastor, *Building Social Capital to Protect Natural Capital: The Quest for Environmental Justice*, Political Economy Research Institute, Working Papers Series Number 11 (Amherst: University of Massachusetts, 2001); Krista Harper and S. Ravi Rajan, *International Environmental Justice: Building the Natural Assets of the World's Poor*, Political Economy Research Institute, International Natural Assets Conference Paper Series 12 (Amherst: University of Massachusetts, 2002).

66. Saskia Sassen, *Cities in a World Economy*, 2nd ed. (Thousand Oaks, CA: Pine Forge Press, 2000).

67. Anthony F. C. Wallace, "Revitalization Movements," *American Anthropologist* 58 (1956): 264–81.

68. Anthony F. C. Wallace, "Mazeway Disintegration: The Individual's Perception of Socio-Cultural Disorganization," *Human Organization* 16 (1957): 23–27; Anthony F. C. Wallace, "Mazeway Resynthesis: A Biocultural Theory of Religious Inspiration," *Transactions of the New York Academy of Sciences* 18 (1956): 626–38.

69. Moran, *Human Adaptability*, 10–11.

70. Charles D. Laughlin, John McManus, and Eugene G. d'Aquili, *Brain, Symbol, and Experience: Towards a Neurophenomenology of Human Consciousness* (New York: Columbia University Press, 1993); Roy Rappaport, *Religion and Ritual in the Making of Humanity* (Cambridge: Cambridge University Press, 1999).

71. Victor Turner, *The Ritual Process* (Chicago: Aldine, 1969).

72. Kenneth Burke, *Permanence and Change: An Anatomy of Purpose*, 2nd ed. (Indianapolis: Bobbs-Merrill, 1965); Kenneth Burke, *The Philosophy of Literary Form: Studies in Symbolic Action*, 3rd ed. (Berkeley: University of California Press, 1973).

73. Robert J. Lifton, *The Protean Self: Human Resilience in an Age of Fragmentation* (New York: Basic Books, 1993).

74. Claude S. Fischer, *To Dwell among Friends: Personal Networks in Town and City* (Chicago: University of Chicago Press, 1982); Benjamin Gottlieb, ed., *Social Networks and Social Support* (Beverly Hills, CA: Sage, 1981).

75. Anthony Giddens, *Modernity and Self-Identity: Self and Society in the Late Modern Age* (Stanford, CA: Stanford University Press, 1991).

76. Robert D. Putnam, "Bowling Alone: America's Declining Social Capital," *Journal of Democracy* 6 (1995): 67.

77. Robert D. Putnam, *Making Democracy Work: Civic Traditions in Modern Italy* (Princeton, NJ: Princeton University Press, 1993), 173; see also Douglas R. Holmes, *Cultural Disenchantments: Worker Peasantries in Northeast Italy* (Princeton, NJ: Princeton University Press, 1989).

78. Theda Skocpol, *Diminished Democracy: From Membership to Management in American Civil Life* (Norman: University of Oklahoma Press, 2003).

79. Craig Calhoun, ed., *Habermas and the Public Sphere* (Cambridge, MA: MIT Press, 1992).

80. James O'Connor, *The Meaning of Crisis: A Theoretical Introduction* (Oxford: Basil Blackwell, 1987), 14.

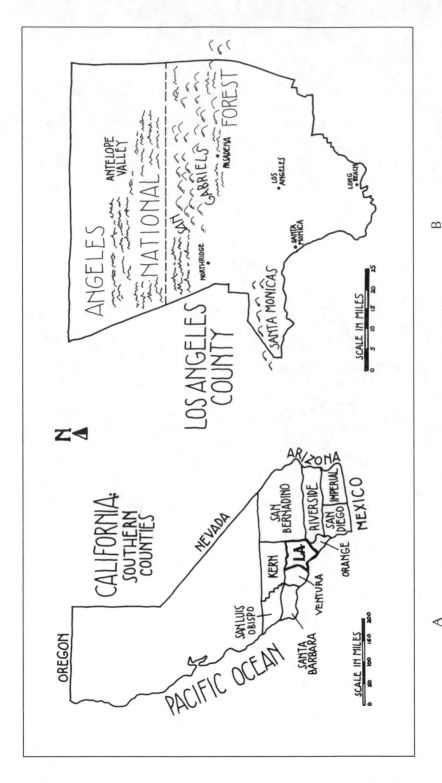

Map 1: (A) The State of California, with southern counties identified. (B) The entirety of Los Angeles County, California; the region below the dashed line comprises the area detailed in Map 2.

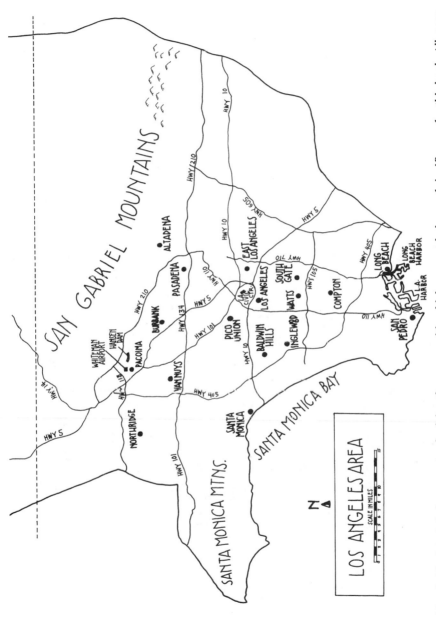

Map 2: The Los Angeles area, emphasizing the communities, highways, and places of significance for this book. All maps were assembled by Barbara Yablon Maida, using information in the public domain.

Chapter Two

Global Economy and Local Dilemma

The second industrial revolution helped to define the technological and organizational networks of American cities that were rapidly becoming transformed into mass production regions during the late nineteenth and early twentieth centuries. Diverse economic and social crises and forms of civic culture emerged with the technological changes brought about, especially with the mass production of the automobile, arguably the most dynamic "engine of change" in twentieth-century economic life. For from the 1920s onward, machine-made goods, like the automobile, began to replace land as the basis of both personal identity and economic security. The production and distribution of automobiles and other manufactured goods would also help define the self-images of cities, regions, even the nation, as its citizens ventured into global markets and met with international conflict.

Automobiles and airplanes were the "heralds of modernity" during the early twentieth century.[1] The application of the internal combustion engine to motor transport and powered flight transformed the industrial economy and the landscape. The rapid spread of the technology revolutionized transportation, production techniques, and warfare in Europe and America. New industries that supported motorized transport and flight, including petrochemicals, rubber, steel, and electrical goods, propelled the growth of entire production regions in the United States and abroad. Industrial cities around the Great Lakes and later in the Far West grew largely as a result of these technologies. These cities were not only pivotal to the manufacturing process, but their freeways and airports attested to the impact of motorization on urban economies and environments. These production regions were comprised of industries with significant economies of "scale and scope" that enabled them to lead the way to multiunit, hierarchical, managerial enterprise.[2]

As "first-movers" in the production and distribution of mass-produced manufactured goods, these corporations practiced a "three-pronged investment" strategy that embodied the modern industrial enterprise. These companies invested in production facilities large enough to exploit a technology's economies of scale and scope. They also built a national and international marketing network, so that the volume of sales would keep pace with production. Their key investment was management—a hierarchy of full-time salaried executives essential to large-scale industrial enterprise.[3] Companies needed to recruit and train managers to administer facilities and personnel, but also to monitor and coordinate production and distribution and to plan and allocate resources for future use. The organizational revolution that would eventually transform all nineteenth-century institutions began in the large corporations. The new managerial elites in these companies were actually information specialists, trained in both the technology and the organization of technical work.

MOTORIZATION AND MODERNITY

By the early 1900s, improved machine tools, a "three-pronged investment strategy," and Frederick Taylor's Scientific Management had revolutionized production techniques. In the 1880s and 1890s, Taylor began to observe skilled workers to determine the precise tasks that made up their jobs. By reducing a job to its elementary operations, Taylor was able to establish the minimum time necessary for workers to complete their jobs. The most efficient workers were rewarded with pay increases, and those that fell behind were let go. Taylor's system paved the way for the rational management and planning necessary for mass-producing industrial goods. Scientific managers and engineers controlled production techniques from above, while workers carried out tasks in compliance with the predetermined work process. The workers' technical understanding of the work process was limited, as their sole function was to carry out certain specialized tasks in the overall production routine.

In 1910, the Ford Motor Company instituted a new system of continuous assembly to produce automobiles at its Highland Park, Michigan, plant. The plant employed about 14,000 workers to produce the low-priced Model T. At first, it took workers twelve hours and twenty-eight minutes to produce an automobile chassis. Ford's mass production techniques used continuously moving conveyors, specialized labor tasks, and rigorous coordination to dramatically increase output of its standardized automobile. As the product moved along the line, the worker experienced few surprises and fewer challenges in this preordained operation. By 1914, the Highland Park plant turned out 250,000 autos a year, with workers taking only one hour and thirty-three minutes to produce the chassis. During World War I, Ford built the giant River Rouge complex, with a steel mill, power plant, railroad, port, and a foundry, that would eventually employ over 75,000 workers. By 1921, Ford's company controlled 55 percent of the automobile market. Its production methods, adopted by numerous other manufacturers, were largely responsible for the corporate growth and higher living standards that gave rise to the mass culture of 1920s America.

Fordism was the term used in the 1920s to describe the mass production techniques used to manufacture consumer goods. The key to Fordist production was standardization. Ford originally produced only the black Model T. Building one model meant lowered costs and increased control over every aspect of production. Ford engineers designed single-purpose machines that required relatively few skills to operate. Workers were trained to perform only a few simple operations, while the machinery determined the pace of work. Although the assembly line was an efficient production method, it was the chief source of worker discontent and alienation. Ford plants experienced high rates of worker turnover, and this proved costly to the company because new employees had to be trained before they could take their position on the line. To counter both turnover and the threat of unionization, Ford offered workers an unprecedented five dollars per day, and reduced their workday from nine to eight hours. As workers became progressively "de-skilled," turning over control of the productive process to the manufacturer, they were rewarded with greater purchasing power and more time to enjoy the mass-produced commodities of the machine age. In 1910, there were fewer than 500,000 automobiles and trucks on American roads. Ten years later, nearly 10 million were registered, and there were over 26 million motor vehicles by 1930. During these years, electrification of American homes created a market for mass-produced household goods, like the washing machine, the mechanical refrigerator, and the vacuum cleaner. The telephone and the radio also became indispensable to life in machine-age America. By 1925, there were 571 radio stations and 2.75 million receivers linking listeners to a network of mass entertainment and advertising. However, telephones and radios also contributed to greater individualism and separation between people in a period of considerable uprooting and resettlement. The phone and the radio were also relatively passive media, requiring only a simple movement to operate, like turning a switch or lifting a receiver. Like the assembly line, they seemed to render individuals more passive in their social relations, expectant of control from above, and dependent upon the guidance and direction of experts.

As large-scale bureaucracies organized more of their daily lives, ordinary Americans turned to advertising to help them decipher the transition. Advertising men were the "apostles of modernity" helping to create new fantasies about "the good life" made possible by industrialism.[4] Advertisers were not simply marketing commodities to workers and their families. They were selling the modern styles and ways of life that Americans were accustomed to seeing in the motion pictures and reading about in mass-circulation magazines. Not content with simply promoting a product's convenience or efficiency, commercial messages also contained moral prescriptions. Advertisers promoted their products as means to overcome personal insecurities and anxieties, and to help individuals reestablish a sense of control and of community lost in the shift toward modernity. Through radio broadcasts and print journalism, mass advertising was instrumental in promoting the consumption ethic that characterized modern America. It helped Americans to change ingrained spending habits of discipline, denial, and thrift, thus paving the way for a new mode of purchasing goods through consumer credit. Not long after this shift away from staid Victorian values, ad creators discovered that consumers were not merely interested in possessing a commodity. They were also willing to regard a product as a means to remake themselves in the image of the advertisement. Advertisers began addressing more sophisticated themes, including progress, individualism, and equality. Their messages were embedded in social vignettes that conveyed fully modern situations to a mass audience. Advertisements mirrored the ideals and aspirations of individuals caught up in the scientific advances and technological innovations of a rapidly changing society. Mass advertising was therapeutic in its emotive content, as ads offered advice and guidance in their messages. However, advertisers were not merely offering uplift and direction, but promoting a commodity in whose use was the promise of personal transformation. Advertising men, like scientific managers and engineers, were successful in controlling from above the most personal values surrounding human needs and the cognitive skills required to satisfy them.

AUTOMOBILE SUBURBS IN TWENTIES AMERICA

During the 1920s, the suburban areas of the nation's ninety-six largest cities grew twice as fast as the core communities. A number of reasons explain why suburbs surrounding older industrial cities chose to emphasize their distinctiveness by incorporating rather than consolidating their relationship with the city by agreeing to annexation. First, legislation passed that facilitated the incorporation of suburban communities, which could now offer residents vastly improved municipal services, including roadways, suburban trolley and train lines, electrical grids, water purification, sewage, wastewater, and garbage removal systems. Second, there was a 150 percent increase in automobile registration over the decade. The automobile was chiefly responsible for the suburban boom, but so were increased wages and lower housing prices.[5] The search for a better quality of life also led affluent, native-born Americans to suburbs far enough away from the foreign and disorderly elements in the city. The country was also strongly segregated along racial, ethnic, and class lines. Kenneth T. Jackson suggests class-based and nativist assumptions were at work in suburbanites' choice not to identify with the metropolis:

> Most important was the changing reality and image of the periphery and the center, particularly with regard to demographic characteristics. With the vast increase in immigration in the late nineteenth century, the core city increasingly became the home of penniless immigrants from Southern and Eastern Europe. And of course, in the early years of the twentieth century, increasing numbers of Southern blacks forsook their miserable tenant farms for a place where, they hoped, "a man was a man." In the view of most middle-class, white suburbanites, these newcomers were associated with and were often regarded as the cause of intemperance, vice, urban bossism, crime and radicalism of all kinds. And as the central city increasingly became the home of the disadvantaged, the number of white commuters rose markedly.[6]

Many early suburbanites were late Victorians and especially suspicious of the divergent lifestyles of "New Negro" communities in New York and Chicago, of Santa Fe's artist colonies, of Greenwich Village's bohemia, and of Los Angeles' amoral movie colony. Above all, it was the "New Women" who were writing, painting, and living their lives in these places that especially provoked them. For it appeared to many that these free-spirited, creative, and outspoken women were not amenable to the forms of control and moral order that had guided middle-class family and community life at least since the Civil War.

Hence, many other middle-class families organized themselves in reaction to these "disturbing" urban social trends. The new Eastern and Midwestern suburbs, such as Grosse Point near Detroit, Elmwood Park near Chicago, and Nassau County on Long Island, offered a respite from the machine-age Babylons that most Progressive Era cities had grown into. As early as 1868, Frederick Law Olmsted wrote in his plan for the town of Riverside outside of Chicago: "The essential qualification of a suburb is domesticity."[7] The suburb was a place of "quiet domestic seclusion" with most of the city's amenities, but without its danger, crowding, or squalor. Even their names, such as Garden City, Lake Forest, and Palos Verdes Estates, suggested a place closer to nature and far away from the city and its industrial blight. Kenneth T. Jackson points out that, in contrast to the numbered streets of most cities, developers named suburban roadways "after the bucolic and peaceful," suggestive of the countryside:

> [T]he enterprising entrepreneur simply combines acceptable word choices (rolling, fields, tall, lake, view, hills, timber, roaring, brook, green, farms, forest) into a three- or four-word combination. The new concoction is never followed by the word "street," but rather by lane, cove, road, way, fairway, or terrace. In California and other parts of the Southwest, Spanish names are substituted for English, but the intent is the same. History, circumstance, and geography are discarded in a conscious attempt to market houses according to the suburban ideal.[8]

The suburb, with its image of tranquility and order, became the perfect setting for middle-class families to continue their Victorian domestic arrangements. For the wife, the suburban household provided a comfortable environment to care for children and to attend to her domestic duties. As men's public lives in business and the professions became increasingly controlled from above, they attempted to remain in control of the one place that they could call their own, namely the suburban home.

Many native-born Americans moved even farther away from the Progressive cities to Far West boomtowns, such as Los Angeles, to establish a home that protected them from new immigrants, new women, and other "disorderly" city types. Few cities could compete with Los Angeles' vast selection of residential property. In the 1920s, the city had more than 3,200 subdivisions, which encompassed 250,000 houses. By the decade's end, 94 percent of the dwellings in the city were single-family houses, a feature essential to a late-Victorian, family-centered existence. Ironically, few other places in the nation exhibited the modernity of Los Angeles in the 1920s. The city relied extensively upon mass motorization for its pattern of settlement, its privatized commuting patterns, and its low-density "automobile suburbs." While the automobile has been credited with giving shape to Los Angeles' metropolitan sprawl, it was the fixed-rail transit system of the preautomobile era that first influenced the city's regional development. The freeways and boulevards to accommodate the automobile were initially built parallel to the railway, and would eventually replace the tracks of Huntington's Red Cars that moved Southern Californians across great distances between the city center and their homes in the suburbs.[9]

Since the 1890s, Americans had steadily migrated to Los Angeles with diverse sets of expectations. Some came for the climate that would improve their physical health. Anxious and tired from the demands of nation building, many native-born neurasthenics also sought emotional health and spiritual re-newal through Asian mind cures and quasi-religious Western sects. But many more harbored other fantasies, including the promise of sudden wealth from the region's oil boom; the experience of ranch life on a waning frontier; a "Mediterranean without Italians"; and the desire to become a part, if only vi-cariously, of Hollywood's image factory. Those seeking land, wealth, truth, and mental and bodily cure in Los Angeles encountered a city establishment that consciously upheld a Victorian ideal of civic life. City boosters, includ-ing real estate developer Harry Chandler and railroad magnate Henry E. Huntington, promoted Los Angeles as a clean, safe, and morally uplifting en-vironment, far from the industrial East and its foreign elements. In contrast to the pluralism of other Progressive Era cities, Los Angeles was homogeneous and remained so through ordinances and laws meant to ensure continuity of a communal and family ethos derivative of its late-Victorian origins. Around the time of World War I, "common interest" homeowners associations organ-ized with the goal of enforcing subdivision deed restrictions, ranging from de-sign homogeneity to the exclusion of nonwhite and frequently non-Christian groups. The industrial conversion of the Vernon Avenue–Central Avenue cor-ridor—the heart of black Los Angeles in the 1920s and 1930s—brought about overcrowding, forcing people to seek housing outside the "white wall" im-posed around their residential area. As middle-class black families sought to buy homes in neighboring communities, white homeowners formed protec-tive associations to uphold restrictive covenants, institute new racially speci-fied block restrictions, and harass potential nonwhite homebuyers.[10] While other big cities accommodated change, Los Angeles' elites still promoted "civic participation" and communal values derived from a synthesis of reli-gion, politics, work, and home.

FORDISM AND AMERICAN LABOR

Fordism had a profound impact on labor relations. The production system based upon long hours of routinized labor, with neither skill nor control vested in the worker, led to worker opposition and sharp resistance from unions.[11] There was high turnover at Ford's assembly plants, which relied heavily upon the continuous flows of immigrant labor and of rural migrants from the Deep South and Appalachia. In 1913, Ford needed to hire 52,000 workers to maintain a workforce of 13,600 on his assembly line. However, all the major industries confronted worker mobility, excessive absenteeism, al-coholism, and avoidable industrial accidents. To address these issues, large manufacturing companies adopted policies of "welfare capitalism," which sought to regularize employee relations from above. These included improvements in plant safety, pension plans, and medical benefits. Management planned ways to create harmony in the workplace through rationalized systems of industrial relations. Some companies operated savings and stock- and home-ownership plans for their workers. Many others experimented with employee representation in the wake of labor unrest during and after World War I. This plan allowed workers to elect representatives to address managers about working conditions and their grievances.

In 1900, big business leaders formed the National Civic Federation to champion the cause of improved labor relations. The body promoted "responsible" and conservative unions, welfare capitalism, and the establishment of workman's compensation laws. Small businessmen also organized during the Progressive Era to counter the threat of organized labor. Organizations like the National Association of Manufacturers (NAM) and the Citizens' Industrial Association openly criticized unions for their tactics. Unlike big businessmen, NAM members strongly opposed welfare capitalism practices that promoted harmony and refused to negotiate with the unions. They instead campaigned for "the open shop," which granted individual workers the freedom to choose whether or not to join a union. Despite these attempts to rationalize industrial relations, there was an upsurge of labor unrest from the turn of the century to the World War I years. The most dramatic strikes were organized by the Industrial Workers of the World (IWW) in the textile mills of Lawrence, Massachusetts, the silk mills of Paterson, New Jersey, and among the hard-rock miners of the Rocky Mountain region. The International Ladies' Garment Workers' Union (ILGWU) organized strikes among semi-skilled immigrant clothing workers in New York, Philadelphia, and Chicago. Labor militancy increased dramatically as Americans attempted a return to "normalcy" after World War I. As President Wilson left for Paris to attend to peacemaking, soldiers returned home to a massive flu pandemic, limited work opportunities, and inflated prices. With production falling to prewar levels, companies tried to roll back the gains that labor unions made in membership and through bargaining efforts. However, the labor movement pushed for wage increases in the face of price inflation. In 1919, there were 2,600 work stoppages, more strikes than in any year in the nation's history. While the president was negotiating the terms of the Versailles Treaty, 4 million workers challenged the legitimacy of both the government and corporate America. This "year of unrest" also witnessed twenty-five urban race riots and numerous lynchings of black people in the South. In the soft-coal regions of Appalachia, 400,000 United Mine Workers walked out of the coal mines. Police and federal troops were called out to maintain order in steel towns like Pittsburgh, Pennsylvania, and Gary, Indiana, after over 300,000 United Steel

Workers idled the mills. In Seattle, 35,000 shipyard workers and 25,000 members of other local unions staged a general strike that paralyzed the city for five days. Policemen in Boston went on strike, leaving the streets to mob violence. Following this action, policemen in thirty-seven American cities joined unions. By 1920, over 5 million American workers had become union members, doubling the size of organized labor before the war.

The 1920s were ushered in by a two-year recession that forced millions out of work for a time. Organized labor lost ground during this period, as companies rewarded workers with improved wages and benefits if they eschewed unions. Although workers lost ground collectively, individuals gained back their purchasing power as the recession ended. The 1920s economy eventually boomed and brought about a flourishing consumer society that increased the living standards of all Americans. Their average life expectancy increased, their nutrition improved and they achieved broad gains in education over the decade. By the decade's end, the nation's gross national product rose 39 percent, and both manufacturing output and corporate profits nearly doubled. In 1929, the U.S. Bureau of Labor Statistics studied the household economies of 100 typical Ford employees living in Detroit. The families earned an average of $1,694, with food expenditures taking up a third of their household budgets. Ford families ate a nutritious diet and lived in spacious housing with modern sanitation and conveniences. Many families owned their homes and most were purchasing modern consumer goods through credit buying plans. At the time of the Great Depression, most unskilled and semiskilled workers in mass-production industries were not organized in trade unions. In the 1930s, two major events signaled the breakthrough to mass production unionism. The Wagner Act of 1933 led to the establishment of the National Labor Relations Board. This legislative sanctioning of collective bargaining rights and the formation of the Congress of Industrial Organizations (CIO) paved the way for unionization of mass-production industries. With the outbreak of World War II, defense production boosted corporate profits, but also the number of union contracts. As a result, industrial workers saw vast improvements in their hourly wages and benefits, in seniority provisions, and in grievance procedures. Membership in the CIO more than doubled between 1940 and 1941. By 1945, most of the mass-production industries had been unionized.

The postwar era was a time of American economic dominance, particularly in industries such as aviation, electronics, and chemical engineering that had boomed in wartime. By 1947, the United States produced half of the world's manufactured goods. It also provided the world with 57 percent of its steel, 43 percent of its electricity, and 62 percent of its oil. The core industrial regions in the Midwest and on the Pacific Coast were the first to be reshaped by federally funded postwar reconstruction efforts. These regions were rapidly transformed by urban renewal, suburban development, and expansion of transportation and communications systems. As regions central to the new global economy, they were a destination for massive flows of raw materials from the rest of the world. Their mills and factories mass-produced goods that would dominate the world market. The global economy linked cities like New York, Chicago, San Francisco, and Los Angeles as financial centers. These cities were pivotal to the control of information generated by a world economy. They were the hubs of banking and information services, but also of travel and tourism services necessary to a growing international culture.

American industrial workers shared in the triumph of postwar Fordism. This was a privileged workforce of predominantly white, male union members. Their affluence permitted them to move their families into suburban homes filled with every modern convenience. They drove their full-sized cars to jobs at modernized plants that were the envy of the world. The automobile, more than any other commodity, symbolized the material abundance and well-being that characterized "the American way of life" in the postwar era. Since Ford's Model T, the auto had influenced how Americans worked, lived, and fantasized about their futures. In the 1950s and 1960s, it was crucial to the suburbanization of American cities. Interstate highways and the drive-in movies and restaurants that catered to the burgeoning car culture further transformed the landscapes and the aspirations of ordinary Americans. Many American families uprooted to take advantage of the "new life out there," presumably in the Far Western cities transformed by the postwar boom. By the early 1970s, there were two automobiles for every three American adults.

Auto manufacturing and its affluent workers were the pride of mass-production unionism. In the postwar decades, the United Auto Workers (UAW) was the nation's premier union. In 1948, it led the way in collective bargaining through an agreement with General Motors. The company agreed to provide autoworkers with an automatic cost-of-living adjustment and a 2 percent "annual improvement factor" so that workers shared in the company's gains. Throughout the postwar period, the UAW negotiated wage increases that set the standard for workers in other industries. The union also greatly reduced wage differences between skilled and unskilled work, and bargained for greater welfare benefits. The UAW was also at the forefront of progressive political movements in the 1960s and 1970s. As a major backer of the 1963 March on Washington, UAW officials stood side-by-side with Martin Luther King Jr. and other civil rights leaders at the largest political demonstration in American history. The union also supported Cesar Chavez and the United Farm Workers in their efforts to organize workers on large commercial farms in California and the Southwest. UAW locals led a score of "wildcat" strikes in the 1960s and early 1970s to oppose what they considered inhumane working conditions on the shop floor. During this period, the UAW openly criticized America's intervention in Vietnam and made concerted efforts to recruit African Americans and other minorities into its ranks. Postwar Fordism ended in 1973 with the Arab oil producers' embargo on shipments to the United States and Western Europe. The rise in oil prices and federally mandated gasoline rationing changed how the nation consumed manufactured goods. Americans drastically reduced their consumption of full-sized cars and other mass-produced commodities. Factory output fell, doubling both unemployment and inflation, and this trend continued over the next ten years. America's dominance in the global economy was also challenged by Japan and West Germany. These countries' lower-priced and often higher-quality products flooded American markets, further eroding the nation's manufacturing base. By the decade's end, the UAW led the way to post-Fordism. In 1979, union officials convinced workers to accept wage rollbacks in a federally orchestrated bailout of the nearly bankrupt Chrysler Corporation. Since that time, the UAW lost 500,000 members as a result of the Big Three automakers' strategy to slash payrolls in the face of foreign competition. American workers, in all industries threatened by foreign imports, lost about $500 billion as their wages and other concessions were bargained away during the economic recession and corporate restructuring that took place in the early 1980s.

A FAREWELL TO ARMS

The postwar boom was the result of both Fordist production and a massive peacetime military establishment. Together with mass-production unionism, military spending propelled the American economy for nearly half a century. In the late 1940s, the United States and the Soviet Union ended their wartime alliance over ideological differences. The ensuing Cold War produced ongoing global political conflict. America militarized its foreign policy commitments to client states in Europe, Asia, and Latin America. The postwar arms race with the Soviet Union also rekindled contractual relationships between the defense department and companies that had done substantial business with the military during World War II. In the face of Soviet power and the threat of international communism, these companies continued to profit from high levels of military production. In the 1950s, military spending increased dramatically, accounting for one-half of the federal budget. Huge government contracts were awarded to aircraft manufacturers and electronic assembly firms. These contracts were the reason why so many industries focused their research and development efforts on military products, such as missiles, guidance systems, bombers, and spacecraft. Production regions like Seattle, Long Island, San Diego, Long Beach, and the San Fernando Valley in Los Angeles were maintained for decades on Pentagon dollars.[12] Their fast-growing economies were linked to high levels of consumption by families spending their defense-funded paychecks. Their local real estate markets boomed along with each increase in defense-related manufacturing jobs. Cities and suburbs became identified with the defense industry plants that bordered them. McDonnell Douglas came to dominate the local economies of Long Beach and Santa Monica, and Rockwell and Lockheed were identified with Canoga Park and Burbank in the San Fernando Valley.

Arms production meant prosperity for millions of defense industry workers, both union and nonunion alike. Pentagon contracts provided them with high-paying blue-collar jobs. In Los Angeles and Orange counties, one-half of all manufacturing jobs were defense related. Aerospace companies were paternalistic in their treatment of workers and their families. They provided generous wages and benefits, including a week off at Christmas. Entire families would often work for the same company. The vast campuslike facilities provided aerospace families with onsite childcare, counseling, and recreation. The lives of many of these families thus revolved around company activities. However, the companies that provided them job security and gave structure to their lives during the boom years pulled the rug from under them almost overnight. The long postwar boom so closely linked with a defense economy ended in 1989, the year the Berlin Wall fell. For the next two years, popular movements in Eastern Europe and the Soviet Union would demonstrate against and eventually oust their Communist governments. These events had profound effects on families a world away in California. The state lost well over 550,000 jobs in the recession of the 1990s, a downturn primarily linked to defense cutbacks. One out of every four jobs lost was in the aerospace and defense industries.

Displaced aerospace workers desperately tried to sell their houses near massive weapons plants in order to escape from "paradise." The forty-five-year global conflict, which had so organized American life, brought a halt to their dreams. These workers, like many others, regarded Southern California as the nation's "ultimate symbol of hope, opportunity and escape."[13] They shared another belief with their fellow Americans, that of the power of science and technology to provide a secure world and secure lives for themselves and their families. Although they acknowledged that the nation's global economic power had been compromised by Japan and Western Europe, their sense of America's political superiority remained unchallenged. Unlike other Americans, aerospace families were shaken to their foundations by the end of the Cold War. Most had embraced the idea that building powerful weapons of mass destruction was somehow connected to a secure future for the nation and for themselves. Perhaps working closely with the components of advanced weapon systems gave them a sense of control and personal security amid the anxiety that most Americans felt over the prospect of total annihilation. However, these prototypical Cold War families have endured greater anxieties since the halt in global confrontation. They are ambivalent and have feelings of self-doubt, having lost both the political consensus and the conformity to the "suburban family ideal" of the Cold War era.[14] For like the containment of communism, postwar families contained their dreams, desires, and discontents in the privacy of their homes. Aerospace work embodied the promise of security, and the promise of abundance was attested to by the plethora of household consumer goods in their homes. These dual sources of well-being have shaped American work and domestic life since the glory days of Fordist modernity. The suburban home and the defense-related job came to represent ideals of love and work for postwar American families. With the ending of the U.S.-Soviet arms race, aerospace families, like many others, have become disillusioned with both domains.

Plant closings and industrial layoffs in basic industries like automobiles, aerospace, rubber, steel, and consumer electrical goods became commonplace in post-Fordist America. Millions of blue-collar workers in aging industrial cities found their jobs abolished or plants shut down because of changing technologies and corporate investment strategies. In the 1970s and 1980s, companies began relocating their manufacturing operations to "right-to-work" Southern states like North Carolina and Texas, and to factories abroad. Between 1950 and 1980, the flow of American capital overseas increased sixteenfold. American companies were investing profits in Asian countries like Singapore and in Mexico's industrial corridor along the U.S. border.

By the 1970s, America's steel, rubber, and automotive industries were hard hit by the loss of sales to imported goods. A decade later, the newer telecommunications, computer, and electronics industries were also facing strong international competition. By the end of the Cold War in the 1990s, the aerospace industry "downsized" as companies converted from defense to civilian production. Unemployment and displacement due to these structural changes have resulted in profound economic and emotional consequences to blue-collar workers and their families in deindustrialized cities throughout the country. Two cases describe how the interplay of the economic and the emotional unfolded in recession-torn Southern California of the early 1980s. The first depicts the issues confronting displaced autoworkers in South Gate, a deindustrialized city in Los Angeles County, when its most notable corporate citizen, General Motors, made the decision to shut down its forty-five-year-old assembly plant. The second discusses the similar plight of warehouse workers at Sears' sixty-year-old regional distribution center near downtown Los Angeles.

SHUTDOWN AT SOUTH GATE

As late as the mid-1970s, a twenty-mile drive along the Long Beach Freeway, between downtown Los Angeles and the port city of Long Beach, revealed the manufacturing base of industrial America. Goodrich, Uniroyal, and Chrysler maintained factories in Commerce, near downtown. A few miles away in Vernon was the fifty-year-old Bethlehem Steel mill, affectionately called "Lady Beth" by the steelworkers. Firestone Tire and Rubber Company and General Motors had factories in nearby South Gate. Located five miles south of downtown Los Angeles, South Gate sat in the center of what was one of the largest industrial areas in the world. A working-class city of Spanish bungalows and small frame houses, factories, water towers, and railroad tracks located along the Los Angeles River, South Gate was home to over 350 industries. That was before the city of 70,000 was devastated in the late 1970s and early 1980s by deindustrialization and corporate flight.

In the 1920s and 1930s, South Gate offered companies like U.S. Gypsum, Bell Foundry, and Firestone a number of incentives to locate factories there. Land was cheap, electricity cost half of what companies were paying back east, and water was also billed at lower rates. In 1936, General Motors began to manufacture automobiles in South Gate. The company produced Buicks, Oldsmobiles, and Pontiacs with 1,000 assembly-line workers earning fifty cents an hour. The South Gate plant was the first to produce several car models on a single assembly line. During the Second World War, its assembly workers built 1,500 tanks for the Army. In the 1940s, General Motors was largely responsible for the postwar transportation revolution that would move Los Angeles away from mass transit to dependence upon the private automobile. The company had bought out and eventually dismantled the Pacific Electric Railway, or "Red Cars," that provided Los Angeles with one of the best public transportation systems in the nation.

After the war, the plant again manufactured full-sized cars on its prewar assembly lines until the early 1960s. Facing competitive import sales, General Motors began producing its compact Pontiac Lemans, Oldsmobile F-85, and Buick Special models on South Gate's assembly lines. The company also continued to assemble full-sized cars at South Gate, until the Arab oil embargo in 1973–1974. Its lines were then overhauled, at a cost of $15 million, to produce the short-lived Chevrolet Vega and Monza Sunbird models. By the mid-1970s, General Motors switched the plant back to assembling the more profitable full-sized cars. But foreign imports from Japan and Europe, coupled with rising gasoline prices and an incipient recession, left the Big Three automakers with fleets of these unsold cars at every dealership. In 1980, General Motors again retooled the plant, idling its 2,400 first-shift workers. After a year, the plant reopened and began producing the subcompact J-car, heralded as the company's response to foreign imports. A second shift of 1,800 autoworkers was added after seven months of production. However, the shift was dropped after one month because of poor sales of the J-cars.

By March 1982, the plant was "temporarily" closed due to high inventories at the dealerships. This closing meant laying off 2,500 predominantly male first-shift workers, half of them African American, and all with at least ten years seniority. During the last full year of its operation, the South Gate plant had a payroll of nearly $77 million and purchased $67 million of goods from California suppliers. On April 20, 1983, General Motors announced that it would be "permanently" closed, deciding that auto sales had not rebounded enough to warrant reopening the plant. The Van Nuys plant, General Motors' other automobile assembly facility in the region, would remain open as a result of an aggressive community-based coalition that threatened the company with a Los Angeles–area boycott of its products.[15] The company was also attempting to concentrate its production in the Midwest instead, closer to its major suppliers, and planned to open two new plants there in 1983.

The city of South Gate turned sixty in January 1983. Its sewers and water lines, roads, and storm drains were badly in need of repair. The city's housing stock was also deteriorating, with sagging walls, peeling paint, and broken windows. Graffiti marking the territory of youth gangs were visible everywhere. South Gate's unemployment rate was close to 15 percent, largely owing to the loss of its three major employers—Firestone, General Motors, and Weiser Lock—over the past three years. Many shops and restaurants on Tweedy Boulevard, the city's "Miracle Mile," were boarded up and the Fed-Mart Store, a major source of sales tax revenues, had closed its doors. Middle-class residents had been fleeing the city for over two decades. Low-income Latino residents, half of them undocumented, now made up 60 percent of the South Gate's population. The city's assessed property valuation was declining, and its tax revenues were rapidly dwindling. As in Flint, Michigan, Youngstown and Akron, Ohio, and other deindustrialized cities in the nation's heartland, the American Dream had shattered in South Gate.

At least half of the 4,300 auto workers displaced from the General Motors assembly plant at South Gate participated in the most ambitious industrial retraining, job placement, and counseling program ever developed in California. Sponsored jointly by the UAW, General Motors Corporation, and the

State of California, the $10 million program was designed to prevent or reduce the social, economic, and personal problems associated with longer-term unemployment. Eight months after the plant had been shut down, a reemployment center providing job service activities and stress counseling was established at UAW Local 216, through the "public-private partnership." Program staff shared limited office facilities at the union hall across from the idle General Motors plant. These cramped arrangements enabled them to develop informal relationships with union officials and the displaced workers. They were thus able to observe firsthand the impact of job loss on the workers' lives. The workers spoke of their financial problems, including confusion over benefits and delays in receiving unemployment insurance checks. The holiday season—the first after the shutdown—added to the family-related stresses. Financial issues, such as accumulating debts, threats of foreclosure, and utility cutoffs, were frequently reported during this period. Rumors spread among workers about the possibility of a mass relocation to assembly plants in out-of-state locations.

These issues and a sense of isolation led displaced workers to seek regular support and guidance from their union "brothers and sisters." Each day, groups of jobless union members gathered to get information and to meet with coworkers. The union hall provided them with a destination where they could socialize with peers and perhaps reduce some of their stress and hostility. At the onset of the program, many of the workers were uncomfortable about seeking help for their problems. Program staff would frequently chat with union members as they congregated at the hall to establish a rapport with them. However, the workers were often wary of these encounters because of the stigma they attached to professional counseling. They were acutely aware of each other's help seeking from the counselors in this open environment. Over time, however, referrals increased as workers' difficulties continued and the services became more visible and less stigmatized. After two months, reemployment activities were moved from the union hall to another location in South Gate. Private offices for all program staff, coupled with less traffic and lingering in the new setting, rendered individual help seeking more confidential. Professional staff provided direct assistance and made referrals to community agencies. They helped workers with unemployment insurance problems by directing them to the proper channels, and thereby deflected frustration and anger. Many workers had problems because their benefits were delayed due to lost or misplaced records. Others needed assistance in filling out the necessary forms for unemployment extensions. The counselors also referred potential retirees to union representatives or General Motors staff members. They also helped workers to obtain assistance from various community agencies to meet their material needs. Peer counselors remained stationed at the union hall and provided information and referral for every kind of material problem, including food distribution programs, utilities, rent, and mortgage payments. Since many displaced workers were in need of food, a food distribution program was developed using government surplus commodities such a cheese and butter, as well as low-cost food packages distributed at the union hall. This program utilized many hours of volunteer time, provided a valuable service to the workers, and was a source of directed activity to many members who were neither working nor in training programs. The union hall also became the center of a free lunch program subsidized by federal funds.

Three months after the start of the $10 million program, General Motors announced the possible relocation of 600 workers. Workers gathered in the union hall and at the reemployment center, and rumors developed even before the relocation notices were actually received and formal interviewing began. They expressed their concerns about the uncertainties of relocation, relocation funds, strained family situations, and the potential disruption of retraining for new skills. In the weeks that followed, interviews and screening of potential workers for relocation to the Oklahoma City plant began in the union hall. These events caused additional anxieties, fed by rumors surrounding the selection criteria for those who would be relocated and whether previous work histories or medical histories would preclude transfer and completion of careers with the company. Rumors also spread about how relocation of assembly workers to other General Motors plants would affect automobile production in Southern California. It was rumored that the South Gate plant would shortly reopen and that General Motors' Van Nuys facility in suburban Los Angeles would close down. There was also hearsay that workers relocating to Oklahoma City would be laid off in ninety days. During these weeks, physical examinations conducted by General Motors renewed anxiety about reassignment to an out-of-state plant. An informal "buddy" system developed, as those who were called for interviews and physicals contacted those close to them in seniority and on the shop floor in order to share information, compare notes, and offer support. Within a week or two following the physical exams, workers were receiving letters asking whether they would accept or reject offers of employment. Approximately eight days after this letter was mailed, telegrams were sent to a small number of workers requesting that they report for work at the Oklahoma City plant, approximately 1,400 miles away, on the following Monday at 6 a.m.

The prospect of relocation resulted in noticeable changes in the workers. An increasing sense of anxiety, nervousness, and worry had been building up in them for weeks. There was more excessive drinking and substance abuse. The workers also showed a lack of concern for their personal appearance and public demeanor. They would often speak aggressively and even threaten staff at the employment center. This bravado masked their concerns regarding separation from their spouses, threats of divorce, spousal depression, and spousal abuse. Workers were also beset by financial insecurities, including house sales, the fate of the spouse's career, and debts relating to relocation. They were troubled about their children finishing school and remaining in the home with only one parent. They were apprehensive of the burden of maintaining two homes when the responsibility for one was already stressful. They were also faced with a dilemma of whether to remain in training or to relocate, and of how to make an informed decision regarding their career prospects in either case. Relocation issues continued to trouble workers throughout the next few months. Unlike the initial Oklahoma relocation notices, subsequent recalls to plants in Louisiana and Missouri were on a more voluntary basis. Workers in retraining programs were able to obtain official postponements of recall in order to complete training. However, many workers were not taking advantage of the training opportunities offered to them. The reemployment center staff began a mail campaign to reach these workers. As a result, a substantial number of them sought assistance for their financial difficulties. The staff would refer them to public entitlement programs, utilities shut-off assistance programs, dental clinics, and financial aid programs for college-age children. Many displaced workers were faced with the inability to pay their monthly rent or mortgage, to afford gas for their cars, and to meet their other bills. Some individuals, especially those with larger households, reported serious difficulty feeding their families. Others had to contend with the problems of delayed unemployment and benefit checks, making household budgeting a difficult task. The most common reactions to these conditions were frustration, anger, and feelings of hopelessness.

An increasing number of individuals were having emotional problems, such as depression, thoughts of suicide, lowered self-esteem, and nervousness. For many, the pressures and demands of retraining, compounded by learning problems, led them to seek counseling. Similarly, the stress of looking for new employment in a tight economy, exacerbated by the upcoming cessation of unemployment benefits, led people to counseling. The most common reactions to these changes and uncertainties were fear, disillusionment, anger, and feelings of powerlessness and hopelessness. For other individuals, the psychological factors associated with being out of work affected their physical health. Workers reported substantial weight gain, sleeplessness, migraine headaches, stomach problems, and general fatigue. There were an increasing number of family and marital problems. Many of these problems first surfaced when workers received letters from the company to report to work out of state. The prospect of relocation, possible family separation, or loss of partial income placed additional strains on family life. Some of the children showed a drop in performance at school and increased behavioral problems, and a few children exhibited illness associated with emotional stress. For workers who were not in training programs and who had low seniority, there was the cessation of unemployment benefits, the depletion of long-held saving accounts, and the inability to rely on extended family for financial support. There were increasing requests for referrals to public entitlement programs. Families were faced with eviction, foreclosure, utility shut-offs, and drastic restrictions on their buying and spending, in addition to marital discord made worse by these financial difficulties.

Many workers and their families were in a stalemate, both financially and emotionally. They had not begun to recoup their financial standing, since the worker had not gone back to work, thereby continuing the uncertainty and confusion about the future. As training programs ended, many workers still had not secured new employment and were faced with two future options: the difficult and frightening task of looking for work in a new trade with only a few months of training or experience behind them, or the disruptive but possibly more secure alternative of accepting or volunteering for General Motors out-of-state relocation. Many workers completing their training programs reported that they would prefer to remain in California and find jobs in their newly acquired trade. However, they also expressed a lack of confidence and a concern that they did not have adequate training or sufficient experience to be hired in new occupations. Relocation became a viable option for hundreds of families. Families separated, with many of the spouses remaining in California, either on a shorter-term or longer-term basis, while their husbands relocated. Many wives sought financial and emotional support at the union hall. They reported difficulty in maintaining two separate households, loneliness, worries about rearing and disciplining their children alone, as well as fears of infidelity or permanent family breakup. With the ending of the retraining program, workers were referred to community services. Although staff had advocated vigorously on behalf of workers with these agencies, very few of them chose to take advantage of the services because many were uncomfortable approaching unfamiliar agencies with their problems. As the intervention terminated, the problems that surfaced were more serious in nature than in the earlier months of the program due to the extended period of unemployment and the continued uncertainty of reemployment and relocation.

LOST WORK FAMILIES

In the years following the deindustrialization of cities like South Gate, Sears decided to close its massive Los Angeles distribution facility. The sixty-year-old Art Deco building was the flagship of Sears' southwest regional operations. It

towered over neighboring blue-collar communities with their flat streets of
small homes, where Sears found its principal clientele. Threats to close the facility had been rumored for years. Although the physical plant and distribution process were essentially outdated, new management techniques were implemented, and there had been claims of increased productivity after quality
circles had been established. Nevertheless, the company made the decision to
close down the distribution center, resulting in the termination of 2,000 employees.

Longer-term managerial and supervisory employees regarded Sears as a
benevolent provider of excellent salaries and benefits, profit sharing, job security, and opportunities for personal advancement. Many had begun their
work lives as older teenagers obtaining their first real job at Sears, and most
had continued to work there for as many as twenty-five years. They acknowledged their positive career tracks within the company, which had provided them with security and advancement opportunities over a long period
of time, and a strong sense of identification as Sears employees. Very few of
these employees expressed immediate financial concerns, perhaps because of
the availability of severance pay and anticipated unemployment insurance
benefits. But at every meeting of the newly unemployed Sears workers, at
least one person would bring up the issue of the loss of the "work family."
Once the topic came up, the workers felt able to talk about their sadness regarding separation from coworkers of many years. Common ties had emerged
through time spent working together and sharing a role with respect to a corporate authority, production modes, and work routines. These employees perceived the workplace as a family or a close-knit network that protected them
emotionally as well as economically. The more strongly attached to this work
family they were, the more traumatic would be the separation process. Many
employees felt a tremendous sense of abandonment and disillusionment when
the closure was announced. However, there was little sanction to express
strong disapproval of the company. All were apprehensive about entering the
labor market because of their secure work environment. Because they were
facing this transition in their middle years, many questioned whether they
could transfer their skills and compete for managerial positions in a competitive labor market. Some stated that affirmative action had enabled them to
progress within the company and that they would most likely face discrimination outside of Sears. The managers thus seemed to feel unready for
change. They were not only dealing with issues of change in their jobs, but
also in their personal lives, as most had worked for Sears for many years.

The impending closure was potentially more catastrophic for the longer-
term, hourly employees in the warehouse. Sears regarded them as part-time
employees, although most worked the equivalent of a full-time workweek.

They had been in this temporary status for many years, without benefits, and upon layoff would not be eligible for retirement or severance pay. However, the company established an outplacement center for the hourly workers a few months before it closed the facility. The workers would roam in and out of the center, viewing job notices and signing up for outplacement services from professional counselors. They regarded finding work as a fairly simple matter, since their tasks, including picking parts, filling orders, and working with heavy equipment, required minimum technical skills. They apparently saw no problems, therefore, in transferring to a similar wholesale distribution center because their skills were so unspecialized. Most of the warehouse workers had regarded their years spent with Sears in positive terms and were very sad about leaving the company. Like other lesser skilled workers, they appeared to derive their job satisfaction from their relatively high wages, and not from the work itself. Their stresses, therefore, were economically rooted, age-related, and less related to skill obsolescence and longer-term career goals. However, they appeared to mask their feelings, perhaps serving to protect their pride before their peers and the professionals at the outplacement center. This masking took the form of denial that anything was wrong or that they were bothered by the impending closure. The effect of the stress may have been more internalized, since these workers concealed their feelings, and may have presented in the form of increased physical symptoms and more use of alcohol and drugs to suppress feelings and emotional confusion.

The warehouse workers usually went to their supervisors when they became demoralized and questioned whether there was "life after Sears." Many of them were anxious, depressed, and suspicious of company policies surrounding their termination. Since the closure was announced, they called in sick more often and expressed fears of downward economic mobility to their supervisors. The key issue for these workers in mostly unskilled jobs was their employability. These blue-collar workers did not share their white-collar colleagues' identification with the company. They displayed less pride in their work than their supervisors, and seemed to have a short-sighted view of a work future. Their lack of future orientation and identification with a skill or a sense of craftsmanship often resulted in less ego involvement around termination from a specific workplace. However, some individuals felt worried about being without a job and experienced a sense of having less of a competitive advantage in the labor market, even though they did not derive gratification from their work. What Sears managers did share with those they supervised was a sense of ambiguity about when the actual layoffs would occur and in what sequence workers would be terminated. They questioned how production goals could be accomplished in an environment of apprehension and uncertainty, and they were concerned about their compromised supervisory role as the layoff date approached. Their past motivational strategy, indicating how poor performance would jeopardize the future of the facility, was no longer effective. Many expressed a need, then, to modify their styles of communication and discipline, which were not working in view of the impending closure. The myth of security that had maintained order and a sense of camaraderie within the workplace was destroyed.

ORGANIZED SUPPORT FOR JOB LOSS

In most job situations, the usual practice had been to notify the employee two to four weeks before termination. In unionized workplaces, management notifies the union of the pending reduction in the workforce. Management and union officials negotiate issues of seniority, benefits, severance pay, and the timetable for layoff or closure. Information regarding these projected actions flows through both formal and informal networks. Media reports on economic issues, such as production flows, mergers, and cutbacks in the industry, usually precede and accompany this process. Many employees begin to seek work elsewhere. Older workers and others who have been with the company for a longer time have a longer-term investment, and are often reluctant to take action during this preliminary stage. In larger companies, for example, there are benefits that will accrue to these longer-term workers at layoff, such as early retirement and severance pay.

Leaders of progressive labor unions appear to have a more enlightened level of awareness and understanding of job loss. The emotional significance of this economic crisis has become commonly acknowledged. Unions have had increased awareness of drug and alcohol problems at the work site. On-site counselors as well as industry-based employee assistance plans have provided union-sponsored substance abuse treatment programs to their members. Union benefit packages often include mental health coverage. Workers themselves are becoming more familiar with counseling services to assist them with family problems and stresses. Increasing numbers of larger companies have subscribed to prepaid mental health plans. Larger unions, such as the UAW, have been at the forefront in providing mental health services to their members through their early involvement with community mental health centers in the 1960s. This has also been true of such unions as the Retail Clerks, which at one time operated its own mental health clinics. The AFL-CIO Federation has sponsored training programs for shop stewards as worksite peer interveners for drug and alcohol problems.

Union leaders have shown a strong sense of responsibility for workers facing layoff. The unions themselves have decreasing power, however, in affecting the decisions leading to plant closures and mass layoffs. These labor organizations, then, are themselves in crisis since they are unable to protect their members from job loss. There are increasingly strong antiunion sentiments among workers in general, and particularly during a crisis period, such as prior to a mass layoff. Workers frequently blame the union for their job loss; it is frequently the union leaders who experience the anger, frustration, and despair of the rank-and-file members, who seek assistance for their constituency. Their motives are often self-protective, since they feel inadequate to respond, both personally and on behalf of their organization, to their members' needs. They fear such catastrophic consequences as suicide and serious psychosomatic reactions. The term "stress" is frequently used, rather than psychological or mental disorder, to describe the circumstances of their membership. Under ordinary working conditions, the shop steward and committee member can utilize peer support systems, onsite substance abuse counselors, or mental health resources. When the layoff occurs, however, the support structure of the worker is gone. Insurance benefits end at layoff or extend for a circumscribed period of time. With some exceptions, the retirement-aged worker may have lifetime health insurance coverage. In anticipation of the impending situation, the more enlightened union leaders become concerned about the repercussions of their members' anger and disillusionment. Many companies acknowledge these same problems in their workforce as layoff approaches, and they hire outplacement firms to assist in résumé writing and job-search workshops. In some rare instances, these companies also offer stress-reduction or other workshops, usually targeted to middle management.

Union leaders and middle management often feel isolated as they observe changes in the atmosphere of the workplace as their coworkers become distressed during the prelayoff period. Many of the workers approach these influentials to voice concerns regarding the layoff and its implications for the course of their lives. Very often, clear information is lacking regarding such issues as the dates of termination and severance pay. This renders these natural helpers essentially ineffective in offering their assistance. Once the decision has been made from the "top down" to close a plant or reduce the workforce the union and middle management have lost their constituency, namely the rank-and-file workers for whom they have served as negotiator and advocate. They are often threatened with termination themselves. In the vacuum, members of action-oriented labor unions will often initiate spontaneous, voluntary self-help efforts, such as food banks, holiday toy campaigns, and outreach within the labor movement. The union hall is a supportive environment during this stage, and its space is "reenergized" with new tasks and roles and the sudden acknowledgment that "we are on our own." New leadership emerges to serve a constituency that is facing an impending crisis, one that the departing leadership is unprepared to manage. There are many questions, for example, raised by rank-and-file members regarding their immediate needs as well as future needs.

Troubled workers who are facing a layoff or plant closure often delay seeking help from outside agencies because of feelings of confusion about what is taking place. There is an initial sense of disbelief and denial. The work situation often places the group of employees in a tightly bound network of relationships. Their work life and, to a certain extent, their social life are spatially and temporally organized around a routine of shift work and car pools, which require fixed behavioral repertoires. These individuals are therefore facing, along with the loss of their jobs, the loss of a pattern of living, a loss marked by changed cyclical rhythms of waking and sleeping, eating, and socializing. The external threat of an impending layoff or plant closure separates the workers from the community, and frequently from their families. These workers' sense of ambiguity and uncertainty results from a process of demoralization that has its origins in workers' declining gratification with their jobs. The worker's dissatisfaction emerges from such factors as the routinized work process, "traditional" management styles, and the absence of intrinsic rewards from job performance. This set of experiences transfers into a sense of demoralization that emerges when a worker must make a decision regarding future options. This lack of enthusiasm that many individuals present for planning their next steps after a layoff needs to be viewed within the context of their prior experiences at work. When work is solely to meet economic survival needs, one job is the same as another. This process of "de-skilling" limits an individual's talents and competencies through mechanized, routinized work function, and lowers an individual's self-esteem, pride in achievement, and sense of self-efficacy.[16] Skill obsolescence for a person whose work task has become obsolete is a particular hazard since that individual may have an underdeveloped work identity. The resulting lack of ambition and motivation attached to skill competencies and lack of pride in personal accomplishment inhibits the individual's ability to maximize the opportunities available to him or her during the layoff transition. The roots of these attitudes go back to early socialization and experiences in the educational system.

It is not unusual for a worker to withhold information about the impending layoff from family members and friends. Some workers have tried to conceal this information, after they have been laid off, by leaving the house each morning and returning home at the end of the day. Union leaders and corporate management often attempt to mask or deny the reality by conducting "business as usual" up to the closing date. Delay, masking, and denial effectively serve to shelter an individual from acknowledging that she or he has a problem and may need help. However, in larger-scale layoffs, where a wider spectrum of workers is affected, reports begin to circulate regarding the fate of those who have already lost their jobs. These reports include suicide attempts, heart attacks, family breakdown, and very often excessive drinking and drug use. Early reports of severe economic problems, such as default on mortgages, are circulated as well.

The initial planning process of the South Gate plant closure involved leadership from the union local, the state Employment Development Department, and key members of the local union executive committee. The UAW local president, Don Evans, expressed the need for stress counseling services. A second meeting was scheduled so that representatives from the California State Department of Mental Health, the local mental health center, and the union local could explore the need for direct services. At this meeting, held at the union hall, union representatives expressed concerns about reported suicides, increased illness episodes, and other stress-related phenomena. This group of union leaders was multiethnic and included younger and older workers. They shared their concerns regarding stress-related problems but disagreed about the type of program best suited to the union members. The benefits representative stated that the members were going to need a great deal of help because of the layoff. The vice president stated that this effort would deplete union funds and added, "they expect too much." The local president then expressed the view that the "older group had nothing to worry about" because of the financial benefits that would come their way because of the union contract.

The concept of "theme interference" is particularly relevant in understanding this meeting.[17] Theme interference describes a process whereby a person, typically a client of a helping institution (in this case a union member), is stereotyped, and as a result, the predicted outcome is negative. These stereotypes may pertain to age, ethnicity, gender, occupational classification, and, in even more general terms, the label of being unemployed. The helper will extend assistance only to those perceived as worthy. Since theme interference intrudes upon their predictive ability, the resulting frustration and anger limits their helping efforts. The theme interference that emerged during this meeting was the "we-they" theme reflected in ethnic stereotyping and ageist biases. The statement took the form of stereotypes by the older union leader (the vice president) regarding the younger ethnic minority workers' dependent attitude with respect to the union's ability to find employment for them. The younger union official attributed blame to the older leader's poor negotiating of contracts that led to the plant closure. In the face of worker "deskilling," demoralization, and the stereotyping that will often accompany many organized helping efforts, individuals coping with job loss require techniques that will help foster self-esteem and a new sense of personal efficacy.

The displaced worker will need to become aware of the impact of workplace demoralization on the ability to make decisions, cope with stress, and become achievement motivated. The individual will also need to begin to recognize the stressors in the workplace that perpetuate this sense of demoralization, with its resulting low self-esteem, diminished achievement motivation, and feelings of helplessness. Personal efficacy results, for example, when individuals who have shared concerns form a mutual support group. Such common concerns as job loss and skill obsolescence bring individuals together who are in crisis and in need of support as a helping force. These groups allow participants to discuss perceived obstacles to training and job loss, to recognize stress reactions, and to cope more effectively early in the transition period.

A union program that developed after a company closed its plant in Chicago offered stress management presentations in union-sponsored, half-day workshops, with information on budgeting, dealing with creditors, unemployment benefits, retraining opportunities, and other help.[18] Support groups, meeting weekly, discussed and sought out retraining opportunities through the union, discovered health insurance options, and educated one another on the status of their pension and on procedures for obtaining unemployment benefits. Discussions were held on such topics as productive daily routine, knowing and communicating work skills and personality strengths, maintaining self-confidence, persistence in job seeking, and handling job interviews. In general, the group moved from having anxiety about being unemployed to making decisions about the future and stepping into various new life routines. One of the unique methods for relieving the stress of job loss was the formation of an "unemployment union" in response to needs of unemployed workers.[19] When the mills along Lake Michigan closed, followed by deterioration of the community, the unemployment union was formed to focus directly on meeting the immediate needs of the workers. Organized like traditional unions, with similar terminology and structure, it acted as a clearinghouse for part-time and shorter-term jobs, helped members negotiate contracts with potential employers, and tried to match service requests with the most appropriate union member. A number of programs to increase skills and build solidarity within the group were developed. Not only was help offered in finding unemployment, but also efforts were made to foster spiritual and physical well-being along with community ties. Immediate needs of the unemployed worker were met by providing a directory of women's health services that would furnish adequate health care; also an emergency food pantry was set up, and Al-Anon and Alcoholics Anonymous programs were offered. Along with medical care, nonmedical services were instituted to improve health status. Teams sent to apartments to observe hazardous living conditions offered counseling on health problems and the reduction of safety hazards. Environmental problems such as the presence of lead-based paints; porches, railings, and stairways in need of repair; need for pest control; and yards or lots requiring cleanup were identified. A nurse practitioner from the local county hospital provided immediate medical attention in an effort to avoid unnecessary hospital visits.

DILEMMA OF COMMUNITY SUPPORT

The emergence of local community support on behalf of displaced workers has been minimal, particularly in the Los Angeles metropolitan area, because of the fragmentation and diversity of interests among the local communities within the region. The heterogeneity of the industries that have been affected by plant closures and layoffs and their work forces has precluded the development of shared interests and community concern for displaced worker issues. When the Bethlehem Steel Corporation closed its Los Angeles plant after a series of layoffs, there were attempts by union members to develop a broader-based coalition of support for displaced workers. They were able to organize a food distribution program collaboratively with other unions in their local region. They were unsuccessful, however, in their efforts at coalition building. The obstacles to community support in this case were due to the lack of concentration of workers in any one community, the gradual erosion of the workforce at the steel mill over a three-to-five-year period, the multiethnic composition of the workers, and the union members' disillusionment with the labor organization as a viable force working on behalf of the interests of displaced workers.

A similar set of circumstances characterized the closing of the General Motors assembly plant in the neighboring industrial community of South Gate. The coalition building that took place prior to the formal closure of the automobile assembly plant became focused on the economic redevelopment of the urban infrastructure, from an industrial base to an economy based on warehouse and tourism services. The autoworkers' identification with the local community was minimal, and they did not identify with the municipality's redevelopment efforts. Their primary relationship was with the plant where they were employed and not with the community itself, despite the fact that the local union hall was located there. Efforts to organize social activities and political rallies were unsuccessful because of the geographic dispersal of the workforce. The retired workers, by contrast, tended to reside closer to the plant and, therefore, maintained a stronger affiliation with the union hall as a social center. Organizational efforts on the workers' behalf were impeded by their disillusionment with the local union leadership, their resistance to returning to a union hall across from the deserted factory to which they had commuted from surrounding cities, and their own unformulated identities as displaced workers. The latter condition may be attributed to the fact that the workers were still subject to recall by General Motors and were receiving union-based financial supplements to their unemployment benefits, and therefore they held a tenuous status.

The socioeconomic base of the communities in which both the steel mill and automobile assembly plant were located was primarily industrial and composed of low-income, minority residents. These communities had undergone population shifts in recent years from predominantly middle-class industrial workers and their families to households composed of newly arrived, monolingual, Spanish-speaking immigrants. There was minimal local expression of concern for displaced workers and no local-level initiatives on their behalf. The ripple effect of these plant closures on local small businesses, ranging from restaurants, bars, and retail outlets to smaller technical operations such as tool and die works and machine shops that maintained a symbiotic relationship with the large industrial plants, created an economic hardship that was evident in the communities. The displaced workers themselves were perceived by residents as outsiders to the community and as "advantaged" because of the economic safety net provided by the unions. The psychological isolation that results from these circumstances discouraged alliance building within the two industrial communities. These commuting workers were alienated from their residential communities as well, since being laid off was an experience that was not shared by their neighbors and friends outside the workplace. This sense of isolation, together with the sense of shame and self-blame often experienced in their encounters within public agencies, served to reinforce negative attitudes toward the unemployed, not only in the community but within the displaced workers themselves. In single-industry company towns, a plant closure is universally experienced as a community crisis similar to a natural disaster. The impact on the individual in a disaster is shared by other community members and is not a source of stigma. After the disaster event, resources become mobilized, mutual assistance emerges, cohesiveness develops around rescue operations, and sharing of concerns for the severely affected evolves, and all of these efforts strengthen community bonds. Psychological stresses affecting the individual, caused by property loss and residential dislocation, physical injury, and perhaps loss of loved ones, may result in immediate and posttraumatic stress reactions. These reactions, however, are buffered by the presence of a common, nonstigmatized, naturally occurring event such as a disaster.

In cities where plant closures are an isolated event, displaced workers, by contrast, experience major difficulties coping with the transition. Their sense

of isolation, personal shame, and even self-stigmatization, coupled with the material issues of unemployment, places them at high risk for emotional problems such as anxiety and depression. The stress of job loss has worsened their family relations and has often led to child and spousal abuse and to divorce. They are also vulnerable to a variety of physical illnesses, including heart disease, stroke, and cirrhosis of the liver. There is even evidence that higher rates of unemployment are related to an increase in suicides, traffic accidents, and criminal violence. In fact, there are more arrests, more admissions to mental hospitals, and more cases of assault and fraud during periods of economic recession.[20] Furthermore, there are similarities between disaster victims and displaced workers in their psychological responses to the traumatic event. The sense of self-blame that both groups report is related to their members' perceived loss of control and self-efficacy. The experience of the loss of a home, and its resultant physical displacement, has its parallel in the longer-term employee's experience of displacement from the familiar terrain of the workplace. Feelings of sadness and disorientation are reported in both instances. The legitimacy of the disaster victim's perceptions and feelings is reinforced by community institutions; the displaced worker's feelings of loss, by contrast, lack such socially sanctioned legitimacy. It is commonly accepted that separation of the disaster victim from the community is sometimes necessary for the reconstruction of the physical infrastructure. The displaced worker's permanent separation from familiar work surroundings and a "work family" has a similar traumatic effect without the extended community support of common acceptance of these emotional responses to job loss.

NOTES

1. Richard Overy, "Heralds of Modernity: Cars and Planes from Invention to Necessity," in *Fin de Siècle and its Legacy*, edited by Mikulas Teich and Roy Porter (Cambridge: Cambridge University Press, 1990), 54–79; Richard Overy, "The Wheels and Wings of Progress," *History Today* (September 1992): 22–27; Pierre Bardou, Jean-Jacques Chanaron, Patrick Fridenson, and James M. Laux, *The Automobile Revolution: The Impact of an Industry* (Chapel Hill: University of North Carolina Press, 1982).

2. Alfred D. Chandler Jr., "Fin de Siècle: Industrial Transformation," in *Fin de Siècle and its Legacy*, edited by Mikulas Teich and Roy Porter (Cambridge: Cambridge University Press, 1990), 28–41; Alfred D. Chandler Jr., *Scale and Scope: The Dynamics of Industrial Capitalism* (Cambridge, MA: Harvard University Press, 1990).

3. Alfred D. Chandler Jr., *The Visible Hand: The Managerial Revolution in American Business* (Cambridge, MA: Harvard University Press, 1977).

4. Roland Marchand, *Advertising and the American Dream: Making Way for Modernity, 1920–1940* (Berkeley: University of California Press, 1985); Jackson Lears, *Fables of Abundance: A Cultural History of Advertising in America* (New York: Basic Books, 1994).

5. Robert A. Caro, *The Power Broker: Robert Moses and the Fall of New York* (New York: Knopf, 1974); Clay McShane, *Down the Asphalt Path: The Automobile and the American City* (New York: Columbia University Press, 1994); David Ward and Olivier Zunz, eds., *The Landscape of Modernity: New York City, 1900–1940* (Baltimore: Johns Hopkins University Press, 1992).

6. Kenneth T. Jackson, *Crabgrass Frontier: The Suburbanization of the United States* (New York: Oxford University Press, 1985), 150.

7. Olmsted, Vaux & Co., *Preliminary Report upon the Proposed Suburban Village at Riverside Near Chicago* (1868), 26, quoted in William Cronon, *Nature's Metropolis: Chicago and the Great West* (New York: Norton, 1991), 347; see also David Schuyler, *The New Urban Landscape: The Redefinition of City Form in Nineteenth-Century America* (Baltimore: Johns Hopkins University Press, 1986); Stanley K. Schultz, *Constructing Urban Culture: American Cities and City Planning, 1800–1920* (Philadelphia: Temple University Press, 1989); Greg Hise and William Deverell, *Eden by Design: The 1930 Olmsted-Bartholomew Plan for the Los Angeles Region* (Berkeley: University of California Press, 2000).

8. Jackson, *Crabgrass Frontier*, 273.

9. Eric H. Monkkonen, *America Becomes Urban: The Development of Cities and Towns, 1780–1980* (Berkeley: University of California Press, 1988), 163–64; see also Scott L. Bottles, *Los Angeles and the Automobile: The Making of a Modern City* (Berkeley: University of California Press, 1987); Kevin Starr, *Material Dreams: Southern California through the 1920s* (New York: Oxford University Press, 1990); Robert Fogelson, *The Fragmented Metropolis: Los Angeles, 1850–1930*, 2nd ed. (Berkeley: University of California Press, 1993).

10. Mike Davis, *City of Quartz: Excavating the Future in Los Angeles* (New York: Random House, 1992), 160–62.

11. Harry Braverman, *Labor and Monopoly Capital: The Degradation of Work in the Twentieth Century* (New York: Monthly Review Press, 1974); David Brody, *Workers in Industrial America* (New York: Oxford University Press, 1980); Tamara K. Hareven, *Family Time and Industrial Time: The Relationship between the Family and Work in a New England Industrial Community* (Cambridge: Cambridge University Press, 1982); Herbert G. Gutman, *Power and Culture: Essays on the American Working Class* (New York: Pantheon, 1987); Lizabeth Cohen, *Making a New Deal: Industrial Workers in Chicago, 1919–1930* (New York: Cambridge University Press, 1990); Martha Banta, *Taylored Lives: Narrative Production in the Age of Taylor, Veblen and Ford* (Chicago: University of Chicago Press, 1993).

12. Gerald D. Nash, *The American West Transformed: The Impact of the Second World War* (Bloomington: Indiana University Press, 1985); Roger W. Lotchin, "The City and the Sword through the Ages and the Era of the Cold War," in *Essays on Sunbelt Cities and Recent Urban America*, edited by Robert B. Fairbanks and Kathleen Underwood (College Station: Texas A&M Press, 1990), 87–124; Roger W. Lotchin,

"World War II and Urban California: City Planning and the Transformation Hypothesis," *Pacific Historical Review* 62 (1993): 143–71; James T. Lemon, "Los Angeles, 1950: The Working Class Thriving on Military Largesse," in *Liberal Dreams and Nature's Limits: Great Cities of North American Since 1600* (Toronto: Oxford University Press, 1996), 191–241.

13. Robert Reinhold, "Nation's Land of Promise Enters an Era of Limits," *New York Times*, August 24, 1993, national edition, sec. 1; see also Patt Morrison, "Payloads, Paydays, Palm Trees," *Los Angeles Times*, December 5, 1993, sec. A; Merry Ovnick, *Los Angeles: The End of the Rainbow* (Los Angeles: Balcony Press, 1994), 15–18.

14. Elaine Tyler May, *Homeward Bound: American Families in the Cold War Era* (New York: Basic Books, 1988), 25.

15. Eric Mann, *Taking On General Motors: A Case Study of the UAW Campaign to Keep GM Van Nuys Open* (Los Angeles: UCLA Institute of Industrial Relations, 1987); Norma S. Gordon, Carl A. Maida, Norman L. Farberow, Nanette Levine, and Alfred H. Katz, "A Psychosocial Intervention Model for Displaced Workers: The Closing of an Auto Assembly Plant," *Innovation* 2/3 (1988): 345–53; Barry Bluestone and Bennett Harrison, *The Deindustrialization of America: Plant Closings, Community Abandonment and the Dismantling of Basic Industry* (New York: Basic Books, 1982); Gregory Pappas, *The Magic City: Unemployment in a Working-Class Community* (Ithaca, NY: Cornell University Press, 1989).

16. Michael Lerner, *Surplus Powerlessness* (Oakland, CA: Institute for Labor and Mental Health, 1986).

17. Gerald Caplan, *Theory and Practice of Mental Health Consultation* (New York: Basic Books, 1970).

18. Jan Drennon, "Responding to Industrial Plant Closings and the Unemployed," *Social Work* 33 (1988): 50–52.

19. Steve Schaps, "Building a Community Unemployment Union," *Health and Medicine: Journal of the Health and Medicine Policy Research Group* 2 (1983): 16–17.

20. M. Harvey Brenner, *Mental Illness and the Economy* (Cambridge, MA: Harvard University Press, 1973).

Chapter Three

Campaign against Stigma

The modern hospital expanded along with other features of the industrial city in the late nineteenth century to become the very model of a helping organization. It soon became the primary place where the crisis of illness was to be controlled, or at best managed, as both hospital facilities and professional staffs became more specialized. Moreover, the culture of the hospital also became universally recognized and accepted by lay people as the preferred context for the resolution of their major life crises of birth, acute illness, and death. To this day, patients and doctors interact and construct their relationships within treatment settings with a distinct cultural context based upon the premises of scientific medicine, epidemiology, and the management of complex organizations. The complexity of the illness itself, but also the social reaction that many chronic conditions carry with them, produce a considerable emotional burden for both the provider and the patient, and this also influences the culture of care. For example, stigma represents one of the fundamental human costs of chronic illness. Its chief emotional consequence is the barrier of psychological and social distance established between stigmatized patients, their health providers, and the rest of society.

Stigma is a sociocultural phenomenon and has its origins in the fact that all, and any, human differences are potentially stigmatizable. It derives much of its force from being embedded in culturally determined beliefs and symbols of illness and deviance. But what is stigmatized in one culture may not be stigmatized in another. Stigma is thus a social construct, in that each society validates what its members regard as a "spoiled identity."[1] Our culture has had a long history of stigmatizing illnesses, such as tuberculosis, polio, leprosy, and more recently, AIDS. In these conditions, where contagion is a factor, stigma leads to some form of restriction. While they are indeed contagious, so is the fear that surrounds them, and, many times, the fear of the disease goes far beyond the epidemiological consequences.

Stigmatized patients, and their families, friends, even their caregivers, suffer the social consequences of the stigma. These include stereotyping, discrimination, social isolation, alienation, and rejection. Patients experience fear and shame as a result of these unfortunate reactions to a stigmatizing illness. In fact, many take responsibility for their devalued identities and blame themselves for their situation. However, others suffering the same stigma turn to self-help groups to redefine their identities as worthy and to learn skills in self-mastery and emotional self-care. As chronic conditions are managed, not cured, and a major component of these illnesses is often stigma, health providers can help to relieve the unnecessary rejection and suffering. Providing nonstigmatized medical care to chronically ill persons requires both clinical and interpersonal skills and a better understanding of the nature of stigma. In this chapter, case studies describe professional and lay initiatives on behalf of persons with end-stage renal disease and lupus to exemplify the difficulties that surround the management of care for patients with chronic medical conditions.

MODERN HOSPITALS AND THE THERAPEUTIC REVOLUTION

In the decades following the Civil War, only the disenfranchised visited hospital clinics and dispensaries when they were sick. Hospitals were stigmatized as houses of infection and contagion and "a place where the poor went to die."[2] Their patients were also stigmatized because disease and social deviance were linked in the minds of the elites of the time. In Victorian America, "moral causes and pathological consequences still fit together."[3] In a society where disease was closely associated with poverty and personal morality, the hospital was "a refuge for the unfortunate and the inadequate."[4]

During this era, most middle-class Americans avoided hospitals, choosing instead to be treated at home. The general hospital was run as a public or private charity to provide care for those in the lowest socioeconomic groups. These included many of the strangers visible in late nineteenth-century American cities, such as immigrants and itinerant workers, the urban poor, and others without familial support. The hospital thus treated people who were new to city living and its risks, including industrial workmen injured on the job. Like the public school, it was a place where those unfamiliar with urban institutions were socialized to comply with the governing elites and their demands for moral uplift. Because it was a charitable institution, hospital staff continually reminded patients that they are expected to be grateful for the privilege of receiving health care. Hospital patients also provided most of the nursing care to their peers and did routine hospital chores like cleaning and maintenance work.

By the turn of the century, many urban hospitals had been transformed from custodial institutions offering mostly care to medical workplaces dedicated to cure. The modern hospital developed through innovations in technology and organization. They grew and flourished within the Progressive Era cities of New York, Philadelphia, Baltimore, and Boston, where the movement for reform addressed not only public health care but also municipal government, public education, social welfare, the penal system, and the mental asylum. The application of Pasteur's germ theory and Lister's antiseptic principles to medical science led to improved surgical practices. The use of X-rays, improved techniques of anesthesia, and the ability to provide blood transfusions greatly enhanced medical diagnosis and treatment. These innovations, along with other rapid advances in medical technology, the professionalization of medicine, and the introduction of formal nursing training, contributed to the therapeutic revolution that transformed the hospital from a charity to a profitable enterprise. Following the lead of English nurse-reformer, Florence Nightingale, upper-class women founded the State Charities Aid Association in New York in 1872 to monitor public hospitals and almshouses. Their efforts in reorganizing the hospital ward and in vigilantly monitoring the institutional environment to diminish the risk of hospital-generated infection led to overall better sanitary conditions. In 1873, the first nursing school was established at New York's Bellevue Hospital, the former New York Almshouse. Nursing education soon flourished as more middle-class women sought out careers in the service occupations. Hospitals grew increasingly reliant upon this cadre of disciplined and skilled student nurses who would work for virtually nothing during their two years of nursing school.

In the early 1900s, progressive reform and corporate philanthropy contributed to the hospital's transformation from almshouse to a center for medical research, teaching, and professional care. The Flexner Commission, sponsored by the newly established Carnegie Foundation for the Advancement of Teaching, investigated abuses in medical education and called for a closer linkage between the medical sciences, the universities, and the hospital. John D. Rockefeller established the Rockefeller Institute for Medical Research in New York to wed the clinic to the laboratory. The medical profession also underwent reform, as physicians reorganized the American Medical Association, formed state licensing boards, and created a more scientifically based medical curriculum. The sum of these measures led more physicians to affiliate with a general hospital, and their patients would more often visit them at the hospital's clinics or in their offices near the institution. As a result, the hospital became the preferred medical workplace and the number of house calls diminished. Throughout the Gilded Age and Progressive Era, the elites supporting these projects envisioned medicine and the modern hospital as scientific enterprises. This followed a trend toward professionalization in such other science-based industries as chemicals, electronics, and production engineering. A concurrent effort to support these endeavors came about through the convergence of government, corporate, and endowment funds. With this support, scientists and physicians began working together in university and industrial laboratories to seek cures for the diseases plaguing humanity. This collaboration yielded breathtaking advances in medical science so that by the first third of the century, the nation's infant mortality declined by two-thirds and life expectancy increased from forty-nine to fifty-nine years. The death rates for many diseases dropped significantly: tuberculosis dropped from 180 to 49 per 100,000; typhoid from 36 to 2; diphtheria from 43 to 2; measles from 12 to 1; and pneumonia from 158 to 50. After the successful eradication of yellow fever and smallpox, public health waged campaigns against malaria, pellagra, and hookworm and similar scourges.[5] Impressed with these advances, ambitious young men entered the modern hospital's wards and classrooms to pursue careers that would afford them prosperity, status, and greater autonomy in an occupational world increasingly being controlled from above by administrators and managers. The middle classes fully supported these advanced hospital facilities with their expanded range of medical and nursing services by electing to give birth, to undergo surgery, and perhaps to die within their white walls. This sense of confidence has not eroded among succeeding generations of middle-class Americans. Their faith in the medical profession and their satisfaction with hospital care increased dramatically with the discovery of antibiotics in the late 1930s. Prior to this, physicians had been powerless in the face of bacterial infections. After 1940, technological innovation and the growth of the pharmaceutical industry further increased the power of medicine to treat a variety of diseases.

As medicine's therapeutic revolution progressed, hospitals became increasingly more bureaucratic in their organizational design. Health bureaucracies have required increasingly more supervisory and managerial personnel to monitor technical and human resources, costs of service delivery, forms of reimbursement, and compliance with government regulations. Between 1946 and 1989, hospital personnel per occupied bed multiplied nearly sevenfold. Since 1980, health care's share of the U.S. gross domestic product (GDP) rose from 8 percent to 16 percent in 2006; by 2017, the U.S. Center for Medicare and Medicaid Services projects that health care will account for 20 percent of GDP. This surge parallels the expansion of the railroads in Victorian America and the ascendancy of the aerospace and defense industries after World War II. The health care industry currently employs 14 million individuals, with wage and salary jobs concentrated in California, New York, Florida, Texas, and Pennsylvania. In postindustrial Pittsburgh, health care has replaced steel as the dominant sector of the local economy. In post–Cold War Los Angeles, the health sector was one of the few places with job openings. This trend is also apparent in New York City. While many production and service jobs have disappeared from New York, the health care sector has expanded dramatically, accounting for most of the growth in employment in the city since the end of the Cold War.

While dominating the local economics of many deindustrialized regions, the health sector has appropriated systems of control that developed in mass-production industries.[6] Technical control methods were used to maintain a continuous flow of production and to increase the output of both the machines and the workers. This form of control is embedded in the design of machinery, the industrial architecture, and the organization of work to maximize efficiency of the physically based aspects of production. Bureaucratic control, by contrast, is embedded in the organizational structure of the company: its job classifications, promotion policies, work rules, and disciplinary procedures. This second form of control stratifies the workforce by creating new distinctions among employees based upon their technical function and their power within the work setting. The number of supervisory personnel also increases because of the need to regularly monitor and evaluate every worker's performance. Supervisors routinely penalize workers who do not comply with company rules and reward those whose behaviors are in accord with established protocols. Bureaucratic control methods are clearly intrusive, as they impose new behavioral requirements on employees. Like the mass-production factory in 1920s America, the hospital is central to understanding how these forms of control are enacted in a core industry of late modernity, namely the care and repair of sick bodies.

IDEOLOGY AND INTERACTION IN THE HOSPITAL

Philip Rieff has observed that the hospital has succeeded "the church and the parliament as the archetypal institution of western culture."[7] As such, it is central to managing forms of behavior that had been previously regulated by familial, religious, and legal domains. In today's hospitals, physicians create and control the symbolic categories of health and illness, organizing diagnostic and therapeutic activities around their images of professional life. A sense of personal autonomy, or individualism, is central to their clinical self-image. As physician-driven institutions, hospitals are likewise organized around an individualistic image of patient care. Central to hospital life is the individual's welfare, so that the patient serves as the reference point for most transactions. This patient-centered attitude is the basis for care and help giving, and both the professionals' and their patients' actions derive from it.

Modern hospitals, like other bureaucratic service institutions, have rules that govern clientship. Both physicians and patients call upon these rules to serve their self-interests. Patients negotiate treatment based on their level of need for health care, but also on their personal attributes. Physicians and other health providers use a central tenet—the individual's return to health—to justify their professional activities. Transactions are negotiated from a core of a few significant rules in hospital care, but the rules are tenuous because it is impossible to project accurately the shifting needs of individuals. An element of uncertainty precipitates countervailing diagnoses and treatment plans, and each health provider operates on the basis of this sense of indeterminacy.[8] The rationale for individualism as a core value can be found in the origins of scientific medicine. Since the late nineteenth century, physicians have sought to understand disease as a process analogous to a mechanical breakdown. The triumph of mechanism and of a naturalistic worldview during the second industrial revolution gave rise to this positivistic conception of the human organism. Since that time, disease has been conceived as an imbalance and dysfunction of the component parts of a machinelike body. Medical intervention proceeds along similar lines, restructuring an individual organism to restore balance or functional regularity. A mechanistic conception of illness, coupled with the germ theory as an explanatory model, led medicine away from a social understanding of disease origins.

Functionalist conceptions of breakdown and intervention to restore homeostasis have also been used to explain patient illness behavior. The "sick role" is a form of ascribed deviance that absolves patients from blame for having become ill but holds them responsible for seeking medical treatment. The explanation of illness as a form of social deviance derives from a mechanistic view of somatic dysfunction "as the incapacity for relevant task-performance."[9] Somatic illness is thus dysfunctional because it incapacitates an organism's productivity in an industrial society. Disease also threatens healthy persons because sick bodies routinely deviate from social norms, producing undesirable and potentially contagious results. However, the sick must rely upon the healthy for care so that they can return to their productive capacities. To control this potentially conflict-laden situation, the physician takes the role of an arbiter and oversees the mutual obligations of the sick and the healthy. The "sick role," a functionalist construct, absolves a person from responsibility for his incapacity and exempts him from normal role or task obligations. A person's illness is deemed legitimate on two conditions. An individual must recognize the role as undesirable, and must take responsibility for seeking care. With the support of family members, an individual must seek only legitimate professional care. The sick are thus obliged to seek help only from physicians and hospitals, and health care providers are equally obligated to treat them. Physicians are required to stigmatize the sick through diagnostic labeling and to insulate them from normal interactions with the healthy to avoid both physiological and behavioral contagion. Despite the threat of contagion, the physician must initiate treatment that compels a patient to depend upon the healthy for care and recovery.

A functionalist framework places intervention in and cure of illness at the center of hospital life. In fact, most hospital routines are negotiated to meet the individual needs of patients whose careers progress from initial diagnosis to intervention in disease processes. A physician decides to intervene based upon symptoms that are presented and noted during a routine consultation. The intervention requires calling on personnel from other specialties to attend to a sick patient's welfare. The emergent team of health care workers establishes a focus and an alliance on behalf of a patient at a specific point in time. However, since hospital life is subject to recurrent crises, these temporary arrangements are terminated, quickly forgotten, renegotiated and forgotten again in a seemingly endless cycle of patient care. The hospital milieu is thus characterized by ongoing conflict and indeterminacy. Professional and organizational interests in medical care are somewhat concealed from the patients and staff because of a common assumption that the hospital's primary function is the restoration of the individual to health. These social interests are most likely concealed, as well, from younger physicians who often enter the profession with similar beliefs. The mystique may result from medicine's success in implementing a professional project that unifies its socialization practices and its cognitive base. The joint production of physicians, as producers and users of medical knowledge, and of the knowledge itself are at the core of this project. Medicine's knowledge base is thus constructed and standardized to assure cognitive exclusiveness and to facilitate training for mastery of a body of specialized knowledge. Medical socialization has a goal of developing a clinical mentality based upon an action-image, rather than solely on a knowledge-image of disease. In medicine, the scientific method is construed as a cognitive process of diagnosing, treating, and managing disease symptoms. Physicians organize a patient's career through labeling behavioral responses to diagnostic and therapeutic transactions. That career is constantly being negotiated because medical decisions change as symptoms manifest, are labeled, and are controlled. Such decisions then are always made with an eye toward treatment interventions, and this blend of cognitive and therapeutic activity has come to define medicine's professional project.

Hospital work is organized as a team effort. Physicians and allied health workers form a team for the purpose of treating a particular disease or condition. Physicians are the highest-ranking team members and therefore wield the most power. Their loyalties are vested in a particular medical specialty and to the clinical chief who oversees their work. By contrast, the loyalties of allied health workers, such as nurses, physician's assistants, dietitians, physical and occupational therapists, social workers, and health educators, are often vested in a specific treatment setting. However, command-and-control styles of management, whereby nurses and other team members receive unilateral orders from physicians, limit their influence in their work settings. They are bound to follow these orders by their contractual obligations to the hospital and in more subtle ways to the physician. The organization of staff as a team that physicians control sustains hierarchies within hospital work settings. Similar arrangements organize the relationships between physicians and their patients. These are dyadic relations between persons of unequal status. While physicians strive to maintain autonomy and control over their work, patients are generally passive and dependent in the sick role. This may explain in part why a physician will remain detached and impersonal when interacting with a patient. For a physician's interest in a particular patient is often determined by that person's compliance to a narrow, professionally defined role. If an individual follows the treatment protocol and maintains this role, conflict tends to be minimized. By contrast, when a patient manipulates the physician or fails to comply with a treatment regime, the physician will often refer the case to other colleagues. Physicians are bound by an ethical code to do everything in their power to maintain alliances with patients who are chronically or acutely ill. However, a patient may breach an alliance because of any number of factors and will thereby become estranged from a particular caregiver.

The physician thus controls medical intervention, the dominant approach to patient care. A doctor views a patient's condition as a technical dysfunction that can be cured by physical and chemical treatment. The physician is active and dominant in the transaction. The health care team is organized such that there is control over the patient, and that the physician's orders are followed expediently. The patient is expected to be passive in the healing transaction. Such passivity may increase the probability of patients becoming alienated from medical professionals and of patients failing to comply with their treat-

ment. Hospitals reflect this mode of care in their organization. Clinical transactions are thus arranged to expedite service delivery within such hierarchies
and most relationships are governed by regulations and sanctions. The ratio-
nales for this impersonal style are treatment success, efficiency, and a lowered
risk of malpractice litigation. Therapeutic intervention, an alternative form of
care, encourages the patient to actively participate in treatment. The physician
is crucial to this approach, but must be prepared to accommodate a patient's
more proactive role in a treatment alliance. Negotiation and reciprocity in the
healing process are central to this approach and these dynamics limit the monopoly of power held by the physician. The patient joins with a team of physicians and allied health workers to realize an alliance. Rehabilitation facilities,
rather than acute care hospitals, are more likely to use this approach to treatment. The demands made upon physicians in acute care facilities preclude the
enactment of a therapeutic intervention approach. The more personal interactions associated with private practice or rehabilitation settings are usually dis-
pensed with or delegated to allied health workers. However, these workers are
usually trained only to perform specific tasks in an efficient and detached
manner. Their education may not have included formal training in counseling
and other supportive techniques. Their limited understanding only increases
their anxieties over not being able to fully handle the emotional aspects of
care. Moreover, they will often view emotional support tasks as those of
higher-paid psychiatric staff that routinely consult to hospital medical services. Allied health workers may also harbor resentment toward the physician
who dropped the matter into their hands without yielding any of the physician's customary demands for sole autonomy in and dominance over the medical workplace. Although the health workers are powerless to act beyond their
specified role, they are expected to undertake the additional tasks of emotional work assigned to them by professionals who have restricted their activities in most other treatment-related domains.

When a patient encounters a physician, the nature of the transaction is usually confined to diagnosis and treatment of physical symptoms. A key element in a clinical transaction is the way in which the discourse flows from the
superior to the subordinate. The physician is expected to control the flow by
actively seeking information from the patient or allied health staff. A diagnostic interview is arranged in a manner such that the physician's legitimacy is
conveyed to the patient but also to subordinates in the setting. The physician
often delegates preliminary routines and social amenities to subordinates—a
procedure that might allow more time with patients—but also displays the
primacy of the physician's role as the key manipulator of the patient as organism. The transaction is further mystified by the physician's down-to-business
style that is sometimes framed by patronizing forms of address and the use of

technical jargon to convey symptoms and diagnoses. A patient may try to regain control of the encounter through confrontation or by actively negotiating treatment. These breaches in protocol may indicate a potential loss of control in front of colleagues and staff. A physician will then usually withdraw from the patient and begin to comment directly to others on the health care team, often referring to the patient in the third person. Hence, medical intervention, as a form of interaction, only reinforces the profession's mechanistic bias and thereby dehumanizes the patient. By narrowly focusing on presenting symptoms, disease is reduced to a strictly organic dysfunction. The patient then becomes an object to be manipulated through one or more task functions. Failure to account for the patient's view of disease symptoms and of the relationship of symptoms to nonorganic factors increases the risk of diagnostic failure and of depersonalization. Depersonalization is symptomatic of a concern for order and efficiency at the expense of flexibility and compassion. It occurs frequently when staff perceive patients as helpless, noncompliant, or not fully cognizant of their condition. Depersonalized care also results from tensions between administrators and professionals over control over treatment. Physicians regard the hospital as a workplace that should be under their professional control. But the hospital is also a bureaucracy operated by administrators where service delivery is formally organized. As such, the hierarchical arrangements characteristic of most bureaucracies may also depersonalize interactions between hospital staff and patients.

ILLNESS "CAREERS," STIGMA, AND SELF-CARE

The goals and assumptions of both medicine and the hospital are embedded in most diagnostic and therapeutic transactions. A patient's career will be constructed to reflect these interests along with the presenting symptoms and health care needs. The hospital as a work organization is likewise influenced by the social interests of its dominant professionals. Physicians have the "legally sustained jurisdiction" to exclusively perform the work of physical healing.[10] This sanction also assures their professional autonomy and right of self-regulation and their technical authority over a body of knowledge and therapeutic skills. These social interests not only dictate standards of professional behavior but also directly influence relations with other hospital personnel and with patients.

Hospitals are places where staff and patients are continually negotiating treatment, and these transactions come to define the life of the organization. Hospital life revolves around numerous "small worlds" created by interactions of health care personnel and their patients. These organizational networks are based upon a set of manifest rules and implicit meanings. For example, physicians expect compliance with their treatment plans. Their initial affiliation is often contingent upon the new patient's acceptance of this responsibility. A "power-dependence relationship" is thus established between professional and client on the basis of control vested in the role of the practitioner. This form of interaction is designed to transform a person into a patient. Repeated clinical visits can thus foster dependency in patients, especially those with a chronic illness. In contrast to the short-term affiliations associated with acute care, chronically ill patients may grow increasingly more reliant on a number of services available to them. They become well socialized in the role of help seeker and learn to use strategies to manipulate the system for a variety of medical and nonmedical services. Patients will negotiate services on the basis of attributes, such as health, age, wage, household size and composition, and their self-presentation. They will typically reinforce their worthiness through deference and other dependent behaviors as an anticipated trade-off for participation in entitlement programs.

Physicians, nurses, social workers, and even administrative personnel will advocate on behalf of a worthy patient to organize and sustain a network of care for their material support. The network usually renders a client dependent upon public entitlements for the satisfaction of his basic needs. The hospital will mediate on behalf of a client for services that governmental bureaucracies routinely deliver to worthy recipients, including disability benefits. A social worker will be assigned to counsel a patient who is incapable of determining a suitable strategy for community living. As case manager, the social worker develops a series of ties with other agencies and negotiates and makes decisions by proxy. Dependent networks of care are thus mobilized on behalf of low-income incapacitated patients who are undergoing a change of status and often lack the requisite skills for negotiating with bureaucracies. These longer-term affiliations give the hospital and its staff greater control over nonmedical aspects of a patient's life. However, a new situation may emerge out of the strategies that patients use to manage their identity as people who are worthy of care. While diversifying demands for health and related services, a patient may become structurally dependent upon many units of the system of health and human services.[11] A number of providers then become committed to the patient's career as a multiple recipient. The institutional field is thereby widened to include exchanges between the hospital and other agencies, including rehabilitation, nursing homes, federal and state disability, and welfare programs. Hospital staff's attitudes toward "dependent" patients, who have become embedded within a nexus of diverse services, can affect their interpersonal relations with them. Allied health workers will often resent these patients who require additional supportive services and record keeping to satisfy government reimbursement guidelines. They begin to withdraw when these patients make continued demands upon them or when they complain to them about poor-quality care. Hospital staff will often state that disadvantaged patients, who cannot afford to pay for their medical care, should be satisfied and grateful for *any* care bestowed upon them. They will often question why general hospitals maintain "semipermanent" patient populations—including those frequently using emergency rooms for primary care—rather than providing short-term treatment and referral to private practitioners.

Physicians and others governing the routines of the hospital organize a patient's medical condition into an illness "career." This is meant to facilitate control of both the disease and any changes in a patient's behavior that are a consequence of the illness. Each stage of this career is managed through both diagnostic labeling and the requisite therapeutic techniques to control disease symptoms. Physicians thus have the legitimate power to understand, label, and intervene in the disease process, and to sanction personal behavior. However, the power of the profession extends beyond physical healing to include the social control of deviance and the stigma that will often accompany an illness. Medicine's status thus permits it to define the need for service and how that need will be organized. In Eliot Freidson's words, "the social organization of treatment may be seen to create the conditions by which the experience of being ill, the relationships one has with others when ill, and the very life of the sick person becomes organized."[12]

As an applied science, the creation of new medical labels will evolve with innovations in medical technology. Each innovative diagnostic or therapeutic technique fosters new careers for professionals and their patients. It is in the best interests of the medical profession to increase the number of diagnostic labels and thereby the range of illness behaviors to which the sick role can be imputed. Medicine's dominant role is thus maintained through such professional expansion, with each new discovery serving to reaffirm its status as the key legislator of healing in the society.

The physician has become a moral arbiter, responsible not only for identifying the cause and prescribed treatment of a condition but also for designating the consequences of a patient's illness behavior on his family, school or workplace, and the wider society. In this role, the physician is often called upon to sequester the sick person, perhaps by temporarily or even permanently prohibiting the individual from engaging in certain routines in the home or in public places. While utilitarian in motive, over time such restrictions in everyday activities may stigmatize a person, render him discreditable, and cause him to lose whatever "social margin" he had attained prior to becoming ill. In the words of Jacqueline Wiseman,

Social margin refers to the amount of *leeway* a given individual has in making errors on the job, buying on credit, or stepping on the toes of significant others without suffering such serious penalties as being fired, denied credit, or losing friends or family. . . . Social margin also encompasses the human resources a person can call upon in case of disaster, such as an incapacitating accident, losing a job, or being arrested. A person with margin can get help from his family, employer, or friends at such times.[13]

Once lost, a person's social margin is difficult to regain, as it is built up over time, much as a credit history. After a while, members of the sick individual's social network may no longer view him as capable of giving or worthy of receiving the benefits accrued through social relations. They will then relate to him according to a diminished set of expectations. When a sick person engages with the world as a stigmatized individual, he may come to expect a certain response from those outside the immediate family or the caregivers within clinical settings. The stigmatized individual may even anticipate such derision and ostracism from former associates as well as from strangers, and this sense of shame may then become a part of his defensive structure. That person will then forge a character that is capable of managing his spoiled identity, and his subsequent behavior will emerge from this defensive stance.

The physician's role as a moral arbiter is evident at the onset of a chronic illness. Upon diagnosis, the patient and family members express fears to the physician regarding the illness and its consequences, the treatment regimes and prognosis, and their concerns to provide for medical care. These are temporary reactions that disturb psychological homeostasis, and they follow Selye's classical paradigm of stress.[14] Coping during this phase means perceiving the illness as a threat, mobilizing resources to meet it, and diminishing the crisis through adaptive behaviors. Although most hospitals are organized around acute care, chronic illnesses affect some 10 percent of the American population, more than infectious or parasitic diseases, and cause 70 percent of all deaths. Patients are hospitalized during the acute stage of a chronic illness and then sent home to manage subsequent phases. Longer-term issues will arise once the immediate crisis has passed. In contrast to the hospital-managed acute phase, subsequent phases of the illness will significantly alter a person's everyday behaviors. Upon discharge from the hospital, a chronically ill person must proactively manage the illness, a drastically changed life situation, and a new personal identity. Home and family life will have to change dramatically in order to accommodate major alterations in everyday routines and vocational activities. However, most chronically ill patients will rely on informal, unpaid caregivers, since two-thirds of those with disabilities do not receive paid home care services.

The primary requirement in chronic illness behavior is adjustment: an individual must adapt everyday life and social functioning to a less-than-normal health status. Coping during this phase will require one to learn how to manage intermittent medical crises and to control symptoms, including pain. Those with a chronic illness will also have to reorder time and the spatial dimensions of their lives, learn to minimize social isolation, and thereby bring about a gradual return to "normal" routines. Chronically ill persons use a variety of coping strategies to enhance their adaptation. However, successful adaptation often requires them to continually work on, test, and modify these strategies. Professional and peer counseling are widely used by patients and their families during the onset and initial treatment of a chronic disease. There has also been a trend toward patient self-care. Self-care describes activities carried out by an individual, sometimes with the help of others, to deal with somatic and emotional problems arising from an illness, to improve health status, or to prevent illness from occurring. The major components of self-care are health maintenance, disease prevention, self-diagnosis, self-medication, and other forms of self-treatment and patients' participation in professional care. Recently, there has been a clear preference for specific stress-reduction techniques, including biofeedback, meditation, visualization, and guided imagery, which help individuals gain more control over the healing process.

There is considerable evidence that psychological attributes play a significant role in mediating health outcomes in chronic illness. Three such cognitive factors are internal locus of control, the sense of coherence, and self-efficacy. Patients who tend toward an "internal" locus of control—those who believe that some control lies within themselves—are more likely to perceive self-care behaviors as efficacious. Similarly, patients with a strong sense of coherence, who view the world as comprehensible, manageable, and meaningful, and believe in the possibility of working through challenging situations and, as a result, that things will work out as well as can reasonably be expected, are thus more likely to engage in self-care behaviors because of their confidence that such efforts will yield positive results. Patients with a sense of self-efficacy are confident in their ability to carry out demanding activities, are aware of their coping strengths, and are therefore more likely to actively pursue self-care behaviors. Chronically ill persons will often participate in health-oriented self-help groups to meet their self-care objectives. These groups are a way to get information about effective coping with both the physical and psychological difficulties associated with their condition. They also provide a setting for obtaining social and emotional support by sharing problems with their peers. Individuals who participate in self-help groups often report increased self-esteem and self-reliance. They appear to have a better understanding of their illness and to be more capable of negotiating and maintaining therapeutic alliances with professionals.

SELF-HELP AND DISABILITY RIGHTS
AS SOCIAL MOVEMENTS

The contemporary impetus toward mutual help and self-care in health has its roots in the women's movement. A central concern of the women's movement was in the area of health. In consciousness-raising groups, women soon discovered that they knew relatively little about their bodies, their sexuality, or the ways medical institutions defined and controlled important phases of their lives. Critical of medical schools' near exclusion of women and of male physicians' condescending attitudes toward their female patients, women's health activists established independent health care clinics run by and for women and lobbied for the legalization of abortion. They established support groups to come to terms with the dependency, sense of powerlessness, and victim blaming that women frequently experienced in health care organizations. Feminists also developed self-help groups focused on particular aspects of health, including know-your-body courses, alternative health care, and postmastectomy recovery. Other self-help groups were established to provide mutual support in parenting and family crises, during menopause and widowhood, and in coping with the range of mental and emotional disorders.[15]

Parallel with the women's movement, people with serious physical disabilities organized self-help groups during the postwar decades. The disabled shared many of the same concerns of the feminists, including stereotyping, stigmatization, and increased dependency on professionals. Both movements flourished in the late 1960s, when people began to view medical care more critically and to demystify its premises and procedures. There was also an upsurge of consumer activism focused especially on the pharmaceutical industry and on the health-related regulatory agencies in the federal government, such as the Food and Drug Administration (FDA) and the Occupational Safety and Health Administration (OSHA).[16] Each movement developed as a result of an increasing mistrust of the professionals sanctioned to look after the public interest in the areas of science, technology, and health, and of the diminishment of personal control as more of people's lives became subject to professional management.[17]

The late 1960s also witnessed the flourishing of self-help organizations of parents of chronically ill and handicapped children, although most of these groups had begun to surface two decades earlier. In fact, by the early 1950s, parent-organized groups developed into state and national organizations as local groups coalesced to publicize their particular condition, especially through the new medium of television.[18] By the late 1960s, many of these disease-specific organizations increased in both membership and influence. The National Association for Retarded Children had over 1,000 local units and a membership of 130,000. The United Cerebral Palsy Associations of America had about 260 local units, over 100,000 members, and more than 50,000 volunteers. The Muscular Dystrophy Association of America had over 400 chapters and 500,000 volunteers.[19] From the early 1970s onward, many self-help organizations spearheaded effective campaigns on behalf of their diverse constituencies in the courts and in state legislatures. They eventually realized their goal of integrated schooling when Congress passed the Education for all Handicapped Act of 1974, which guarantees the right to public education for all children with a physical or mental disability who are living in the community.[20]

The 1970s brought about the creation of a new type of self-help group: the independent living organization. Usually organized by young adults with a variety of disabilities, these local groups provide mutual support and specific help with a range of problems. As they developed, they offered many of the services of established health and welfare agencies and added some innovative ones. They took a critical posture toward the conventional forms of service delivery and had a strong orientation toward advocacy and social action to achieve changes in policies. In Berkeley, California, the prototypical Center for Independent Living (CIL) originated in 1970 among a group of physically disabled students at the University of California who organized to obtain more accessible buildings, classrooms, laboratories, and other academic facilities so they would not be hampered in pursuing an education. The students' success in bringing about changes in the university's facilities led them to extend their activities into the community on behalf of other persons with disabilities. By the mid-1970s, the Berkeley CIL had become a major resource for independent living, jobs, and personal services for young adults with disabilities who were living in the San Francisco Bay Area.[21]

As soon as these local-level, self-help organizations banded together to form national coalitions, they realized considerable political influence. The National Council of Independent Living Centers (NCILC), a coalition of over 200 local self-help organizations of persons with disabilities, lobbied hard to improve the quality of life for disabled persons. The national organization campaigned for improved procedures for disabled Social Security recipients, and for the recruitment of personal attendants for disabled persons. It also worked to ensure that public transportation and housing facilities were wheelchair accessible and for increased job openings for persons with disabilities. The NCILC's extensive campaign on behalf of the Americans with Disabilities Act (ADA), including several years of lobbying, public education, media campaigns, and mass demonstrations in Washington, D.C., and in state capitals, eventually led to the act's passage in 1990.[22] Like the NCILC, the National Alliance for the Mentally Ill (NAMI) was established along self-help lines to provide assistance to discharged patients and their families. Originally a loosely structured coalition of small family groups, the NAMI established a strong policy advocacy presence through its campaigns on behalf of the civil liberties of the mentally ill and for improved conditions in both community treatment facilities and in the state hospitals. By the late 1980s, the NAMI had nearly 1,000 affiliates and an annual budget of over $1 million. Its fully staffed national office in Washington, D.C., was established for the purpose of policy advocacy, most notably through the National Institute of Mental Health (NIMH), on behalf of federally funded social programs that benefit the mentally ill, such as Social Security and the Community Support Program.[23]

By the late 1980s, AIDS activists went beyond each of the considerable achievements of the other activist groups in spearheading policy advocacy on behalf of patients with a condition that the medical profession was virtually powerless to cure.[24] In the AIDS epidemic, gay activists clearly indicated that such passivity should not be taken for granted. They numbered among their members articulate individuals with considerable intellectual skills who also had experience in political activism. Their counterparts in the lesbian movement brought similar skills and experiences, but also feminism's fundamental questioning of the motives of health care providers. Both groups share a fundamental ideology of personal efficacy and of control over their own health care. Together with other constituencies, such as parents of persons living with HIV, especially children, they created a powerful coalition that could not only organize but also deliver funds, protesters, and votes. Clearly, the politicization of health has challenged notions of stigmatization for at least these specific subcultures and their supporting institutions. Because of their involvement in, and access to, the arts and other cultural institutions, AIDS activists had developed the skills to present their definitions of the epidemic and to express what it means through powerful images. In the area of research, AIDS activists with scientific training were also able to influence all aspects of the research process, from the funding to the conduct of clinical trials. More significantly, they have been able to influence what constitutes good science in AIDS research. They mobilized public interest in the ways persons living with HIV are treated, antiretroviral therapies and other AIDS drugs are marketed, AIDS-related research is funded, even how the epidemic is defined. The powerful AIDS lobby convinced Wellcome to slash prices on the controversial drug AZT and persuaded the Food and Drug Administration

(FDA) to release unapproved drugs that were thought to be effective in treating AIDS. Advocacy groups obtained the release of information about experimental treatments, "overcoming the FDA's insistence that to do it would violate commercial confidentiality."[25]

What weaves together these diverse social action practices is the resurgence of populism in the social movements of the late twentieth century. Like its nineteenth-century predecessor, the "new populism" implies a reliance on self-initiated activity, based on both participatory democracy and experiential forms of knowledge. Most contemporary movement organizations emphasize the creation of social environments, such as self-help groups, support networks, and experiential learning situations, where participants solve problems by "taking action together." Within these settings, the change process is relational, rather than individualistic, emphasizing the connectedness and mutual involvement of participants in meaningful activities. This emphasis may account for the success of many voluntary social action initiatives, from neighborhood organizations to broad-based citizen coalitions.

Similarly, the "social model" programs that frequently emerge from populist initiatives differ considerably from their professional counterparts because of their experiential knowledge base. These programs strive to transform the knowledge, gained through life experience rather than that of experts, into an institutional ethos that is shared by all participants. While they appear similar in their organizational and administrative structures to the more formal expert-driven programs, social model programs differ with respect to their perspective toward a specific issue or situation. Their alternative approach, based largely upon populist values of self-control and self-determination embedded in their practices, is itself continually transformed and reconfigured through the open-ended experiences of participants.[26]

The following cases describe how patients with chronic conditions obtain support from self-help groups. The first case describes how one such group helps renal patients cope with the move from hospital-based hemodialysis to CAPD, a self-care modality that gives them greater independence and control over their treatment. The second case describes how self-help groups help persons with lupus achieve greater emotional self-care as they learn to adjust to the cyclical flare-ups and remissions characteristic of the disease.

PARTNERS IN HEALING

End-stage renal disease (ESRD) is a chronic, life-threatening condition that requires ongoing medical treatment.[27] Renal disease indicates that a person's kidneys, as the body's filtering system, are unable to remove metabolic waste products from the blood. Chronic renal failure was once considered untreat-able, and its sufferers faced a slow death. However, major advances in med-ical technology in the 1960s diminished the threat of death to renal patients. Multiple dialysis treatments with an artificial kidney machine, once reserved for only acute and potentially reversible cases, have become standard therapy for all ESRD patients. Another key breakthrough is the arterio-venous shunt. Usually implanted in the forearm, the shunt provides access to the blood with-out permanently damaging the vessels. Renal patients are now kept alive through dietary management, medication, and long-term dialysis techniques, and in some cases, organ transplantation. The major cost of treatment for kid-, ney failure is borne by publicly financed Medicare and Social Security pro-grams. In-center hemodialysis (HD) is the predominant treatment for adults with renal disease. Patients must visit a hospital three times a week to use a mechanical kidney; the treatment requires about four hours to complete. Dur-ing this time, a patient is passive and dependent upon the machine and the hospital staff. The patient remains immobile in a reclining armchair while his blood is pumped through clear plastic tubes to an artificial kidney that re-moves impurities, controls electrolyte levels, and eliminates excess fluids.

Continuous Ambulatory Peritoneal Dialysis (CAPD), an alternative dia-lytic technique, uses the natural lining of the abdomen, called the peritoneum, as the dialysis membrane to filter wastes and fluid out of the body. CAPD cleanses a patient's blood by filtering it through a solution in the abdominal cavity. The technique uses a small tube or catheter to infuse and drain the ab-dominal cavity of a cleansing liquid. The tube is surgically inserted into an in-cision in the abdomen. After surgery, patients learn how to dialyze themselves during a five- to ten-day training course. They are taught how to filter their blood by running a sterile solution through the catheter. The infusion takes up to thirty minutes to complete. Several hours later, the patient extracts the old chemical solution and inserts a new supply of the liquid. CAPD patients usu-ally have fewer fluid and diet restrictions, but must perform the fluid ex-change procedure three-to-five times a day. There are complications associ-ated with CAPD, especially peritonitis, an infection in the abdomen, but also back pain, hernias, and accumulation of high levels of fat in the blood. ESRD patients are required to perform a daily regimen that may be restrictive and unpleasant. This varies from dietary restrictions to performance of dialysis exchanges to taking a number of medications. Patient noncompliance with the HD regimen is quite common. ESRD and chronic dialysis are associated with acute and chronic adverse biological effects on almost all organ systems. Many patients have impairments that limit both their performance of routine physical activities, including self-care, and their ability to work. Restrictions on social and leisure activities and vocational disability are ubiquitous in chronic HD patients. They frequently have psychological symptoms of anxiety and depression, but also more severe psychiatric syndromes. HD patients' family lives are marked by serious marital conflicts resulting from decreased libido and sexual dysfunction, and their children also experience high levels of psychological distress.

CAPD patients are able to engage in more routine physical activities. Because they are not dependent upon the hospital dialysis unit, they have more independence and control over their treatment. They can set their own schedules and travel without making special arrangements. They have a less restricted diet. Although these patients express boredom with performing CAPD exchange procedures, they have increased freedom and ease of travel and are thus capable of sustaining a fuller vocational life. As a result, their families suffer less treatment-related stress. However, CAPD patients report both chronic pain and fear associated with peritonitis. They show little improvement in sexual function even though many men report a greater libido and many women see the recurrence of their menstrual periods. These patients must also cope with a changed body image as a result of the two-inch-long catheter protruding from their abdomen. The abdomen will often distend as a result of the procedure, and patients will usually gain weight because of their increased caloric intake. Although they are capable of performing a wider range of activities, CAPD patients report only marginal improvements in their psychological mood, sense of well-being, and overall life satisfaction. This probably results from the initial apprehension and malaise that accompany the transition to self-dialysis. As renal patients move out of the dialysis unit, they relinquish a world of caregivers who have surrounded them since the onset of their illness. Patients become a regular part of a unit three times a week, very often for years. They grow attached and dependent upon staff for their medical, nursing, dietary, and rehabilitative care. The social worker mediates many of these transactions within the hospital, but also with the federal agencies that finance dialysis and other entitlement programs. This network of emotional support and "hands-on" care is expected and delivered to them whenever they enter the hospital. Once they initiate CAPD, however, they lose the ongoing support of the health care team and will often become anxious about their ability to handle the physical crises that are a part of renal disease.

The dialysis unit is also a place where patients routinely gather to discuss their condition and other aspects of their lives. Patients tend to rely on the unit for more than their health care needs. It is a source of ongoing support, providing both social relationships and a sense of belonging. Patients routinely socialize and discuss various aspects of their treatment. They frequently compare notes about members of the staff and discuss at length their family lives.

After so many years of thrice-weekly visits, patients tend to find their primary support on the unit where close friendships evolve and are celebrated on birthdays and other occasions. As patients switch to CAPD, they become isolated from their peers and thus relinquish the support provided them by the dialysis unit as a "treatment family." This is particularly distressing at a time when they are confronting an altered physical appearance and doubts about whether they are capable of managing self-dialysis.

Harry Brey and Joyce Jarvis established a support group to help HD patients cope with the transition to CAPD.[28] The group met twice each month at a community hospital in the New York metropolitan area. Patients joined the group during the training period just after surgery to insert the catheter. However, some joined the group after they decided to adopt CAPD but before they made the change to the new treatment. Group members shared medical information about CAPD and confronted the challenges of self-care. They also took turns recounting their struggles with renal disease and their treatment experiences. Strong emotions would often accompany the retelling of their medical histories, and the group was a source of support and clarification of these emergent feelings. As patients disclosed more of themselves in the group, they began to experience a revived sense of themselves as individuals.

The individuation process begun in the group was especially important. These patients had grown dependent upon a hospital treatment milieu for their continued survival. They also accrued "secondary gains" from their illness. These included an increased dependency upon members of their social networks, but also upon the hospital-based network of care and entitlement programs that became available to them. For many patients, dialysis resolved many of the conflicts that had beset them before becoming ill. For example, they would use the sick role to justify abdicating both work and family responsibilities. The group discussions thus validated and supported their newly felt sense of personal autonomy as they moved toward greater self-responsibility for their treatment. This independent stance was an essential part of the move away from the dialysis unit and its myriad forms of support.

Self-care meant going home to a life apart from the medical setting. As patients engaged more in their treatment, issues that had been resolved or at least occluded by dialysis resurfaced. As CAPD reduced their opportunities to further accrue secondary gains, patients were forced to confront their personal lives. The group encouraged greater independence in resolving treatment-related difficulties. Peers helped each other adjust to their changed family worlds now that they were spending more time at home. Members also reinforced one another's greater engagement with the world outside of the home and the hospital. They supported each other's search for part-time and full-time employment, but also for volunteer opportunities. Perhaps the most important forms of support were provided in the areas of body image and sexuality. While some reported an increased libido after their catheter was implanted, others had difficulties accepting a changed body image resulting from abdominal distention. Just as the challenges of self-care and of survival apart from the hospital focused earlier phases of the group, help in resolving predialysis issues of intimacy and family life formed the basis of later phases. During each phase, however, the emphasis was clearly on the possibilities of living independently of the medical environment and of seeking and gaining mutual support from peers in coping with the change. The support sought by the CAPD patients may be compared with that sought by the lupus patients who formed groups to help one another to cope with a chronic disease, one that requires them to gain control over their emotions and their physical limitations, as they attempt to gain control medically, as well, over an unpredictable and unpleasant disease.

Systemic lupus erythematosus is a chronic, inflammatory autoimmune disease; it damages the connective tissues and can affect any organ of the body.[29] Lupus occurs in all races and ethnic groups; it is far more common in women than in men. Typically, the onset of the disease occurs during the childbearing years. Those with lupus develop blood cell abnormalities, including the overproduction of the antibodies that normally help protect the body against infectious environmental bacteria and viruses. In the absence of outside infectious agents, these antibodies attack the body's healthy cells, setting off an allergy-like reaction. In effect, the body's immune system turns against the body itself, attacking and sometimes destroying bodily tissue. Like arthritis, lupus causes swelling and inflammation of muscles and joints. It often affects the kidneys, but it can also involve the heart, lungs, central nervous system, liver, or other organs or systems. Patients experience extreme fatigue, lose hair, develop mouth sores and skin rashes, and run low-grade fevers. Swelling of the hands and feet; pain in the joints; and sensitivity to the sun, heat, and cold are also common.

To date no cause of lupus has been established. Because there is no single pattern of onset and no single set of symptoms, the diagnosis may take several years. Lupus is difficult to diagnose because early indications are vague and diffuse. Patients often experience symptoms long before there is physiological evidence from blood tests or other clinical assessments. If there is no change in organ functioning or blood tests are normal, physicians may conclude there is no real disease. Until a definitive diagnosis is made, patients receive no specific corroboration that something is physically wrong with them. Lupus patients report that some physicians described them as "hysterical," "nagging," "inquisitive," "demanding," and "anxious." Before the diagnosis, patients may thus doubt their own judgment and feel that their problems are psychosomatic and self-induced. Although there is no single laboratory test to determine whether a person has lupus, in 1982, the American College of Rheumatology established eleven criteria for diagnosing lupus. These criteria include both the results of routine laboratory tests, specialized tests related to immune status, and physical symptoms. If a patient has four or more of the symptoms on the list, a diagnosis of lupus is made.

The symptoms of lupus are unpredictable and erratic. One day, the patient feels relatively well and energetic, but the next day, he or she feels ill and enervated. The erratic course tends to evoke counterproductive behavior in patients. On "good days," patients attempt to accomplish as much as possible to compensate for past and future "bad days." The tendency to overdo things exacerbates their symptoms, causing them to feel ill for several days afterward. This "vicious cycle" may even be life threatening, and it usually prevents patients from achieving a relatively normal way of life. Because of the cyclical exacerbations and remissions, lupus creates stress for patients and their families. The chronic stress with which lupus patients live helps create episodic "flare-ups" of the disease and adds to the discomfort of the symptoms. The physical pain can cause severe fatigue and interrupted sleep. The prescribed medications alleviate or control specific symptoms but often produce adverse physiological and emotional changes and troublesome side effects. Differentiating physical and psychological symptoms caused by the disease and from those caused by the treatment is, at best, difficult.

Cortisone is most frequently prescribed to alleviate or control specific symptoms. The corticosteroids, however, will often produce adverse physiological and emotional changes, and side effects that are experienced as distressing. These include mood swings, insomnia, depression, nausea, weight loss and gain, increased appetite, bloating, water retention, personality changes, anxiety, memory impairment, mood lability, mental deterioration, obsessive reactions, and sometimes psychosis. If the dosage of the corticosteroid is changed, abnormal behavior is apt to occur, ranging from "steroid psychosis" to physiological withdrawal symptoms. Because cortisone both stimulates and simulates bodily stress, the drug also detracts from the body's natural ability to counteract stress and to maintain the fight/flight response.

Lupus is a serious and presently incurable illness. To a great extent, the prognosis depends on the patient's psychosocial adjustment, since the state of mind, emotional stress, and immunological factors are closely linked in the disease process. Patients frequently have psychological or technically psychiatric symptoms. These symptoms are of two kinds: a mild form of emotional distress that is manifest in neurotic depression, anxiety, tension, phobias, or obsessional behaviors, and a severe form that manifests in such florid symptoms as hallucinations, delusions, disorientation, and psychosis. Depression is pervasive. As was just noted, medications used in the treatment of lupus may have depressive effects. Some clinicians believe that the patient's anger at having lupus is expressed in a depressive style or in self-destructive behavior: anorexia, the tendency to be suicidal, noncompliance with medical regimens, the abuse of medication, and the denial of physical limitations imposed by the disease. Patients experience a loss of positive self- and body image, lowered self-esteem, heightened stress, and depression. They fear that they will be rejected by others and hence, isolated.

People with any chronic illness have periods of reactive depression. At the point of diagnosis, patients with lupus may need help in coping with the unpredictable assaults of the disease on the body and with the associated psychological distress. Anxiety, fear, and stress tend to be greater when the causes and nature of the illness and the prognosis are unknown. Lupus is mysterious and unpredictable, and many who encounter lupus patients react negatively to it. Some withdraw because they are afraid of "catching" the disease; others deny its impact on the patient.

Withdrawal by others is not the only form of isolation the patients with lupus experience. Because of physical pain, exhaustion, and emotional fatigue, these patients may isolate themselves. Divorce rates among patients with lupus are higher than the norm, in part, because of the limitations or inability to engage in sexual relations, either owing to pain or to the tendency of medications to suppress the libido. Sexual dysfunction may add to reluctance of unmarried patients to socialize or to become involved in intimate relationships. Another reason for this flight from intimacy is the fear of bearing children who might have lupus too. That genetic forces play an important role is clear, in view of the fact that lupus develops regularly and spontaneously in certain inbred strains of mice. In humans, there is a moderate tendency for lupus to occur in more than one family member. Many patients with lupus experience anxiety and distress about the financial burdens that the disease imposes, both the direct medical costs and the loss of income arising from the erratic course of the disease, which makes regular employment difficult. Patients who are employed full-time fear the consequences of missing too much work. Those who can no longer work full-time experience distress about having to rely on others for financial help. Those with family obligations may feel they have failed when they cannot provide consistent financial support for their dependents.

Local chapters of the Lupus Foundation of America, a nonprofit voluntary health organization, hold regular meetings and organize support groups for patients. Members of these local self-help organizations also develop and implement community outreach programs and work with hospital staffs, professionals, and the local media. The goal is to transmit accurate scientific information about lupus. The local chapters, in sum, help the individual members through traditional self-help techniques that support peer relationships in dyads and group settings. They develop a cadre of members who, despite their illness, develop and use skills in community organization, mutual support, and the education of patients; thus, they are a model of the self-help principles of the importance of activity to overcome stress and anxiety and the reciprocity of giving and receiving help. Groups of lupus patients may be dichotomized into two main types that function differently according to the characteristics and needs of their primary members. The first type, which may be termed "primary support" groups, are made up of members who, for a variety of reasons, are not receiving support from their immediate families and intimate friends. The second type, which may be termed "supplementary support" groups, consist of people with relatively intact and satisfying primary supports but who wish to establish and maintain contact with peers who are experiencing a similar problem. The Lupus Foundation set up self-help groups in two Southern California locations: a large urban neighborhood and a smaller suburban community. The urban group was largely a "primary support" group and the suburban group was mainly a "supplementary support" group. The two groups differed in such aspects as the breadth of participation, the proportion of trivia to significant content, and the frequency of conflicts or disagreements. Probably because of the greater homogeneity and personal security of its members, the suburban group allowed for rapid and intense discussions of significant issues surrounding the illness, rather than for a focus on procedural and status questions, as in the urban group. There was also a more positive mood at the end of the sessions in the suburban group, and members reported greater satisfaction with the group process than in the urban group.

The urban group had a higher proportion of small talk than "significant" talk during its sessions compared to the suburban group. In fact, group procedures were frequently discussed in the urban group. These procedural issues, nonsubstantive so far as the disease is concerned, involved such questions as who should be invited to address the group, who should do the inviting, the frequency of meetings, and so forth. Furthermore, the startups of the discussions were more difficult in the city than in the suburbs. Fewer members participated in the urban group's meetings than in the suburban group. Antagonistic, critical, or indifferent moods were observed at the end of many of the urban group's sessions, but none in the suburban one. Such differences in content, level, and functioning of the group discussions and group functioning as a whole are related to differences in the composition of the two groups. The majority of the urban group's members were single, separated, or divorced women, most of whom had to work. Their various kinds and levels of situational life stresses were substantial and continuous, and this situation was reflected in the often-acrimonious group sessions. In contrast, the other group's members were mostly married, lived in middle-class suburbs, and generally had supportive husbands; fewer of them worked, not because they were too ill but because they chose not to.

The participation of lupus patients in health-oriented, self-help organizations is a form of emotional "self-care." The purposes of such participation are several: to get information from others with lupus about how to cope effectively with psychosomatic difficulties; to obtain emotional and social support by sharing problems in a group setting; and to bolster self-esteem and self-reliance, both in understanding one's illness and in relationships with the health care system and its professionals. Although conscious self-care, in the form of necessary changes in lifestyle, is required to improve their physical and social adaptations, the lupus patients' major problems seem to be in the mental health sphere. Self-care cannot "cure" the disease or change its course, but participation with others in self-help activities seems to alleviate the greatest stresses of lupus and to improve the patients' ability to cope with the disease. Self-care is not a substitute for needed medical interventions; rather it is a desirable form of parallel social treatment for this severe, often life-threatening, chronic disease.

Medical self-care is thus sustained through active participation in close-knit networks of care, including self-help groups and mutual aid organizations.[30] Self-care skills learned through these networks include symptom recognition, treatment of minor illness and injury, and negotiation and advocacy skills. Individuals may also decrease their dependency by engaging in self-care activities, such as risk reduction, health promotion, and preventive health practices. The sum of these skills and activities can empower chronically ill persons to take greater control over their bodies and their lives. Knowledge of self-care practices is especially important to informal caregivers because they provide most home care services for persons with a chronic illness or disability. By participating in self-care networks, family members and other informal caregivers can also learn how to recognize, encourage, and employ lay resources in managing everyday routines. Lay caregivers will then be better informed and capable of supporting individuals as they learn to use problem-solving and other self-management skills. Self-help, self-care, and other lay initiatives clearly affect a person's morale. They have also been found to provide important emotional sustenance because these resources offer models of successful coping. Together with such cognitive factors as self-efficacy, internal control, and the sense of coherence, they foster an individual's sense of mastery of the skills necessary for a return to productive living. Studies suggest that self-care, motivated through a support group, is more effective than individually practiced self-care. The most promising outcomes of self-care and peer self-help groups in chronic illness are those that convey stress-buffering, supportive, and socializing effects. These are processes that encourage a sense of personal efficacy through modeling healthy behaviors and engaging in voluntary action. Those who mobilize self-care networks or who participate in self-help groups may thus have found additional resources that enhance their resistance to emotional and somatic disorders. Many participants who join support groups may have realized a sense of community, as well, albeit one that is more fluid and emotionally focused than their families and neighborhoods.[31] As self-help and social support groups emphasize the primacy of caring over more instrumental styles of helping, they appear to have replaced traditional forms of attachment—to place and kin—for many contemporary urbanites, especially those coping with life-threatening illnesses and addictions.

NOTES

1. Erving Goffman, "Stigma and Social Identity," in *Stigma: Notes on the Management of Spoiled Identity* (Englewood Cliffs, NJ: Prentice-Hall, 1963), 1–40; Robert B. Edgerton, *The Cloak of Competence*, rev ed. (Berkeley: University of California Press, 1993).

2. Charles E. Rosenberg, *The Care of Strangers: The Rise of the American Hospital System* (New York: Basic Books, 1987), 116.

3. Rosenberg, *The Care of Strangers*, 120.

4. Rosenberg, *The Care of Strangers*, 120; see also Charles E. Rosenberg, "The Therapeutic Revolution: Medicine, Meaning and Social Change in Nineteenth-Century America," in *Explaining Epidemics* (Cambridge: Cambridge University Press, 1992), 9–31; Charles E. Rosenberg, "Disease and Social Order in America: Perceptions and Expectations," in *Explaining Epidemics* (Cambridge: Cambridge University Press, 1992), 258–77; Paul Starr, *The Social Transformation of American Medicine* (New York: Basic Books, 1982); Rosemary Stevens, *In Sickness and in Wealth: American Hospitals in the Twentieth Century* (New York: Basic Books, 1989).

5. Samuel Eliot Morison, Henry Steele Commager, and William E. Leuchtenburg, *The Growth of the American Republic*, vol. 2, 7th ed. (New York: Oxford University Press, 1980), 469.

6. Richard Edwards, *Contested Terrain: The Transformation of the Workplace in the Twentieth Century* (New York: Basic Books, 1979); Michael Burawoy, *Manufacturing Consent: Changes in the Labor Process Under Monopoly Capitalism* (Chicago: University of Chicago Press, 1979).

7. Philip Rieff, *Freud: The Mind of a Moralist* (Garden City, NY: Doubleday Anchor, 1961), 390.

8. Anselm Strauss, Leonard Schatzman, Rue Bucher, Danuta Ehrlich, and Melvin Sabshin, "The Hospital and Its Negotiated Order," in *The Hospital in Modern Society*, edited by Eliot Freidson (New York: Free Press, 1963), 147–69.

9. Talcott Parsons, "Definitions of Health and Illness in the Light of American Values and Social Structure," in *Patients, Physicians and Illness*, edited by E. Gartly Jaco (New York: Free Press, 1972) 107–27; Eugene B. Gallagher, "Lines of Reconstruction and Extension in the Parsonian Sociology of Illness," *Social Science and Medicine* 10 (1972): 207–18.

10. Eliot Freidson, *Profession of Medicine: A Study of the Sociology of Applied Knowledge*, 2nd ed. (Chicago: University of Chicago Press, 1988).

11. Don Handelman, "Bureaucratic Transactions: The Development of Official-Client Relationships in Israel," in *Transaction and Meaning: Readings in the Anthropology of Exchange and Symbolic Behavior*, edited by Bruce Kapferer (Philadelphia: Ishi Publications, 1976), 223–75.

12. Freidson, *Profession of Medicine*, 302.

13. Jacqueline P. Wiseman, *Stations of the Lost: The Treatment of Skid Row Alcoholics* (Chicago: University of Chicago Press, 1970), 223.

14. Hans Selye, *The Stress of Life* (New York: McGraw-Hill, 1976).

15. Alfred H. Katz and Eugene I. Bender, *Helping One Another: Self-Help Groups in a Changing World* (Oakland, CA: Third Party Publishing, 1990), 35–36.

16. Robert N. Mayer, *The Consumer Movement: Guardians of the Marketplace* (Boston: Twayne Publishers, 1989), 49.

17. Lowell S. Levin, Alfred. H. Katz, and Erik Holst, *Self-Care: Lay Initiatives in Health* (New York: Prodist, 1979), 20–21.

18. Alfred H. Katz, *Self-Help in America: A Social Movement Perspective* (New York: Twayne, 1993), 14.

19. Katz and Bender, *Helping One Another*, 17–18.

20. Katz, *Self-Help in America*, 87.

21. Alfred H. Katz and Carl A. Maida, "Health and Disability Self-Help Organizations," in *Working with Self-Help*, edited by Thomas J. Powell (Silver Spring, MD: NASW, 1990), 149–50.

22. Katz, *Self-Help in America*, 88.

23. Katz, *Self-Help in America*, 47–49.

24. Steven Epstein, *Impure Science: AIDS, Activism, and the Politics of Knowledge* (Berkeley: University of California Press, 1996).

25. *The Economist*, "Tomorrow's Doctoring: Patient, Heal Thyself," February 4, 1995, 19.

26. Thomasina Borkman, "Experiential Knowledge: A New Concept for the Analysis of Self-Help Groups," *Social Service Review* 50 (1976): 445–56.

27. Carl A. Maida, Alfred H. Katz, Deane L. Wolcott, John Landsverk, Gayle Strauss, and Allen R. Nissenson, "Psychological and Social Adaptation of CAPD and Center Hemodialysis Patients," *Loss Grief and Care* 5 (1991): 47–68.

28. Harry Brey and Joyce Jarvis, "Life Change: Adjusting to Continuous Ambulatory Peritoneal Dialysis," *Health and Social Work* (1983): 203–9.

29. Carl A. Maida, Alfred H. Katz, Gayle Strauss, and Cecilia Kwa, "Self-Help, Social Networks and Adaptation in Lupus," in *Self-Help: Concepts and Applications*, edited by Alfred H. Katz, Hannah L. Hedrick, Daryl H. Isenberg, Leslie M. Thompson, Therese Goodrich, and Austin H. Kutscher (Philadelphia: Charles Press, 1991), 165–85.

30. Levin, Katz, and Holst, *Self-Care*; Katz and Maida, "Health and Disability Self-Help Organizations," 141–51.

31. Robert Wuthnow, *Sharing the Journey: Support Groups and America's New Quest for Community* (New York: Free Press, 1994); Ronald C. Kessler, Kristin D. Mickelson, and Shanyang Zhao, "Patterns and Correlates of Self-Help Group Membership in the United States," *Social Policy* 27 (1997): 27–46.

Chapter Four

Facing Crises through Culture

Many residents of low-income communities are dependent upon health and human services funded by the public sector. Low-income families have had to learn the rules and expectations of government-funded health programs as they adjust to both economic pressures and illness. Caregivers within these programs have created a supportive nexus to ease the emotional burdens of chronic illness on patients and their families. These networks of care are mobilized on behalf of patients who lack both support during health crises and skills for negotiating services in medical bureaucracies. As pathways to care, they are the means through which patients sustain alliances with health care providers. A network of care in South Central Los Angeles helped hypertensive patients cope with their illness through support groups, peer counseling, and education.[1] The staff, volunteers and patients in the network often related to one another in a quasi-familial manner. Caring through an extensive network of kin and close friends is an expression of African American urban ethnicity. Quasi-kin relationships are the ways that poor blacks have always dealt with severe deprivation and the disruption of family life after migration and urbanization. Extended and augmented households emerged as black families ascribed a familial status to close friends who rendered support and mutual aid. Known as fictive kinship, it was an attempt to sustain extended family ties in the city. Black families embraced this style of mutual support during their mass migration to the North in the early years of the twentieth century.[2]

THE GREAT MIGRATION:
CULTURAL CHANGE AND CONTINUITY

By 1890, the Southern United States had undergone significant shifts from traditional agriculture and cottage industry to more capital-intensive modes of production. The agricultural village and small town had been transformed by industrialization, and cities of the "New South" became central to the region's economic growth. These changes brought about a major population shift as African Americans migrated from the rural South to cities in the North and Midwest at the time of World War I. Between 1915 and mid-1917, nearly a quarter million black southerners moved North to take jobs left unfilled by men who had been drafted, or by immigrants who had returned to their families in Europe. The first wave of the "Great Migration" continued until 1930, with more than one million people leaving the South, moving as far west as Los Angeles.[3] This was followed by a second wave of rural black families migrating to Northern and West Coast cities on the eve of World War II, making this decades-long population movement perhaps the largest voluntary uprooting in history. These passages from the Southern countryside created new forms of community life, but also sustained distinctly African American styles of culture in host cities.

At the time of the Great Migration, Northern labor agents recruited Southern blacks for janitorial and domestic services but also for work in the meatpacking, auto, and steel industries and as strikebreakers in periods of labor unrest. Migrant families traveled to unfamiliar cities because of the promise of good jobs, better schooling, social opportunities, and the political rights denied them in the South. The "New Negroes" settled into Northern cities and worked in unskilled and semiskilled jobs at the fringes of an expanding industrial and commercial economy. They were unprepared for the slum conditions they faced in Northern cities. They endured these conditions, however, in order to fully emancipate themselves from the virulent racism of the New South.

The Northern city promised a minimum wage, legal rights, and social services to black migrant families. These benefits were the outcome of the Progressive reform movement led by artisans, workers, and small property owners as a response to industrial conditions and urban chaos. Public health and social service agencies established strong footholds in Progressive Era cities. Municipal reformers constructed fireproof and steam-heated model tenements in urban slums. Public health workers conducted evening courses on tuberculosis prevention, nutrition, and sanitation. Settlement houses, staffed by social workers, offered services ranging from temporary shelter and child care to instruction in music and art. Housing and employment bureaus located clean homes and steady jobs for the newcomers. Public schools and libraries were powerful socializing influences for young African Americans and for the immigrant children of European origin who often shared these neighborhood resources. Two influential Progressive reform organizations that provided impetus to the African American struggle for equality in the city—the National Association for the Advancement of Colored People (NAACP) and the National Urban League—would become central to the post–World War II civil rights movement.

These reform efforts, as well as indigenous businesses, civil rights organizations, mutual aid, and neighborhood improvement associations, including black Protestant churches, sustained urban black community and cultural life in the North and on the West Coast. From the 1920s, the Central Avenue area was the hub of black Los Angeles, with two black-owned newspapers, banks, insurance companies, churches, community organizations, and numerous other smaller black-owned businesses.[4] Central Avenue's legendary nightclubs, such as the Club Alabam, the Downbeat, the Memo, and the Last Word Cafe, showcased jazz, blues, and R&B musicians from the "Southwest Circuit" of Texas, Oklahoma, Kansas, and Louisiana—states from which the majority of black migrants emigrated to work in the region's defense plants.[5] An enthusiasm for building and sustaining indigenous institutions was especially evident among the writers, artists, and musicians of the Harlem Renaissance—a 1920s cultural movement in New York's premier black community—whose works and lives had come to embody the sensibility of "the New Negro."[6] Writers and artists such as Langston Hughes, Zora Neale Hurston, Jacob Lawrence, Thomas "Fats" Waller, and Edward "Duke" Ellington conveyed the African American encounter with big city life in experimental verse, colloquial styles of narrative and painting, and jazz rhythms celebrating the enthusiasm and the pathos of migration and resettlement. Black artists and intellectuals drew their inspiration from the range of Harlem's community resources, including the 135th Street Branch of the New York Public Library's Division of Negro History, Literature, and Prints, now known as the Schomburg Center for Research in Black Culture, as well as the vaudeville and dance acts performed at the Apollo Theatre and the vernacular rituals and routines of street corner life.

Other segments of the society prospered from the Progressive Era measures that had transformed urban life at the time of the Great Migration. The public and the corporate sectors gained significant political and social control of densely populated industrial cities. A new middle class of professionals and managers emerged to document and regulate institutional life in these cities. Regulatory and welfare organizations in the expanding public sector employed clerical workers and supervisors. The large corporations that controlled the sophisticated new technologies of production hired engineers and managers. The scientific management practices in the industrial workplace required supervisors to employ similar techniques to monitor and to regulate workers' productivity. Social service occupations requiring casework used social scientific techniques, such as case histories, surveys, interviews, and observations, to document their clients' lives. The specialist occupations that emerged to distribute social welfare and manage risk in the industrial city were empowered to identify disorderly and threatening individuals, to place them within defined physical and social institutions, and to design treatment regimens for their rehabilitation.[7]

The social contracts negotiated between in-migrating black families and members of this new managerial class have certain resemblances to the dependency relations of the South. In the agrarian setting, sharecroppers and laborers were bound by economic contracts with wealthy landowners. A semifeudal patronage system, comprised of family heads, local political leaders, and landowners, organized power and exchange in the countryside. African American families freed themselves from the constraints of this rural nexus after migration to the city. However, the dependency relation was frequently transferred to union leaders, political bosses, work supervisors, and caseworkers. Upon migration, black families yielded their traditional functions, including moral regulation and sanction of occupational role and domestic partner, to professionals and managers who administered to their basic needs. This new set of patron-dependent relations disrupted the strong interpersonal ties that sustained traditional African American family life. Domestic conflicts intensified as the moral economy of the extended black family was compromised by city life. These families, then, had to redefine their traditional kin obligations, group affiliations, and modes of friendship and mutual support in view of the urban situation. Extensive networks of black kin and friends emerged as a response to the pressures of uprooting, resettlement, unemployment, and deprivation characteristic of inner-city life; these strategies for personal and cultural survival continue in contemporary African American communities.[8]

THE AFRICAN AMERICAN STRUGGLE FOR EQUALITY

The modern American civil rights movement began in the 1950s, a decade that celebrated affluence and was fired by a consumption ethos. By the 1960s, the decade marking the centennial of the American Civil War and the Emancipation Proclamation, movement leaders portrayed an image of a segregated society and, in Michael Harrington's words, of an "other America" of the poor and disenfranchised.[9] Poorer African Americans in the rural South had been denied the right not only to vote, but also to use resources held commonly by all residents of a community, namely parks, swimming pools, and other recreational facilities; transportation; schools; housing; eating places; and even water fountains.

As it was necessary for organizers to direct public attention to conditions in the American South, that region became the primary arena for early movement actions. In December 1955, seamstress Rosa Parks, the secretary of a local chapter of the NAACP, refused to give up her seat in a segregated bus in Montgomery, Alabama. After four black students from North Carolina A & T College took seats at a Woolworth's lunch counter in Greenborough, North Carolina, on February 1, 1960, 70,000 others participated in such "sit-ins" that year. In 1961, the Northern-based Congress on Racial Equality (CORE) organized "Freedom Rides" to the South to test the recent court rulings that mandated the integration of Southern bus terminals. In 1963, Martin Luther King's Southern Christian Leadership Movement (SCLC) focused its efforts on the desegregation of Birmingham, Alabama. The SCLC organized mass meetings in the city's largest Baptist church and mass demonstrations to disrupt business in the downtown commercial district. Both CORE and Student Nonviolent Coordinating Committee (SNCC) organized the 1964 Freedom Summer voting rights campaign in rural Mississippi. Inspired by the Algerian-born French philosopher Albert Camus, Robert "Bob" Moses, SNCC's first field representative in rural Mississippi, often stated that the Negro should be "neither victim nor executioner." And like the Algerian masses under French colonial rule that he read about in Camus' works, Moses "experienced the American South as an occupied territory with a terrified, yet submissive population."[10] Moses brought 1,000 primarily white activists from Northern universities to spend their summer in rural Mississippi to help with voter registration.

However, the urban North was responsible for contributing far more than an army of idealistic student activists. While the South continued to be the regional arena for most actions, civil rights leaders called upon the inherited traditions of American political culture, notably the ideas and strategies of the Progressive movement. For the most part, these traditions and ideas were maintained in the organizations inspired by or founded by Progressives in Northern cities. Martin Luther King learned about the "social gospel" tradition within American Protestant thought as a college student in the North. This school of thought emerged in the Gilded Age, when liberal theologians came under the sway of Darwinism, but flourished in Progressive America. Inspired by reformers such as John Dewey and Jane Addams, who encouraged "learning by doing," this form of urban Protestantism united with social

workers, labor activists, and municipal reformers to build "progressive" in-
stitutions, such as the public school, and to enact social welfare legislation.[11]
Ella Baker, who became the first associate director of the Southern Christian
Leadership Movement in 1958, also had roots in Progressive civic culture.
Like King, she grew up in a Southern family of ministers, and was educated
in its Negro colleges before moving to New York in the 1920s. During the
New Deal, Baker worked as a consumer educator in the Works Progress Administration (WPA) and also organized consumer cooperatives in Philadelphia and Chicago. By the late 1930s, she had become national field secretary
for the NAACP and organized local chapters in the South and the Southwest
throughout the next decade. Clearly, Baker as a SCLC organizer, and King
and other ministers in their work with Southern black church congregations,
used Progressive styles of participatory democracy to inspire initiatives for
school desegregation, and to transform these local struggles into a mass-
based social movement.[12]

Following the success of African American struggles for equality, grassroots movements flourished in Chicano communities in California and the
Southwest, in the Puerto Rican neighborhoods of Chicago and New York
City, and among Native Americans on reservations and in urban enclaves.
The women's liberation movement also developed in the image of the civil
rights movement. Postwar feminists modeled their struggle for gender
equality on the NAACP's successful use of the courts and legislatures to
fight racial discrimination. The National Organization for Women, founded
in 1966, lobbied hard to enforce the ban on gender discrimination in employment and public accommodations included in the 1964 Civil Rights
Act. This new wave of American feminists advocated for corporate and
government-sponsored child care centers and greater wage parity in the
workplace. The following case study examines the mutual influences of the
civil rights and the women's health care movements on a community-based
initiative to increase access to needed care for low-income patients with cardiovascular disease.

SOUTH CENTRAL LOS ANGELES: A COMMUNITY IN CRISIS

The 1980s brought only trouble to South Central Los Angeles.[13] At the beginning of the decade, the city of Los Angeles had nearly 3 million people. It
was fast becoming a destination for thousands of Central American immigrants seeking high wages or fleeing political repression at home. South Central's traditionally black neighborhoods, such as Compton, Lynwood, and
Watts, were being rapidly transformed by the influx of Latino immigrants.

For example, Watts would be 50 percent Latino by the end of the decade. Immigrant families lived crowded three to a dwelling formerly occupied by one black family. To black residents, a telling sign of the change was the disappearance of grass in the yards of their Latino neighbors; groups of children playing on the front lots of homes wore out the lawns that the previous tenants had striven to maintain. These neighborhoods were part of the West Coast's fastest growing Latino barrio. Korean immigrants were also streaming into the city, renting stores and operating small businesses in every South Central neighborhood. Longtime black residents were troubled by the reshaping of their community and apprehensive about the future.

Tom Bradley, the city's first African American mayor, was serving his second term in office. During his tenure, the downtown skyline would be fully transformed by high-rise development, and the city would serve as host to the 1984 Olympic Games. Los Angeles was struggling with budget cuts forced by the passage of Proposition 13, the statewide taxpayers' revolt against increased public spending, two years earlier. The inflation rate in the city soared to 15.8 percent, and unemployment was at 6.6 percent. Over 500,000 Los Angeles families were receiving welfare benefits for their dependent children. The Southern California aerospace industry had been in decline since the end of the Vietnam War. Following a national trend away from heavy industry, companies would close their South Central plants, leaving thousands of blue-collar workers jobless. In March, 1980, Firestone Tire and Rubber Company announced plans to close its fifty-two-year-old plant in nearby South Gate. Over the next two years, Bethlehem Steel would shut its fifty-two-year-old South Central mill and General Motors would close its giant South Gate assembly facility. Just as they were beginning to recover from the ravages of civil unrest in the 1960s, communities in South Central Los Angeles faced ongoing economic recession, deindustrialization, and well-publicized epidemics of homelessness, crack, and AIDS.

HYPERTENSION: A DISEASE OF ADAPTATION

For African Americans in Los Angeles, these stresses exacerbated another epidemic: hypertension. It was much less obvious, but nonetheless insidious and dangerous. High blood pressure is linked to a number of stresses in the urban environment, such as crowding, high noise levels, pollution, and dietary patterns.[14] As a rural people urbanize, their blood pressure levels change as they find ways to respond to these stresses of city living. The incidence of hypertension, for example, is seven times greater in African Americans than in the white population. Accounting for this striking difference are a number of risk factors for African Americans, including a genetic predisposition, a diet high in fats and salt, psychosomatic disorders, and higher stresses from the combination of urbanization and racism.

Hypertensive patients need to adhere to a complex therapeutic regime in order to control their high blood pressure. The hypertension clinic at a general hospital in South Central Los Angeles provides diagnostic and therapeutic care to patients who have been referred from community screenings, the emergency room, in-patient units, and other specialty care clinics at the hospital. The health care team includes physicians, nurse practitioners, nurses, a medical social worker, a dietitian, health educators, and clerical staff. The clinic operates four mornings each week. Upon referral, a baseline is established for each patient through lab work and other diagnostic techniques. The clinic uses a graduated therapeutic regime for hypertension control. Patients are kept under regular medical supervision and are scheduled for follow-up diagnostic and therapeutic evaluation at periodic intervals.

A high percentage of those who have been identified as hypertensive discontinue treatment after the first or second clinic visits. Those who continue in treatment must significantly alter their lifestyle, which includes adapting to the therapeutic regime and its short-term effects, including lethargy, impotence, decreased libido, sleeplessness, and increased blood sugar and uric acid levels. Hypertensive patients often fear being stigmatized by others whose folk conception of the illness sees it as a nervous condition caused by social stress. The patients themselves frequently perceive the disease and its treatment as inconsistent with their beliefs about health and illness. Seeing a physician only once every two months, for example, rather than frequently as they would during a routine illness, fosters the belief that the disease is not very important. Prolonged dependency on antihypertensive drugs may also confuse patients who are accustomed to short-term, quickly effective drug therapies, like antibiotics. Such differences in treatment style, coupled with the fact that the hypertensive label does not bestow disability benefits, render patient compliance central to clinical care.

NOTHIN' ALONE: HELPING ONE ANOTHER STAY HEALTHY

Seeking to help hypertensive patients stick to the regimen, a coalition of clinicians and health activists established a network of care, including peer counseling, health education, and stress management groups in South Central Los Angeles. The caregivers strove to increase patients' awareness of their disease and its treatment, and of their responsibilities for health maintenance. They also established a broader-based coalition of support for high blood pressure control in the region. The Hypertension Control Project consists of a cadre of volunteers providing support and peer counseling to hypertensive patients. They spent each morning phoning patients scheduled for clinic appointments on the following day. The phone call was a reminder of the appointment and acted as a channel for the communication of any barriers to service utilization, such as transportation to and from the hospital. Volunteers also made follow-up phone calls to determine the reason for broken appointments. The project was established through both grassroots community action and political patronage in a manner similar to the founding of the community hospital and its affiliated medical school. Central to this institution-building process was Sadie Brown, who was a member of the national Democratic Party Committee and a leading African American political figure in South Central Los Angeles in the 1970s and 1980s. Ms. Brown also directed the federally funded Comprehensive Employment Training Act (CETA) program, which provided stipends and subsidized training for unemployed persons in South Central Los Angeles. Through the program, Brown had a key role in planning and staffing the hospital in the early 1970s, as CETA participants were eventually placed in the hospital jobs. The CETA program was also the initial funding agency for the affiliated medical school. Through a $3 million grant, the agency was able to identify the school's deans and chairmen. Under her direction, nine committees were formed to develop the structure of the medical departments based upon both affirmative action policies and community health care needs. Sadie Brown also headed a local black caucus that put pressure upon state and local representatives around consumer issues in health care. She had an office in a building immediately adjacent to that housing the Hypertension Control Project.

The project drew upon the resources of Sadie Brown's office for a number of its needs. Her office provided CETA placements, copying and printing facilities, and political advocacy in Sacramento, where Brown sat on the state committee that oversees the project's funding. Her daughter sought elected office in a local city council race, and the campaign was sponsored by her mother's political caucus. Two of the project's paid staff were active throughout the campaign, spending their days off in canvassing efforts on behalf of the candidate. The Southeast High Blood Pressure Coalition was also organized with Brown's grassroots political support. The coalition extended the power and responsibilities of the project by creating a community advisory board made up of representatives of professional and consumer interests in the region.

The project's volunteer cadre developed through loose and open-ended agreements with hospital staff. Participation and recruitment occurred through word of mouth, rather than through notices or advertisements. Volunteers had a vested interest, either because they were hypertensive or someone close to them had the disease. They underwent an initial training program and weekly continuing education workshops. These workshops sustained volunteers' interest in the program and updated them on recent developments in high blood pressure control. Health care professionals and volunteers discussed issues in hypertension management based upon their common experiences with patients. Through this forum, volunteers broadened their knowledge, and the ties of affiliation between these responsible laypersons and professionals were strengthened. These bonds reinforced the professionals' trust in the volunteers' capacity to communicate middle-class norms to patients. While these norms of prevention and self-care are individualistic and may result in victim blaming, they clearly possess value for enhancing the quality of life of all Americans. The volunteers were mostly middle-aged women. Teenagers, who were usually relatives of the volunteers or hospital staff, appeared during the summer when they were out of school. The volunteers had their own room in the office where they made the phone calls. They left the office at midday and walked together as a group to the hospital cafeteria to have lunch together. The volunteers were provided with a complementary hot lunch and minimal funds for transportation. Although the extrinsic incentives and rewards were minimal, the sense of shared purpose and pride was intrinsically derived through relationships with fellow volunteers and with patients.

Two paid staff members were charged with ongoing recruitment, supervision, documentation, and planning for the volunteer project. The coordinators were also responsible for its primary mission, peer counseling, whether or not the volunteers were present. Flora Sanders, a middle-aged black woman, handled overall coordination, recorded the daily census of phone calls, and carried out general administrative and outreach activities. She had been active in local politics and youth groups and had previously managed her own business. Flora Sanders used an informal style to coordinate volunteer participation. She often spoke to volunteers in a black dialect, conveying a folk-quality in her relations with them. Ms. Sanders also formally addressed them as Mr. Jones or Miss Fairchild in the manner of her Southern upbringing. These manifest gestures of respect were both expected and consciously performed to maintain the volunteers' loyalties. Their participation required ongoing reinforcement through these mannerisms but also through more explicit acts of gratitude such as certificates and awards. Flora also solicited their opinions on the direction of the project and asked them to suggest ways to expand the volunteer pool. In Flora Sanders's words, "We don't do nothin' alone; we all makes decisions." Flora Sanders's coworker, Joyce Clayton, was articulate in standard English and highly skilled in administrative duties. She coordinated the weekly continuing education workshops and carried out phone surveys of local physicians. She was also active in community high blood pressure screenings at local churches, schools, and worksites. Ms. Clayton had previously worked in corporate settings, where she became adept at communicating across ethnic and class boundaries. Her informal style expressed that of a younger generation of African American women raised outside of the South. She conveyed a sense of warmth and openness through a compliment, an extension of her hand, or a hug after a particularly exhausting phone call.

Joyce Clayton also planned and orchestrated the annual Hypertension Workshop. The event took place in the hospital auditorium. Hospital staff and faculty at the affiliated medical school participated in it. Volunteers prepared and served a "heart-healthy" soul food luncheon in the hospital cafeteria. The audience was composed of high school students, hypertensive patients, and providers in the region. Clinnie Ashford, D.S.W., a social worker and administrator of the Hypertension Control Project, welcomed everyone to the workshop. Daniel Sayers, the hospital director, also gave welcoming remarks, noting the emphasis on youth participation in this year's workshop and citing the presence of honor roll students and the youth chorus from two local high schools. At least half of those attending the workshop were community youth. One of the project's goals is screening teenagers in high schools and community colleges for elevated blood pressure readings. Sayers then pointed out how grassroots action within the African American community led to the establishment of both the project and the hospital. He then addressed the necessity for community screening and the involvement of volunteers and community leaders like Sadie Brown. He reiterated the importance of the project to the community and asked the youth to consider volunteering their time to it. Dr. Ashford then introduced Sadie Brown, the National Democratic Committeewoman. Ashford cited the political leader's continuing interest and dedication to community health issues and mentioned that Ms. Brown had asked her to be a part of the project since its inception. Ms. Brown stood at the podium and addressed the audience, invoking a traditional "call-and-response" from her audience:

> Good morning . . . good morning . . . good morning . . . good morning [not stopping until she received an emphatic response from the audience]. Where are you this morning? What's the name of this auditorium? The H. Claude Hudson Auditorium. You got to know where you are in order to get things done. Dr. Ashford said she was invited to be a part of the project. We told her to take over this project, and she said I was moving along, well, first it was Clinnie Ashford, social worker, then Clinnie Ashford, director of social services, then regional director, and now it's Dr. Clinnie Ashford. She's got a degree in streetology. The project and the community volunteers, everybody's a doctor, a specialist. We don't need any more doctors; now that's power, isn't that right? I want you to

change the myth about what Martin Luther King Hospital ain't to what Martin Luther King Hospital is, right! I was a patient here a few months ago. I'm able to say that I got great care here. As I move off this scene, one day, you'll be here at a conference and I won't be here. But I want you to know that I've helped to bring together a few communities around here. Join hands with each other and say: We've come a long way. We've come a long way. We've come a long way. We've come a long way [the audience is joining hands and repeating the phrase after her in unison]. Thank you.

Ashford then recognized the honor students from Lynwood High School and asked them to raise their hands. She directed everyone's attention to the blackboard beside her where photos of two of the project's volunteers were posted and explained to the audience that both had died during the past year. The program was dedicated to the memory of these two volunteers, one the son of Flora Sanders, the other a woman who had hosted the annual Christmas party for the volunteers at her home. There were also photos of the workshop's guests of honor, Mr. and Mrs. Wilson, who were patients at the hypertension clinic, and of members of the Wilson family.

Dr. William Hill, the director of the United High Blood Pressure Foundation, was introduced and thereafter presided as master of ceremonies. He introduced the Compton High School Chorus. Their choral program began with the assembly standing and singing together the Black National Anthem, "Lift Every Voice and Sing," and continued with a number of gospel songs. Vincent Sowell, a clinical psychologist and researcher at the historically black medical school, then spoke to the assembly on stress in the family:

> Problems within the family may give rise to problems in the rest of our lives that we are increasingly less able to handle. How can we be sure that our families are stress-free as they can be? We must take a look at our impact on the resolution of problems in the family. Look at how families define and cope with problems. Families develop coping styles in handling problems. Many blame and shout: the aggressor style; others take on the blame: the martyr style. . . . We are caught up in a cycle where the home, the school, and the street become a problem place, and what's left?

Hill then introduced Sadie Brown's daughter, Terry Brown, the youngest person to run for a seat on the Lynwood City Council. Hill compared her campaign to that of the Reverend Jesse Jackson and urged the youthful audience to "vote and take some responsibility in your community." Terry Brown also directs a community acting ensemble, "Sisters in Black," which has performed in both Los Angeles and Chicago schools. Their performance depicted causes of patient noncompliance. Sadie Brown then appeared on stage to introduce Mervyn Dymally, the former lieutenant governor of California and, at the time, a candidate for Congress in the district. Dymally stressed the importance of his candidacy to the future of the medical school. He also presented the service awards to the project staff and others who had volunteered their services during the year. After the presentations, Dr. Alphonse Jackson, chief of the hypertension clinic and the "dean" of high blood pressure control efforts in South Central Los Angeles, introduced the guests of honor. The Wilson family had been his patients through the years. Jackson stressed how familial coping and genetic predisposition were important aspects of high blood pressure control. After another performance of the Sisters in Black and more gospel songs by the high school chorus, which had the audience standing and clapping their hands, Sadie Brown closed the program.

The workshop was a "crossroads" event that brought together patients, professionals, and politicians for a brief time. It displayed black accomplishments in disease control by dramatizing familiar situations and attendant stresses of African American life. Speakers and performers appeared on the stage with minimal introductions. The boundaries between performances faded as political oratory, lecture, theater piece, and choral arrangement immediately followed one another. Political leaders, clinicians, and youth appeared on stage within minutes of each other. Each performed, lectured, or demonstrated before the other group. The distance between audience and performer was thereby minimized in the fast-paced spectacle. Like a Mardi Gras or carnival festivity, roles were reversed and hierarchies were temporarily leveled. Any resulting discomfort, however, was reduced through the humor that pervaded the event and through hand clapping and dancing in the aisles during gospel music performances.[15]

The workshop also recognized the contributions of leaders in the hospital and the local African American community. Black politicians and health care reformers presided over this event and had the clout to improvise and to use the occasion for their own ends. They recounted their part in the struggle for community-based health resources. They credited themselves for winning these resources, many of which were displayed at the workshop: the printed health education materials and films communicating African American themes, hardware ranging from medical instruments to musical instruments, and the hospital itself. White politicians had previously controlled access to these commodities. Youth in the audience had not directly experienced the Watts riots and could not remember the hospital's emergence out of the civil rights movement to become a major teaching institution of over 500 beds, with an annual census of over 10,000 inpatients. They had benefited, however, from the web of community-based institutions that emerged from these struggles. The event's core message was, in the words of one politician, "We've come a long way." An indirect message, "respect your doctors and comply with their orders," was conveyed through tributes to physicians, lay volunteers, and exemplary patients. These dual messages, restated throughout the event, were meant to shape the symbolic landscape of a new generation.

The Hypertension Control Project was a peer-counseling program generated by a cadre of people who had a vested interest in high blood pressure, either because they were hypertensive or someone close to them had the disease. It operated as a loosely knit project within the formal structure of a public community hospital. While the medical enterprise operated through specialized roles and technical activities, the lay initiative achieved its goals through informal measures. In this case, middle-class norms of patient behavior were communicated through telephone conversations, community gatherings, gospel music, and soul food luncheons.

WORKIN' TOGETHER: LEARNING HEALTHY WAYS

Community health educators also deliver targeted services to patients with high blood pressure as part of the Hypertension Education Project. They have acquired insight into factors relating to treatment compliance through years of screening, counseling, and education of patients with high blood pressure. As a result of this experience, they were able to identify patients who were likely to resist treatment and to determine the potential sources of noncompliance. These "indigenous" peer health educators sometimes used unconventional methods to inform patients of the risks associated with noncompliance. They consulted with hypertensive patients hospitalized after a heart attack or a stroke in a style suggestive of a close friend or family member. The health educators also intervened directly into daily clinic routines. On the clinic's walls, they had painted murals depicting risk factors associated with high blood pressure. In their lectures, they used stylized forms of address, including metaphor, joking, and insults, to motivate patients to adhere to their treatment plans. In these ways, health educators established a niche in the setting. A familiar part of any hospital visit, they were the most visible and accessible sources of support that patients encountered in the clinic's public areas. They showed films, tested clients' knowledge of their disease and its treatment, and often relieved the boredom of the long wait characteristic of public hospital visits. In this manner, they helped patients to hold more rational beliefs about high blood pressure and to share responsibility for their treatment. Paraprofessional community health educators used an informal folk style of presenting information about disease prevention, alternating between standard English and black vernacular speech in the talk:

If there ain't no salt on the table, the table ain't set. Why should we modify our salt intake? The big problem is we have to stop eating something that we like—fried chicken, greens, beans—you know what I do: I make mustard greens with chicken wings without salt. Otherwise, we wind up a human salty dog [laughs].

They also used distinctly African American modes of rhetoric to address the audience. They would frequently use signifying, an African American mode of metaphoric speech that combines verbal dueling and coded meanings.[16] The dueling, or "sounding," common in children's speech games like "the Dozens" has two opponents hurling insulting spontaneous word associations back and forth. The encoded messages or meanings in conversations are conveyed implicitly and indirectly through facial expressions or variation in vocal tone. The verbal dueling of children is an adaptive response to a dangerous inner-city world. Signifying in adult speech makes indirect references to the changing character of African American life. The following passages illustrate how the speaker, Calvin Jones, an indigenous peer community health educator, signified to his audience that change was at hand in the clinic:

How many people love colors? Black and white are my favorite colors. . . . High blood pressure is a very serious disease. You cannot jive with it because it does not play with you. . . . Thirty-five million Americans have high blood pressure; one-half don't even know they have it. It can lead to death. . . . It can lead to death. Let's get that clear. It takes a team effort—you and your doctors, the community workers, health educators, and the social services. We're all working together to control your high blood pressure. . . . Fat people have more high blood pressure, and many persons with high blood pressure are overweight. The combination of high blood pressure and being overweight has been shown to lead to greater chances of having heart disease. . . . So stay away from junky foods. Americans and Californians are junk food junkies. We cannot wait to have a decent hot-cooked meal. I'll say this: the fried chicken places are like liquor places; they're cropping up on every corner [laughs]. I think they're workin' together [laughs]. I think they're working together.

Overtly, these were Calvin's routine remarks to the patients, persuading them to comply with their treatment, to modify their diets and to exercise. Encoded in this passage, though, was an additional message. Despite his rhetoric of inclusiveness—"We're all working together"—Calvin was telling his listeners about what he perceived, namely the precariousness of his autonomy within his current work situation. Prior to his presentation, social work professionals and paraprofessional community health educators had met to discuss ways to gain greater access to hypertensive patients during their clinic

visits. Calvin's supervisor, Tom Jergensen, a white health education professional, informed Calvin that the meeting was to seek cooperation between the
community workers and social workers affiliated with the clinic. The social
worker called the meeting to explore how to introduce stress management
groups in the clinic. The group facilitator, Sherry Hawthorn, a white social
work professional, remained after the meeting to watch Calvin's presentation.
She had intended to address the patients after his talk. However, Calvin's
lengthy monologue forestalled her; he spoke until all of the patients had been
called for their appointments.

Calvin routinely "warmed up" his audience by engaging in word play, joking, and friendly banter. This time, he carried on with them for quite a while
before starting his formal talk. Calvin established his program's legitimacy by
reading its goals and objectives to patients. He later acknowledged its seven-
year tenure in the clinic. By signifying, however, he cued his audience to
what, for him, was a potentially threatening situation. His phrases, "Black and
white are my favorite colors" and "I think they're workin' together," and bodily gestures indirectly signaled his need for the audience's display of support.
The audience evidently grasped his meaning, for many patients began to read
aloud from the printed health education materials, at times jumping in to complete his sentences. While the new state of affairs was not a cause for the patients' alarm, it did threaten Calvin's role as the dominant persona in the setting. He had felt marginalized, and perhaps betrayed, by the two white
supervisors who were planning to permit other caregivers into what Calvin
had defined as his arena. The introduction of groups meant that staff from two
programs would be "competing" for patients during clinic visits and the professional social workers seemed likely to win.

The following day, social work administrator Clinnie Ashford called a joint
meeting of both projects offering services to hypertensive patients. She
wished to address the ways that staff could cooperate with each other. Stating
that social workers had decided to revive patient stress management groups,
Ashford assured the health educators that she did not wish to saturate patients
with information but to compliment their efforts. She emphasized the need for
both projects to acknowledge their shared mission of serving the hospital's
hypertensive patients. She informed them of prior efforts to introduce groups
in the clinic and how these groups led to closer ties between health educators
and social workers. At the meeting, Tom Jergensen cited problems encountered when health educators introduced formal classes for hypertensive patients, from scheduling rooms to arranging transportation. Health educators
also found themselves competing with medical and nursing staff for patients'
time and attention. Health educators then moved their sessions directly into
the clinic waiting area to engage patients on a drop-in basis. Calvin inter-

jected that the patients often preferred to watch soap operas while they waited for the doctor, rather than taking part in any formal presentation. Jergensen then suggested that the stress management groups could best happen on the first and third Friday of each month, the times when health educators had not scheduled clinic presentations. He also offered to lend his film on relaxation training to the social workers conducting the groups. Ashford convened the joint meeting after Calvin had publicly "signified" his disapproval of his supervisor's decision to cooperate with the social workers in their efforts to reintroduce stress groups. Jergensen at first stood behind Calvin by citing the failure of the formal classes. However, he eventually supported the competing project's enterprise, suggesting days and times that would not interfere with Calvin's presentations and thereby would reduce any territorial conflict. Despite their manifest agreement to complement one another, each project retained its exclusive knowledge and practice base. The inherent territoriality between the two projects points to broader organizational conflicts within public hospitals.

The conflict between the two projects emerged around issues of workplace autonomy. Both projects were designed to promote patient adherence to a difficult therapeutic regime. The social workers perceive their roles as providers of support to patients and their families. The community health educators perceive their roles as "indigenous" teachers and peers who provide information that reduces the risks of serious trauma in a potentially noncompliant patient population. However, they are limited in their professional autonomy and have minimal control over their work situations. They are members of a health care team that is organized on a therapeutic interaction pattern and controlled by medical staff. The Hospital Social Services, by contrast, is managed by social work professionals who, in this case, have attempted to increase their presence in the clinic. Social workers have traditionally aligned with bureaucratic reform efforts at their worksites. In this case, they have won access to state funds in order to implement changes in clinic protocols. The state health services department thereby granted them the authority to introduce new forms of supportive care. The threat to the health educators' autonomy was even more pronounced in view of the new group leader's credentials. Sherry Hawthorn was a member of management, herself a controlled hypertensive, and a licensed professional with extensive experience in group work. Similar to the social workers, indigenous health educators routinely conveyed the familiar message of "follow your doctor's orders." However, they served another function within the hospital, which was subtler. They were cultural brokers, or go-betweens, who had the dual capacity to translate scientific medicine into understandable messages and to alert their audiences to changing situations in the milieu. This was an important role in a hospital with a commitment to using paraprofessionals to sustain helping alliances with patients. However, like Calvin Jones, indigenous workers had only minimal control within their work environment. Their jobs would remain only so long as middle-class professionals had career interests in maintaining organic ties with the community through projects of this nature. These ethnically based alliances of professionals and indigenous workers are constantly challenged, as in the above case, by ongoing fiscal crises and changing ideological commitments within the public sector.

WORKIN' WITH MY MIND: STYLES OF MANAGING STRESS

Stress management groups convened weekly in the clinic. These groups were held in the clinic waiting room and were composed of patients who participated as they waited for their appointments. The groups focused on a common disease and offered patients support during the anxiety-provoking routine of seeing the doctor. The group typically began with the facilitator's introductory remarks:

> I'm Sherry and I'm a controlled hypertensive and I've had to learn a few things about how to handle stress. Let's first introduce ourselves by our first names. [Each states their name.] Let's talk about, first, the kinds of things that upset us. What upsets me is when someone cuts in front of me on the freeway and if my grown children don't call. Phil, what upsets you?

After all the participants had related a source of stress, Sherry asked them to state their usual style of coping:

> I want you to see that we all have worries. We all have problems. There's nobody in this life who doesn't have problems. Sometimes you see people and you think they have everything, but they have their problems too. When you get upset, Emma Lou, what do you do?

After everyone had related how they usually coped, Sherry introduced a style of coping that worked for her, namely talking with kin and close friends. Sherry invited participants to use the group as a medium for working on their problems:

> The worst thing that you can do is hold it in, and one of the easiest things to do is to sit down and talk to someone about it. . . . This is the place where you can discuss things among people who are not close family and who can help each

other: I had this little old lady here in the group and she was so mad at the doctors for keeping her waiting in the room for a long time, and she was cold. She got it all out in the group.

Group members verbalized a variety of stresses and coping styles in the group. Stresses from family problems, illness, and city living were predominant responses to the question: What upsets you? These are the issues that troubled the older adults who came to the clinic during the morning hours. Their primary concerns were with the loss of family role, the problems associated with chronic illness, and stresses of the urban environment. Issues associated with working, parenting, marriage, and money were voiced by the younger patients, a group who visited the morning clinic less frequently than the older cohort.

Participants indicated that suppression, that is, "pushing the thought from my mind," was the best way of coping. Physical activity, usually cleaning the house or walking, and prayer or Bible study were second and third preferences. Anger was the fourth most expressed coping style. Reading, television, and radio combined represented a fifth preference. Sleep, food, alcohol, and drugs were not widely expressed coping pathways. Group members indicated that they talked with their families and close friends during crises only after hearing Sherry's message that talking was her best way of coping. They may not have associated talking as an effective coping style because they were not cognizant of its role in stress management.

Sherry used informal learning styles to help patients to cope with the onset of their illness. Patients often experienced greater anxieties at this stage because of the need to change their lifestyles to comply with treatment regimens. Clinical staff at the hospital expected their patients to behave within the norms and roles that were congruent with those of professional medicine. However, these middle-class expectations often increased the anxieties of patients adjusting both to the treatment milieu and to professional demands. Sherry thus used social learning, or modeling, techniques to reduce the dissonance that patients experienced during critical stages of their careers.

Modeling, or observational learning, is based upon identification with the attributes and behavioral patterns of significant persons in the social world. Identification has three aspects: first, there is an emotional and cognitive similarity between the learner and the model; second, there is a motive or desire on the learner's part to be like the model; and third, there is a process through which the learner comes to emulate the model. Identification is not a unitary process because the learner is exposed to a diversity of models through observational learning in a variety of contexts. Complex behavioral sequences are learned through observation, synthetic recombination, and integration of behaviors for future use in an appropriate situation. An element of discriminative judgment is requisite for future action, otherwise the modeling process would be analogous to instinctual activities. The factor of discrimination rests in the learner's choice of whether or not to imitate and adopt a model's behavior. The characteristics of the model, such as nurturance, power, and similarity to the observer, affect the learner's choice and enhance the chances that he will successfully imitate and learn the observed behavior.

Three styles of social learning were used to introduce new patient norms. First, the facilitator directly confronted participants who related a style of coping that clearly deviated from the norm being socialized in the group:

Sherry (the facilitator): Frances, what upsets you?

Frances (the grandmother): Everything. Anything upsets me.

Sherry: Do you have high blood pressure?

Frances: Yea, I have high blood pressure.

Sherry: Anything in particular bother you?

Frances: The record player and the radio.

Sherry: Who's playing the radio?

Frances: My sons. They really keep my blood pressure up. It's my three sons.

[Laughter]

Sherry: What do you do, Frances?

Frances: I do everything. I even hit.

Sherry: You even hit out?

Frances: That's right, I fuss and holler. Everything. I talk, talk, talk, but it only upsets me more to talk.

Ralph: The more you talk about it the madder you get.

Sherry: What about you Sandy?

Sandy (Frances's granddaughter): Well, let me see, my uncle Benny, he make me mad sometime.

Sherry: What do you do?

Sandy: I run. He hurts my hand sometime.

Leader: What do you do when he does that?

Sandy: I hit.

Sherry: So you're like your grandmother. Frances, you know you serve as a model for your child.

Frances: I know.

Sherry: What about you Jim?

Jim: I throw up. But that ain't the only thing. I wore out a hundred pencils like this [demonstrates how he twirls a pencil].

Sherry: Well pencils don't hurt anyone.

Frances: Are you tellin' me that doin' something like that helps?

Sherry: Hittin' people is going to cause people more problems. Some people walk away from problems, like Sandy. What do you do Sally?

Sally: I do my yoga. I'm mostly workin' with my mind. . . . You have to sit there and focus your mind on something beautiful. It's mostly like prayin'. . . . I sing. I have a guitar and I sing and people tell me my voice is best when I'm upset.

Sherry: I once knew someone who would paint all of his problems out in those pictures and that was his way of expressing something.

Sandy: My Uncle Tommy, he's an artist, and he paint all his troubles all over his walls.

Sherry: We're going to stop for today. We gave you something to think about.

Frances: Well, you gave me something to think about.

A second style of social learning occurred when the facilitator deliberately elicited support from the group to help a member work on a stressful problem:

Sherry: What upsets you Wilson?

Wilson: The things that really upsets me is that as long as I've been married, I haven't been able to really communicate with my wife.

Sherry: How many children do you have?

Wilson: Four. Two by a previous marriage, twenty and eighteen, and two girls at home, nine and eleven.

Sherry: Wilson, do you have someone to talk to when you are upset?

Wilson: Sometimes I talk it over with my oldest son. He's a good listener. I try not to lay my troubles out too much.

Sherry: Does anybody have any advice to give Wilson?

Effie: Do you try to take her out?

Wilson: I tried.

Effie: Do you ever watch TV together?

Wilson: I tell you, we're not compatible. I try to go to church with her but she don't like to. My children do but she don't. She only likes to go to bars and drink. I don't drink because of my health.

Mrs. Stevens: Some people, like you say, you can't communicate with them. You can't please them no matter what you do.

Sherry: Some people need counseling.

Mrs. Stevens: Yes they do, some people need counseling.

Wilson: We tried counseling, but after the counseling ended, it went right back to the way it was before.

Mrs. Stevens: I've been married thirty-five years. . . . [She goes on a diatribe about the value of church attendance in holding a family together.]

Wilson: I have a daughter who is supposed to be getting married in November, and I told her that you have to have understanding between you.

Sonia: Even if you're married, you can be lonely.

Willie: More lonely.

A third form of learning happened as participants spontaneously helped one another solve their problems. This occurred when it looked as though the speaker had reached a barrier and was so emotionally involved with a situation as not to be able to see a solution:

Sherry: What upsets you, Flo?

Flo: My kids.

Sherry: How do you deal with it?

Flo: I leave the house. I be hollerin' at 'em. I get in my car and leave the house.

Sherry: You run away. When we have a problem we usually use flight or fight.

Flo: Well, just this morning, I said, "I'm going to take my friend to the hospital." I just tell 'em, "I'm going." My fifteen-year-old son mumbled: "It's always me," and I took a broom to him. I told him to get up since he's the oldest and he should set an example for the younger ones.

Theresa (addresses Sherry): Could I ask a question? I'm thinkin' about her.

(Sherry nods in the direction of Flo.)

Theresa: You say your son is fifteen. How do you feel when you hit him with a broom?

Flo: I feel bad. My husband passed about three years ago and I don't want no back talkin'.

Theresa: Have you tried givin' the Bible to him? I have five boys . . .

Sherry: But fifteen-year-olds are hard to raise.

Flo: He's not a bad boy.

Sherry: Does he sometimes . . . sometimes when they lose their dad, we put responsibilities on them . . . the oldest son . . . they become the man of the house.

Theresa: Just read the scriptures to them, you know, how the child should respect their mother and father, and go to church.

Sherry: I think what she's saying is find a way to cope. You may not have time to read scriptures to them. You're surrounded by children and you have to act right away.

Stress management groups offered clients a model of coping that was consistent with modern group theory and stress management techniques. The group facilitator endorsed seeking support from family and close friends during crises, but also accepted more traditional forms of coping, such as prayer, church services, and pastoral counseling. Older participants were encouraged to offer advice to younger ones based upon their prior experiences. This style of learning, through personal narrative accounts, was effective in helping younger participants resolve family conflicts. When a participant's responses deviated significantly from the group's norms, the facilitator usually intervened directly. When it became clear that a person could not see any solution to a problem, advice was solicited from other participants. They would often advocate coping through religious conversion, prayer, scripture reading, and church attendance. Although the group socialized a secular model of coping, the facilitator remained open to traditional cultural styles of resolving conflicts. The group has encouraged patients to reorient their personal roles and coping styles through a model of mutual aid. It provided the framework to participants who experienced increased stress during a life transition, that of chronic illness and disability. A model of coping, based upon self-responsibility, empowered them to take charge of their illness. Participants shared their individual coping strategies in a familiar setting with peers who shared similar ethnic backgrounds. This helped situate the chronically ill, older patients within local networks, reintroducing a tri-generational scheme to coping and social problem solving. The support group enabled these patients to develop new roles and coping strategies based upon their cumulative experiences, restoring a sense of community as the ground for aging and healing.

SOUTH CENTRAL COMMUNITIES TRANSFORMED

Latino immigrant families have resettled communities in South Central Los Angeles, such as Watts and Compton, where African Americans have resided since mid-century. The resulting social transformation has forced black-run municipal institutions to reorient in the face of an altered demographic mix. Watts was called "La Colonia" when it was settled in the early twentieth century by Mexican railroad workers. After World War II, African Americans migrated into Watts and developed a separate culture contiguous with that of the Latino residents. During the postwar decades, South Central's Latino population moved eastward into the San Gabriel Valley, especially after the 1965 civil unrest. By the 1970s, African Americans gained control of municipal institutions that were run for decades by white minorities. In the 1980s, immigration again transformed communities like Watts and nearby Compton, where Latinos represent over half of the population. New immigrants find cheap rents in South Central's high-crime neighborhoods but also access to the Los Angeles job market. Local landlords prefer to rent to these monolingual, often undocumented immigrants, in order to minimize complaints about substandard dwellings that violate the housing code. Two or sometimes three in-migrating families will live crowded together in what was once a single-family household. These depressed circumstances are a result of the labor conditions in the downtown garment industry, which employs large numbers of undocumented immigrants and pays them less than a living wage. Male day laborers also receive substandard wages without benefits in working conditions that place them at greater risk of job-related injuries.

Meeting Latino immigrant families' demands for services has increased conflict within the area's municipal institutions. The disproportionate number of families per dwelling unit has put pressure upon all of these systems, from schooling to health and social services. In Compton's 28,000-pupil school district, Latinos make up about 70 percent of the student body. African Americans occupy most administrative posts within the district, and account for most of the certified teaching staff. At South Central's general hospital, which closed in 2007, Latino patients have surpassed blacks in hospital admissions, and 85 percent of children born in the hospital are Latino. Today, Latinos outnumber African Americans by nearly two to one in Los Angeles' Second Supervisorial District, an area of 2 million people in Watts, Baldwin Hills, and the Crenshaw District, which was primarily black until the 1990s.[17] Intergroup conflicts in both the school and the hospital have heated up over cultural differences between the African American staff and an increasing Spanish-speaking clientele. Latino leaders have accused the black middle-class professionals running Compton's municipal institutions of stereotyping the recent immigrants as noncitizens with limited rights. Some outspoken black leaders have even opposed further bilingual education in the city's financially troubled school district. Cultural stereotyping complicates matters at the local general hospital where some staff members have questioned whether recent immigrant patients are worthy of costly treatment protocols. Black staff will often perceive the increasing Latino presence as an encroachment on their community and its institutions, and view the Latino patient's cultural dissonance as an obstruction to the flow of hospital protocol. The fact that many Latino patients are undocumented immigrants, making demands upon an understaffed public hospital, has fostered further resentment and staff alienation. The Latino staff counters such claims with the retort that blacks believe the hospital "belongs to them."

The Spanish-speaking staff has learned to manage problems of communication and translation at each step of the health care process. Latino staff members report particular frustration when they are expected to develop an instant rapport with a patient solely on the basis of linguistic heritage. A staff nurse related how her situation, as an assimilated Latino working with a predominantly immigrant clientele, was a source of conflict. She had difficulty interpreting the disease symptoms of those who spoke in regional dialects. Mexican patients often made irrational demands upon her, for benefits and preferential treatment based solely on language. When she explained that their expectations were unrealistic, these patients often made derogatory remarks about her identification with the Americans. They would call her *Chicano* or *pocho*, labels that she disdained because they did not apply to her self-image. She prefers to be called a Latino, which, she claims, is a universal term that more appropriately describes her heritage, which is a blend of Mexican, Puerto Rican, and Spanish descents. Intergroup conflicts also arose between Latino and African American staff in the obstetrics and gynecology clinic. Many young Latinas choose to have an abortion on the basis of financial need. This decision develops out of a series of pregnancy counseling interviews between the patient and the health care team. Spanish-speaking nurses serve as interpreters during these interviews and often withhold relevant information about the patient's choices, namely to continue or to terminate a pregnancy. The Latino staff is predominantly Roman Catholic and frequently advocate a "pro-life" stance against abortion.

Social support is problematic because Latino patients bring different needs and expectations into a treatment setting. This was apparent in a support group for patients with high blood pressure (*presión*) that convened weekly in the internal medicine clinic. African American participants were skilled in articulating personal problems to the group. Latino participants were initially resistant about relating their problems to the group. They would sometimes deny that any problems existed in their lives that caused them stress. They often expressed that their only problems were physical ones related to their illness:

Susanna (the Spanish-speaking co-leader): How about you Juan, what bothers you?

Juan: I was sick in the hospital and I had some surgery and my heart is bothering me and I worry about my wife and my kids.

Susanna (to the group): He's got plenty to worry about. What about you Mrs. Ramirez?

Mrs. Ramirez: Just my sickness. It worries me. That's all I worry about. My health, my heart.

Susanna: What has been bothering you lately, Lucy?

Lucy: I have high blood pressure and that's what is bothering me. I work in the cleaners and the lady who is sitting next to me, that's my daughter, and I'm concerned about her.

Susanna: What bothers you Anna?

Anna: I'm a diabetic and I have high blood pressure and that's what is bothering me.

Susanna: What about you Sonny?

Sonny: I am sick from the heart and that's what is bothering me.

Susanna: How about you Marina?

Marina: I have a heart condition too.

Spanish-speaking participants thus responded to the question "What upsets you?" with a somatic rather than an emotional complaint. Most probably assumed that life's traumas and difficulties are to be endured with dignity (*dignidad*) and courage (*valor*). Susanna, the Spanish-speaking co-leader who is of Afro-Cuban heritage, acknowledged her initial difficulties in finding the correct term in colloquial Spanish to convey the notion of stress as an emotional construct, and changed her approach. When she translated "stress" as *esfuerzo*, rather than *tension*, participants answered in more interpersonal terms. She redefined "coping" more concretely, as talking with family and close friends, and found that participants quickly responded to her suggestions:

Susanna: I hear from these people the physical ailments. What I'm talking about is the things that bother us and then we get excited and that raises our blood pressure.

Lucy: Now I'm waiting to see the doctor and I'm upset.

Susanna: By telling us that she is upset, by this she is alleviating stress. This is one way —talking about it.

Susanna: Who do you talk with Paula?

Paula: Well, I talk to the Lord and I read the Bible.

Susanna: What do you do Lucy?

Lucy: I do the same thing, I pray and read the Bible.

Susanna: Lucy, do you have someone to talk to?

Lucy: I'm from Guatemala. I don't have any family here, just me and my daughter. But when I'm at home [in Guatemala], I talk to my friends.

Susanna: There are several ways of getting rid of that upsetness. One is physical—bake bread, do exercise, or fix your car. There's also a way of running away, like drugs and alcohol, but that doesn't deal with the stress. But when you get it off your chest . . . but you have to have someone who will listen.

Lucy (spontaneously to the other members of the group): When I get upset, I go and talk with my daughter and my daughter talks to me.

The difficulties associated with any group situation, namely resistance and denial, are exacerbated when there are language and cultural barriers. These obstacles often affect the kinds of responses that participants choose to verbalize. To be effective, both leader and interpreter had to be cognizant of participants' culturally prescribed modes of expressing subjective stress and attitudes toward illness, stigma, and help seeking. One important cultural factor is "familism," the idea that individuals are encapsulated within a close-knit kinship network. This pattern of intense family involvement is frequently cited as the key mediator in illness behavior and the pathway to care for Latino patients.[18] A person will consult close relatives for help in understanding the meaning of symptoms. Group consultation is the preferred mode of evaluating the severity of symptoms and the degree to which they interfere with everyday activities and familial responsibilities. The family, rather than the individual, is thus central to the initial diagnosis and the decision to seek treatment. For many recent immigrants, there is the additional burden of living within a split "transnational family" with one spouse living in the home country and the other in the United States.[19] The situation contributes to the sense of loss, isolation, and emotional abandonment felt by many recent immigrants. The following dialogue with a woman and her daughter alludes to the multiple stresses that transnational families must cope with in the new country. It suggests how Latino clients can be reached by better understanding their intrafamilial help-giving arrangements. In this case, Susanna enlisted the patient's trust by establishing a rapport with her daughter. By triangulating the helping relationship, Susanna demonstrated her respect (*respeto*) for the importance of the family in health consultations. Familial consultation may even have accounted for the patient's fuller participation and acceptance of the model of coping in subsequent groups:

Susanna: Isabella, what upsets you?

Isabella: I need to be alone when I'm upset.

Susanna (to Eva): I want you to tell your mother what we've been talking about and ask her if she ever talks to anyone about her problems.

Eva: When it first happens, she wants to be alone, but later she wants to talk things over with someone.

Susanna: Who does she talk with?

Eva: Her children.

Susanna: When there's a problem with one of the children, who does she talk about it with?

Eva: She has many children.

Susanna: How many children does she have?

Eva: Eight children.

Susanna: Does she have a husband?

Eva: He's in Mexico.

Susanna: Any lady friends?

Eva: No.

Latino clients may feel uncomfortable discussing personal issues with strangers in a group since the dominant cultural framework for problem solving in Latin American societies is dyadic and private. Catholic religious tenets hold that prayer to a transcendent deity and confession to a male priest in the privacy of the chapel are the acceptable modes of resolving intrapsychic conflicts. Then there is the belief that one keeps one's suffering to one's self. This "tragic sense of life," in the words of philosopher Miguel de Unamuno, is represented in images of the suffering Christ and in pastoral homilies entreating the laity to "bear their cross" in silence. Both constructs reinforce acceptance of earthly suffering as part of the bargain of life. The poet Octavio Paz laments over his fellow Mexicans' sense of isolation and powerlessness in the expression, "our silence and apathy, our reticence and gloom."[20] This "labyrinth of solitude" will often inhibit dialogues and objectification of personal conflicts in a group situation. Because life is a "veil of tears" and the world outside the home a "sphere of distrust, questionable loyalties, conflict and violence," many people turn to supernatural beings to intercede on their behalf. Eric Wolf and Edward Hansen explain how the cult of the saints is a part of everyday life for many Latin Americans:

> In Catholic belief the saints receive the prayers of the faithful and present these petitions before the throne of God. Similarly, the Mother of God is thought to be able to intercede for men with her son, Jesus Christ, God the Son. Men therefore turn to these supernatural intermediaries when they seek to connect their personal lives with the greater power beyond. They approach the saints and the Virgin as friends and patrons, just as in real life they seek both friends and patrons.[21]

Individuals, households, and communities have patron saints to whom they offer goods and devotions in return for help in financial, health, and personal problems. These payments are regarded as a way of reciprocating supernatural intercessors for their ongoing protection from the darker aspects of the human condition. Such hierarchically sanctioned modes of problem solving are clearly dissonant with group process and Western scientific thought, and pose significant challenges to health care providers focusing on the psychosocial needs of chronically ill Latino immigrant clients.

AN AFRICAN AMERICAN NETWORK OF CARE

In South Central Los Angeles, as in many low-income urban areas, chronically ill patients are often unable to reenter community networks in a functional capacity. They have difficulties coping with their lost work and family roles and their increased dependency on service institutions. Also lost is the extended family that facilitated support and coping during crises. This ethnically based network of care communicated new roles and coping strategies in ways both familiar and comprehensible to low-income African American patients. The support groups encouraged participants to reformulate their personal roles and coping styles. A cadre of community volunteers provided supportive care through peer counseling and transportation to and from the hospital. Health educators used stylized forms of address in their presentations, including metaphor, joking, and insults, to help patients develop rational beliefs about their condition. The interpersonal strategies used at this network of care differed significantly from those used in other public agencies in the same community where staff would frequently alienate

clients because of their unrealistic expectations and their demands for compliance with unfamiliar norms. Health care workers socialized compliance by
using social learning, or modeling, techniques to communicate with their patients. The role model in the network was often a staff member or a volunteer
who possessed attributes that were similar to those of the patients. The model
was a grassroots community leader with an interest in health care issues, a
professional interested in broadening her political base, or a paraprofessional
with a particularly charismatic affect. Volunteers and support group participants, who nurtured and counseled others experiencing difficulties with their
treatment, were usually controlled hypertensives themselves. These modeling
activities communicated a sense of interdependence or connectedness among
patients and staff through both traditional and modern forms of speech and
action. African American health care workers appropriated symbols and
styles of ethnic heritage to address sophisticated concepts of disease and its
treatment. Professional staff adopted these cultural styles to foster alliances
between the patients and themselves. Paraprofessionals often shared many of
the problems of urban adaptation with the patients they were trained to help.
Because of this identification with the problems and needs of the patient population, help giving by many paraprofessional staff often took the form of
quasi-familial bonds. A sense of fictive kinship thus developed within the network because of the need to build alliances between caregivers and patients
at the onset of a life-threatening chronic illness.

Fictive kinship is an adaptive strategy that many urban families have used to
maintain the extended family ties that were severed after migration to the city.
As a continuity of ritual kinship—a significant mode of alliance in traditional
societies—fictive kin are bound together for any number of material ends. In
folk communities, these bonds shape interpersonal relations within the village.
People will call upon fictive kin for mutual economic, social, and emotional
support. Fictive kinship thus serves as an informal means of social integration.
In periods of rapid social change, fictive kinship serves as a transitional social
identity that can be adapted to new conditions, such as urban living and industrial work. For example, persons marginal to urban lifeways often lose the
thread of continuity or a sense of past and future because of the city's impersonal forces. They will thus establish interfamilial ties within the new urban enclave. Fictive kinship was used within the network of care to enlist the loyalties
of patients and to sanction adherence to a demanding treatment protocol. The
quasi-familial ties were especially functional to older patients, whose social
identities had developed within a more traditional, and often rural, African
American cultural framework. These bonds offered them a sense of belonging
and identity in a nonalienating framework that blended traditional sentiments
with knowledge about modern health care. Moreover, the organizational frame-

work within which these bonds functioned provided a sense of coherence and of interdependence. The sense of interdependence was most fully celebrated during the annual hypertension workshop. The event conveyed a folk-conception of cultural identity to participants. Black religion, gospel music, soul food, and community politics were blended together, and kinship, friendship, and neighborliness are the underlying themes. The workshop honored the efforts of volunteers who were pivotal to the success of disease control in a community with a high incidence of hypertension. It also celebrated the success of reform-oriented professionals whose efforts in the civil rights struggles of the 1960s led to the establishment of the medical facility. In the hospital's formative period, there was a sense of inherent pride and identification with the needs of the black residents of Compton, Lynwood, and Watts. The initial recruitment of clerks and nurses was from these same communities, in response to political pressures to employ and train local residents in skilled occupations. Since staff and patients shared a common set of institutions, a sense of familiarity developed. The African American population of South Central Los Angeles thus identified with the hospital on the basis of its emergence from the civil rights movement, as well as its location.

Health care reform efforts continued in this African American community so closely associated with the movement for equality. In fact, the coordinators of hypertension-control efforts in the hospital used their exemplary positions, as role models to patients, to extend their power. They forged a political coalition to lobby for more funding for efforts to control high blood pressure on behalf of the city's African American community. They enlisted the support of hospital physicians and private medical providers to ensure continuing support for their efforts as leaders of community health programs. These urban "big men" built a coalition of cultural and political interests through the establishment of patron-client bonds, based upon help giving, with older members of the African American community. Physicians in private practice and program administrators from three government-funded programs to control high blood pressure formed the Southeast High Blood Pressure Coalition. They combined efforts because of state budget cuts that threatened the status of their programs. The provider coalition planned a referral system that would be mobilized after a community screening to direct patients with elevated readings to their clinics and private practices. They discussed ways to establish a federally funded hypertension research center at the public community hospital. Their most immediate concern, however, was to challenge the findings of a state-funded impact study. The report found the incidence of hypertension among African Americans in the region to be significantly lower than previous estimates. Program administrators were apprehensive that state health planners would use these statistics as a rationale to cut their funding. They undertook a phone survey of physicians in private practice and an audit of community screenings in order to verify their estimates that one out of five individuals in the region had an elevated blood pressure reading. The administrators' motivations for coalition development were to maintain current funding levels.

Physicians were motivated by a different set of interests. They proposed that unified standards of treatment be established and maintained by physicians in the region. They planned to establish a statistical database and a patient tracking and referral system. They also planned to have a uniform treatment protocol with which a physician would have to comply in order to qualify for referrals from community screenings. The protocol would focus on state-of-the-art treatment modalities and patient compliance strategies. The physicians thus envisioned a regional network that would coordinate screening, referral, treatment, education, and research in high blood pressure control. The professionally driven coalition attempted to move a low-income urban community toward a middle-class standard of care. The smaller nexus of lay activities shared many of the same goals. Patient-centered activities encouraged individuals to explore their beliefs, personal experiences, and coping resources through culturally familiar modes of speaking and acting. All were carried out in the public spaces of a community hospital, where social relations cut across class, racial, and ethnic domains. These activities and the institutional setting itself represented rational, secular, and modern approaches to health care. This African American network of care thus conveyed active images of health maintenance and social problem solving to those on the boundary between the lifeways of the countryside and its small towns, and the city.

NOTES

1. Carl A. Maida, "Social Support and Learning in Preventive Health Care," *Social Science and Medicine* 21 (1985): 335–39.

2. Carol B. Stack, *All Our Kin: Strategies for Survival in a Black Community* (New York: Harper & Row, 1974).

3. William Trotter Jr., ed., *The Great Migration in Historical Perspective: New Dimensions of Race, Class, and Gender* (Bloomington: Indiana University Press, 1991); Nicholas Lemann, *The Promised Land: The Great Black Migration and How It Changed America* (New York: Knopf, 1991); Milton C. Sernett, *Bound for the Promised Land: African American Religion and the Great Migration* (Raleigh, NC: Duke University Press, 1997).

4. Morris Newman, "New Riffs for a Street Linked to Jazz," *New York Times*, March 23, 1997, national edition, sec. 1; Ted Gioia, *West Coast Jazz: Modern Jazz in California, 1945–1960* (New York: Oxford University Press, 1992), 7.

5. Mike Davis, *City of Quartz: Excavating the Future in Los Angeles* (New York: Random House, 1992), 64; Gioia, *West Coast Jazz*, 3–9.

6. Nathan Irvin Huggins, *Harlem Renaissance* (New York: Oxford University Press, 1971); Henry Louis Gates Jr., "New Negroes, Migration and Cultural Exchange," in *Jacob Lawrence: The Migration Series*, edited by Elizabeth Hutton Turner (Washington, DC: Rappahannock Press, 1993), 17–21; Ann Douglas, *Terrible Honesty: Mongrel Manhattan in the 1920s* (New York: Farrar, Straus and Giroux, 1995); George Hutchinson, *The Harlem Renaissance in Black and White* (Cambridge, MA: Harvard University Press, 1995).

7. Frances Fox Piven and Richard A. Cloward, *Regulating the Poor: The Functions of Public Welfare* (New York: Random House, 1971); Andy Alaszewski, Mike Walsh, Jill Manthorpe, and Larry Harrison, "Managing Risk in the City: The Role of Welfare Professionals in Managing Risks Arising from Vulnerable Individuals in Cities," *Health and Place* 3 (1997): 15–23.

8. Herbert G. Gutman, *The Black Family in Slavery and Freedom, 1750–1925* (New York: Pantheon, 1976).

9. Michael Harrington, *The Other America: Poverty in the United States* (New York: Macmillan, 1962).

10. Ron Eyerman and Andrew Jamison, *Social Movements: A Cognitive Approach* (University Park: Pennsylvania State University Press, 1991), 131–32.

11. Jane Addams, *Twenty Years at Hull-House* (New York: Macmillan, 1910); Allen F. Davis, *Spearheads for Reform: The Social Settlements and the Progressive Movement, 1890–1914* (New York: Oxford University Press, 1967); Rivka Shpak Lissak, *Pluralism and Progressives: Hull House and the New Immigrants, 1890–1919* (Chicago: University of Chicago Press, 1989); Mina Carson, *Settlement Folk: Social Thought and the American Settlement Movement, 1885–1930* (Chicago: University of Chicago Press, 1990); Theda Skocpol, *Protecting Soldiers and Mothers: The Political Origins of Social Policy in the United States* (Cambridge, MA: Harvard University Press, 1992); Shannon Jackson, *Lines of Activity: Performance, Historiography, Hull-House Domesticity* (Ann Arbor: University of Michigan Press, 2000).

12. Eyerman and Jamison, *Social Movements*, 128.

13. Mike Davis, "Who Killed L.A.? The War Against the Cities," *Crossroads* 32 (1993): 2–19.

14. Frank A. Finnerty Jr., Edward C. Mattie, and Frank A. Finnerty III, "Hypertension in the Inner City: I. Analysis of Clinic Dropouts," *Circulation* 47 (1973): 73–75; Frank A. Finnerty Jr., Lawrence W. Shaw, and Clifton K. Himmelsbach, "Hypertension in the Inner City: II. Detection and Follow-up," *Circulation* 47 (1973): 76–78; William W. Dressler, James R. Bindon, and Yasmin H. Neggers, "Culture, Socioeconomic Status, and Coronary Artery Disease Risk Factors in an African American Community," *Journal of Behavioral Medicine* 21 (1998): 527–44.

15. Lawrence W. Levine, *Black Culture and Black Consciousness: Afro-American Folk Thought from Slavery to Freedom* (New York: Oxford University Press, 1977).

16. Claudia Mitchell-Kernan, "Signifying, Loud Talking and Marking," in *Rappin' and Stylin' Out: Communication in Urban Black America,* edited by Thomas Kochman (Urbana: University of Illinois Press, 1972), 315–35.

17. Michael Finnegan, "L.A.'s Black Politicians Face Changing Landscape," *Los Angeles Times*, May 27, 2008, sec. A.

18. Janet M. Schreiber and John P. Homiak, "Mexican Americans," in *Ethnicity and Medical Care*, edited by Alan Harwood (Cambridge, MA: Harvard University Press, 1981), 316–17.

19. Leo R. Chavez, *Shadowed Lives: Undocumented Immigrants in American Society* (Fort Worth, TX: Harcourt Brace Jovanovich, 1992), 119.

20. Octavio Paz, *The Labyrinth of Solitude: Life and Thought in Mexico*, translated by Lysander Kemp (New York: Grove Press, 1961), quoted in Eric R. Wolf and Edward C. Hansen, *The Human Condition in Latin America* (New York: Oxford University Press, 1972), 115–16.

21. Wolf and Hansen, *The Human Condition in Latin America*, 110.

Chapter Five

Strangers in the City

Immigration and resettlement are crises that affect newcomers, their families, and even the institutions providing health and social services to immigrant and refugee communities. Both the physical trauma and the psychological impact of uprooting will often lead to a variety of conditions that require medical care. Because of limited English-language skills, lack of medical insurance, and limited knowledge of how to obtain health care resources, recent immigrant and refugee families remain medically underevaluated and undertreated. Many public and private agencies of potential help to immigrants do not know how to identify, reach, and work effectively with immigrant populations. Newcomers from Latin American and Asian nations face troubling life circumstances that include substandard housing, poor working conditions, language barriers, and racism, which increase their apprehension about using public health services in the host society. Tighter cost controls, especially on capital spending, have led to rationing of health care resources in the form of waiting lists and closures of public hospitals and clinics in cities with large immigrant populations. These tighter fiscal controls on health care keep poor clients, including new immigrants, out of the health care system. Experiences in troubled homelands and in the North American metropolises clearly affect their ability to seek help from established institutions during crises.

TRANSNATIONALISM AND THE NEW UPROOTED

The mass migrations across national borders of recent decades have redefined the meaning of immigrant identity and network formation. Transnationalism describes a process whereby migrants construct a social field that spans diverse geographic, cultural, and political boundaries. Through their social networks, transmigrants are simultaneously linked to the homeland *and* to the host society.[1] They make decisions, form associations, and seek support within a social field that encompasses both countries. Their national, ethnic, and personal identities are similarly constructed upon these multiple involvements within two or more geographically distinct places.

The lives of transnational migrants are closely related to global economic and political transformations, specifically to the behavior of multinational firms. Corporations operate transnationally when they simultaneously maintain an organizational presence in more than one country. These global firms view the world as a single economic unit and manage their diverse financial arrangements, technologies, and labor forces accordingly. Immigrant resettlement usually follows transnational routes that mark the corporate search for cheaper ways to produce and market commodities. Transmigrants supply the labor for the global assembly line of production regions spanning various national cultures and political jurisdictions. These globally integrated economic activities, including manufacturing but also specialized producer and financial services, are highly concentrated in large urban centers, such as New York and Los Angeles.[2]

As unskilled and semiskilled workers, transmigrants will be offered the lowest-paying, often most dangerous, manufacturing and service jobs. Because they participate in the low-wage and casual employment sectors that receive few fringe benefits, the immigrant workforce will depend more upon publicly funded housing, health care, and social welfare. Transmigrant households will nevertheless acquire globally produced commodities, such as televisions, stereo systems, radios, and even designer-labeled clothing, promoted through an urban public culture. They will likewise consume global services, such as telecommunications, air travel and transport, mass entertainment, electronic gaming, and other impersonal indicators of leisure and recreation. Transnational identities are shaped within this flux of people and material goods in global cities with their characteristic mix of traditional and modern sensibilities.

The bifocal nature of transnational migration requires its sojourners to forge identities and ego defenses to weather the insecurities within both home and host countries. Many are refugees from political and economic repression, compelled to reorient to unfamiliar and frequently life-threatening environments. Before coming to the United States, they often suffer from the extreme traumas of war, forced relocation, malnutrition, parasitic and infectious diseases, and minimal medical care. The psychological manifestations of these traumas include depression, anxiety, somatic responses, and substance abuse.

The transnational passage is anxiety provoking, as immigrants inevitably present themselves to officials charged with enforcing border policies. Those arriving at a port of entry with the requisite papers experience this as a necessary inconvenience that moves them a step closer to their destination. For the undocumented immigrant, however, crossing the border zone is like negotiating a "war landscape." As with any other dangerous place, the border's terrain and the officials charged with its surveillance appear ominous to the person crossing illegally. Navigating this unknown territory challenges the more conscious mental processes, like planning and strategizing, but also intensifies an individual's sense of fear, apprehensiveness, and anxiety.

Transmigrants will initially resettle in ethnic enclaves where high rates of crime, crowding, and disorganization mix with familiar lifeways. Hence they can speak, worship, and watch television broadcasts in their native language or dialect and shop in ethnic markets selling familiar foods and other commodities of their homeland. Beyond their neighborhoods, they may encounter unprovoked gestures of fear, disdain, and ridicule. Newcomers immediately sense their otherness when they approach municipal agencies for health care or schooling for their children. They will often be unduly stigmatized and deemed unworthy by service personnel—"gatekeepers" who may themselves dwell at the cultural periphery of the host society. Their own marginality will often predispose them to view the newcomers through a prism of territoriality, competitiveness, or fear of contagion.

These attitudes frequently derive from the nativist thinking of elites within the society who have mounted aggressive campaigns to limit immigrant rights during recent waves of transnational migration.[3] The current nativist reaction to the size and diversity of immigrants residing in the nation has triggered demands for restrictive legislation and calls for more aggressive enforcement measures. These include denying a driver's license to undocumented immigrants and issuing a national identification card to discourage them from seeking jobs and benefits. A group of environmentalists and population control advocates launched the Federation for American Immigration Reform (FAIR) in 1979 to pressure Congress to curb immigration.[4] FAIR sought to protect both the environment and American jobs and wages, to reduce crime, and to improve education. The group believed that unrestricted transnational immigration further imperiled working people and the poor in America. Its board members included ecologist and University of California professor Garrett Hardin, former Colorado governor Richard D. Lamm, former New York City mayor John V. Lindsay, and former senator Eugene McCarthy. FAIR fought the amnesty provisions of the 1986 federal Immigration Reform and Control Act (IRCA), but lobbied hard for that law's sanctions against employers who hire illegal immigrants. In fact, a former Immigration

˙and Naturalization Service (INS) commissioner served as a lobbyist for the organization. FAIR also lobbies for state legislative measures, such as the California Proposition 187, which the "Save Our State" movement placed on the November 1994 ballot. Californians approved by 59 to 41 percent the ballot initiative that denied the state's illegal immigrants their rights to non-emergency health care, welfare, and public schooling for their children. The day after the election, a state judge blocked enforcement of the provisions that would deny access to schooling until they are tested in court. The Los Angeles Unified School District voted unanimously to challenge the initiative's legality and the American Civil Liberties Union filed a lawsuit charging that Proposition 187 interferes with federal jurisdiction over immigration and denies immigrants their constitutional rights by encouraging others to discriminate against them.

There has been a marked change in Americans' attitudes toward the immigration question. National telephone surveys conducted by the Gallup Organization and by the *New York Times* and CBS News in 1993 found that two-thirds of Americans favored a decrease in immigration. In 1986, the year IRCA was enacted, almost half preferred a decrease; in 1977, 42 percent of Americans favored restrictions; and the 1965 poll shows that only one-third called for a decrease. These responses reflect a trend in attitudes related to changed economic conditions. Conservative populists, having sensed this changed national mood, rally a culturally disenchanted and economically anxious middle-class to oppose open immigration and free trade within the hemisphere. In California, the nativist arguments are economically driven. According to the director of the Center for U.S.-Mexican Studies at the University of California, San Diego, "the economy has created the reality and perception of a zero-sum game in which citizens see themselves pitted against immigrants."[5] The anxious economic environment at the end of the Cold War was the result of massive corporate restructuring, economic dislocation, and downward economic mobility for several hundred thousand California workers. Mass demonstrations, or "Light Up the Border" rallies, were staged at the U.S.-Mexico Border in San Diego to express populist discontent with national migration policies. At least once a month in 1989 and 1990, at the time of mass layoffs of San Diego's aerospace and defense workers, scores of San Diegans lined up their cars and shined their headlights at the border to symbolically state their opposition to illegal immigration. They also displayed slogans such as "Order on Our Border" and "Support the Border Patrol." Such negative sentiments toward the increasing numbers of "strangers in the land" are not unlike those expressed during an earlier period of massive immigration to American shores. For not since the turn of the twentieth century has the United States tried to absorb so many people at one time.

IMMIGRANTS IN URBAN AMERICA, 1880–1930

In the mid-1880s, immigrants from southern and eastern Europe began to arrive in this country. From 1880 to 1930, 4.5 million people emigrated from Italy; 4 million came from Austria, Hungary, the Balkans, and Greece; with another 4 million arriving from Russia and Poland. By 1910, 38 percent of America's foreign-born population originated from these countries. Transnational migration within North America also increased after the turn of the century. Between 1900 and 1919, 185,000 Mexicans crossed the border to work primarily as casual laborers in the cotton, rice, and beet-sugar fields of the Southwest, particularly Texas, California, Arizona, and Colorado. Over the next decade this number increased to about 750,000. Mexicans also worked for the railroads and in the mines, with some moving on to take industrial jobs in the Midwest. By 1930, 1.5 million English-speaking and French Canadians had crossed the border. Most Canadians came to work in the forests of the Great Lakes and the Far Northwest, but also in the textile mills of Northern New England.

These immigrants were the new workforce for an expanding industrial economy. Very few spoke English, and many were semiliterate in their own language. Most were primarily unskilled peasants and agricultural workers. They left European agricultural regions that were unable to compete with new commercial farming techniques of the United States, Canada, and Argentina. The majority arrived in this country without the money to buy land or the machinery to succeed in commercial agriculture. Without a trade or a craft, they took jobs as miners, as railroad and factory laborers, and as meat packers and cannery workers. Unskilled immigrant women found low-paying jobs as domestic workers. Those with manual or clerical skills found work in urban garment and retail shopping districts.

Immigrants of every skill level clustered together in "villages," primarily in the manufacturing cities of the East and Midwest. By 1930, three-fourths of the foreign born were living in towns and cities. Immigrant families concentrated in the tenements and wood-framed houses of a city's working-class district. As most homes lacked space and privacy, the ethnic neighborhood became a "street corner society" where children played in its streets and adults socialized on porches and sidewalks. These "urban villagers" created a coherent public space and a cultural life for themselves within the nation's shabbiest industrial districts. They opened boardinghouses, grocery stores, and saloons that catered to the needs of their countrymen. Entrepreneurs founded foreign-language newspapers, ethnic clubs, and fraternal organizations to offer mutual assistance and cultural support to other newcomers.

Even as they sought to establish a sense of order within their communities, the newcomers aroused the suspicions of native-born and rural Americans. In

1890, 62 percent of the foreign born lived in cities, compared to only 26 percent of Anglo-Americans born of native parents. The nativists viewed immigrant enclaves as congested and corrupt places occupied by transient foreign-born males who led lives of crime.[6] As most of the new immigrants had come from non-democratic societies, nativist groups feared that their unfamiliar cultural traits would undermine the nation's republican values. Because the newcomers were mostly Roman Catholics and Jewish, many American Protestants became alarmed enough to harbor conspiracy theories. This paranoia translated into a wave of anti-Catholic agitation by the nativist American Protective Association, and of political anti-Semitism, particularly during the economic depressions of the 1880s and 1890s. Other critics adopted more virulent ideologies to darken the debate over the unlimited entry of immigrants in American society.

Nativist social theorists appropriated Charles Darwin's concept of the competition between unequal species to challenge assimilationist ideas.[7] Social Darwinists believed that nations, like species, were engaged in a struggle for survival. They held that certain races were more inherently fit to succeed in a system of free enterprise and democratic government. Researchers measured the cranial capacity of skulls from various ethnic groups to determine which members of the species were the most fit. Racial nativists described the new immigrants as "subcommon" and "beaten men from beaten races" who would destroy the nation's Anglo-Saxon heritage. Theodore Roosevelt would even scold the American upper and middle classes for heading toward "race suicide" by restricting the number of their offspring. Many of the nation's elites feared that the lower classes, presumably the unfit, were gaining a competitive edge through their excessive breeding. Followers of the pseudoscientific eugenics movement believed that intermarriage between old-stock Americans and "genetically inferior" Mediterranean or Slavic races would lead to mongrelizing and national deterioration. These biological reformers advocated immigration restrictions to protect the gene pool by keeping out "degenerate breeding stock." Alarmed and encouraged by this powerful ideological rhetoric, the American Federation of Labor, the Daughters of the American Revolution, the patrician-established Immigration Restriction League, and nativist interest groups pressured Congress to reform the nation's open immigration policies. The Dillingham Commission, a joint Senate-House committee, was established to investigate all aspects of the new immigration. Its forty-one-volume report, released in 1911, found that the newcomers were less intellectually, physically, economically, and culturally fit than earlier settler groups. The Commission recommended a literacy test and legislation that would restrict immigration based upon nationality. That same year, anthropologist Franz Boas conducted experiments to refute racial nativist dogmas by measuring the skulls of new immigrants and their offspring to determine changes in the slope of the cranium. He showed that environmental factors, such as nutrition and improved living conditions, not heredity, were responsible for modifying this particular racial characteristic in second-generation immigrants.

By 1915, a new voice was beginning to be heard in a nation divided on the immigrant question and on whether to enter the European war, that of the newcomers' political radicalism. The Great War disrupted transatlantic travel and also the lives of many transmigrants who had planned to return to their homelands with the money earned in this country. They found themselves stranded in the nation's slums and locked into low-wage jobs. Many who had labored in urban sweatshops for years without protest began to take collective action to change their working conditions. Immigrant workers, who had been exposed to trade unionism, socialism, and anarchism in their homelands, engaged in labor militancy. Progressives like Theodore Roosevelt, along with the more extreme nativists, called for a loyalty crusade to challenge immigrant radicalism. As the nation mobilized to enter World War I, "Americanization" campaigns supported by settlement houses, the YMCA, civic groups, and government agencies pushed for mass citizenship efforts, including English and civics classes. Many large corporations, such as the Ford Motor Company, taught English to their immigrant workforce and required "American" forms of dress and behavior. The corporate campaigns encouraged foreign-born workers to become citizens to enhance their chances for career advancement. In fact, many immigrants did improve their lives by upgrading their jobs during the wartime labor shortage. Others volunteered for the armed forces and fought in Europe. The immigrants in uniform and those working in the war industries realized a greater sense of belonging and a stronger identification with their adopted national culture. Many influentials in immigrant enclaves throughout the nation began to embrace the ideals of Americanization, even the lawyers, shopkeepers, and other small businessmen who previously showed little concern for the assimilation of their clientele.

Amid the rising anti-immigrant sentiments and Anglo-Saxon nationalism of the period, Randolph Bourne's "Trans-national America" appeared in the July 1916 issue of the *Atlantic Monthly*. As America prepared to enter the Great War, many insisted on unconditional political loyalty and cultural allegiance from members of southern and eastern European immigrant groups. Bourne, in contrast, argued for an acceptance of these immigrants' dual citizenship and transnational cultural identities, rejecting the idea of assimilating newcomers into the emerging mass culture of industrial America:

> Those who came to find liberty achieve only license. They become the flotsam and jetsam of American life, the downward undertow of our civilization with its

leering cheapness and falseness of taste and spiritual outlook, the absence of mind and sincere feeling which we see in our slovenly towns, our vapid moving pictures, our popular novels, and in the vacuous faces of the crowds on the city street. This is the cultural wreckage of our time.[8]

Bourne called for accepting the folk cultures of recent European immigrants into the American tradition. He envisioned that ethnic communities would regenerate a national culture that had placed commercialism and industrialism at its center. Bourne's alternative ideal of a "Beloved Community" was founded upon a new set of experiences that "would centralize American culture into a new cosmopolitanism by first releasing the potential of the nation's ethnic and racial subcultures."[9] The transnationalist community would blend America's emergent sense of modernism with the best of traditional cultural expression from European folk life.

Nationalist appeals triumphed over transnationalist ideals in the World War I era. The period of unlimited entry into the United States ended when Congress passed the Immigration Act of 1917, which established literacy requirements. Because southern and eastern European countries had higher illiteracy rates, the measure amounted to a de facto quota. Despite appeals for cultural pluralism by leftist intellectuals, settlement house workers, and new immigrant voters, the restrictions begun in wartime were made permanent over the next decade. Senator William Paul Dillingham, whose 1911 report set the nativist political agenda, drafted a bill in 1920 that would reduce the total number of immigrants from southern and eastern Europe. His quota system would be the cornerstone of the Immigration Act of 1921. The legislation limited the number of immigrants from each group who could be admitted to the United States each year. It provided an annual quota equal to 3 percent of the total number of foreign born of that group residing in the United States in 1910. This ensured that most of the 350,000 new immigrants would be admitted from northwestern Europe.

An even more restrictive system was imposed by the Johnson-Reed Act of 1924, which excluded immigrants, especially from Asia, who were not eligible for citizenship. It also reduced the annual quota from 3 to 2 percent and used the 1890 census as a basis. This revised the scheme of European immigration by allotting 85 percent of the total quota to northwestern Europe. The 1929 National Origins Act reduced the number of immigrants admitted to the United States to a total quota of 153,714 distributed among the various European countries equal to their proportion of the American population of 1920. This act left hemispheric immigration untouched; however, officials worked covertly to impose a quota on Mexican immigration. The consulates of both countries agreed to enforce old regulations when issuing visas, thereby restricting the number of immigrants crossing the border. The United States adopted a form of administrative restriction so as to not alienate the revolutionary government's relations with American companies doing business in Mexico. This arrangement left open the possibility of issuing temporary work permits to Mexican laborers when there were labor shortages, for example the *bracero*, or guest-worker, program established during World War II. The policies, reflecting the attitudes and political power of native-born elites of the early twentieth century, have helped to shape contemporary national immigrant reform legislation, as well as the state regulations guiding the provision of health and welfare services to recent immigrants and their families.

THE CITY AND THE BORDER

The IRCA included major provisions in the areas of employment and legalization for persons residing in the United States without government permission. The legalization component, commonly referred to as amnesty, allows these persons to become legal residents once they have met specified criteria. However, the IRCA's civil and criminal sanctions against employers who hire undocumented immigrants have failed to stem the flow of illegal immigration. The Illegal Immigration Reform and Immigrant Responsibility Act (IIRIRA), enacted in 1996, imposed severe restrictions on the political asylum process that generations of newcomers had used to gain entry into the United States. The law makes it difficult for illegal immigrants who are longtime residents to avoid deportation under a humanitarian waiver when their expulsion would render "extreme hardship" to themselves. To avert deportation under the new rules, the applicant must have been living in the United States for ten years and prove that expulsion would cause extreme hardship to a legal resident spouse, parent, or child. The ruling also severely restricts administrative hearings and judicial review of INS decisions — processes that have allowed deportation cases to go on for years.

Despite federal attempts to limit newcomers' ability to gain entry to the country, inexpensive immigrant labor is the mainstay of California's agricultural and manufacturing economies; hence, the state is home to 27 percent of the nation's immigrants. California's foreign-born population has increased dramatically: between 1970 and 2005, the number of immigrants increased more than fivefold, from 1.8 to 9.6 million. Of the estimated 11.1 million illegal immigrants in the nation, 25 percent live in California. By 2005, 27 percent of the state's population was foreign born. However, fewer than half of California's foreign-born residents are citizens. More legal and undocumented immigrants settled in Los Angeles than in any other metropolitan area except New York. Over a third of Los Angeles' population is foreign born, mainly from Latin American and Asian countries, but also from Armenia, Russia, Lebanon, and Iran.

These diverse groups have maintained their cultural traditions in ethnic neighborhoods throughout Los Angeles. The huge pool of immigrant labor has also transformed the Pacific Rim metropolis into a global city with a massive production-dominated artisan economy, driven by the region's design-oriented manufacturing, entertainment, and multimedia companies. The six-county metropolitan region is the nation's largest manufacturing zone, employing workers in thousands of small companies producing goods ranging from furniture to personal computers to artificial heart valves to giant turbines used in the natural gas industry, as well as in the apparel or garment industry, which is the largest industrial employer in Los Angeles.[10] Although the state and its municipalities gain some tax revenues, the federal government is the major beneficiary of immigrant workers' taxes; yet little of these tax dollars return to the state in the form of needed health care and other public benefits.

There are currently a number of barriers to accessible health care for working poor and indigent residents of California's immigrant communities. The increased federal role in welfare and child health insurance reform has led the state to reevaluate its safety net policies, and to experiment broadly in health and welfare reform as a result of the greater flexibility of federal funding streams.[11] In 1996, the Personal Responsibility and Work Opportunity Reconciliation Act (PRWORA) and the IIRIRA consolidated a number of public welfare programs, including Aid to Families with Dependent Children (AFDC) and emergency assistance funding streams, into a block grant to states for cash assistance and child care. Under the legislation, those coming to the United States after August 1996 were barred from federally financed government benefits, including full Medicaid eligibility, during their first five years in the country. It was left to the states to decide whether to cover the costs of those benefits; California decided to spend its own funds to extend Medicaid to all legal immigrants regardless of when they entered the United States.[12] The State Children's Health Insurance Program, passed in 1997 under the Balanced Budget Act, authorizes states to provide health insurance to the nation's uninsured children in low-income families through expansion of existing Medicaid programs, a separate children's health insurance program, or a combination of both Medicaid expansion and a separate program.[13] Under the "New Federalism," the decision to separate welfare from Medicaid eligibility, coupled with restrictions on legally admitted immigrants' eligibility for Medicaid, led to unexpected declines in Medicaid caseloads, placing many children at risk of losing their eligibility for Medicaid coverage.[14]

Survey data indicate that over half of low-income immigrants are uninsured, roughly double that of the native-born citizen population, perhaps up to two-thirds for California's illegal immigrant population. They rely upon safety net providers, such as public and nonprofit hospitals and clinics, for their health care. However, many immigrants will often avoid or delay mainstream care, choosing instead alternative sources of care, including unlicensed health care providers, folk healers, and prescription drugs smuggled from abroad.[15] Some also seek lower-cost health care and pharmaceuticals on their trips back to Mexico or Central America, before attempting to cross back into to the United States. While California has sought to increase the number of insured families through the expansion of Medi-Cal (California's Medicaid program) and Healthy Families programs, a consistently large number of immigrants statewide remain uninsured.[16] The numbers of immigrant children and the children of immigrants have been steadily increasing in the United States, and they represent a rapidly growing population in California. Their immigration status or that of their parents places them at increased health risk, for they experience greater residential mobility, have fewer familial and social supports, and realize less health care access than their non-immigrant counterparts.[17] A study of Mexican American children in two Los Angeles communities found that immigrant families had fewer economic resources and were less likely to be insured or have continuous Medicaid coverage than citizens in the same communities.[18] Children of citizens, by comparison, realized better health care access and more outpatient visits; they were more likely to have received well-child care in a health maintenance organization (HMO) or private office and less likely to have put off seeing a health provider for financial reasons.

Two factors may account for the recent decline in the number of eligible California residents seeking public benefits. First, the arbitrary time limits placed on receipt of welfare benefits under the 1996 PRWORA and IIRIRA laws, and state welfare reform efforts, such as CalWORKs, have resulted in the loss of Medi-Cal coverage. Second, under Proposition 187, passed in 1994, California sought to prohibit use of state funds for undocumented aliens' public benefits, and worked with the INS to force immigrants to repay Medicaid benefits based on public charge issues. Under federal law, a person may be barred from entering the country or moving from temporary to permanent status if government officials determine that she or he may become a public charge. As a result, hundreds of thousands of noncitizen children would lose their Medicaid eligibility, and many citizen children of noncitizen parents appeared to be jeopardized as well.[19]

A statewide survey of 5,000 newly legalized immigrants undertaken in the 1980s—a decade that witnessed an extraordinary demographic shift in the

Southwestern borderlands—determined that the general health of the respondents was better than that of a general sample of comparably aged Latinos in California.[20] Approximately 90 percent of this group of newly legalized respondents, as compared to 78 percent of the general population of Latino Californians, said they were in excellent or good health. About half of those who resettled before 1982 and 30 percent of the agricultural workers said that they had health insurance. This contrasts with a finding that about 63 percent of California's general adult Latino population has health insurance. Further, survey findings suggested that respondents did not seek medical care as frequently as the general population of Latinos in California. The general low incidence of health insurance in the sample surveyed, as well as their superior reported health may partly explain why newly legalized immigrants do not seek medical care more frequently. However, new immigrants encounter poor working conditions, language barriers, and racism, which increase their apprehension about using health services. Policies emphasizing tighter fiscal controls on health care may serve to keep poor clients including new immigrants with limited English-language skills out of the U.S. health care system.

A regional survey of immigrant health in Southern California was also undertaken at the end of the 1980s.[21] Over the decade, undocumented immigrants crossed the Mexican-U.S. border in greater numbers because of Mexico's economic crisis, which reduced real wages for most workers by 40–50 percent. The survey of 104 men and 96 women in the study was representative of the wave of Latino immigrants who resettled in urban Los Angeles and in border towns of predominantly rural Imperial County. The majority emigrated from Mexico; however, about 20 percent came from Central America, and 2 percent migrated from other Latin American countries. The mean age of respondents living in Los Angeles was thirty-nine, and thirty-five for those in the Imperial Valley. The city dwellers had been living here for fifteen years, compared to thirteen years at the border. They had crossed the border as young adults to seek a new life. Despite their considerable tenure in this country, over 60 percent of those in Los Angeles spoke little or no English, while 80 percent of those in the rural towns had limited or no English language skills. Two-thirds of the immigrants had fewer than ten years of formal schooling. These newcomers, on average, earned less than $260 per week, since legalization. Nearly 65 percent of respondents in Los Angeles had steady work for most of each year since they were legalized, compared to just over 55 percent of those at the border; one in four in the city were minimally employed, having worked less than thirty weeks each year since legalization, compared to about 15 percent of those in the countryside.

A third of the newcomers to the Imperial Valley indicated that they had learned about the availability of health services for legalized immigrants in their English classes, at rural health centers, and at hospital emergency rooms and clinics. Only a handful (5 percent) of those living in Los Angeles said they had received this information. The most prevalent health conditions reported by the respondents were hypertension (10 percent), back problems (8 percent), heart disease (4 percent), diabetes (4 percent), and high cholesterol level (3 percent). Fifty percent of the respondents reported miscellaneous other health problems. Almost 40 percent of individuals suffering from these maladies did not seek medical care. Half of those with high blood pressure and a third of those with back problems, although aware of their conditions, had not sought care. Those who did seek care reported dissatisfactions with high costs, long waiting times, and insufficient time spent with the physicians.

About 40 percent of respondents in Imperial County reported only limited satisfaction with the health care they received before legalization, compared to about a third of those in Los Angeles. High costs were the source of dissatisfaction at the border, while long waiting times burdened urban respondents. Since becoming legalized, a third of the newcomers in both the city and the countryside were not fully satisfied with their health care, citing these same concerns. Over 85 percent of those living in Los Angeles did not think that the quality of their health care services would improve after permanent residency, compared to 20 percent of those in the Imperial Valley. While those at the border expressed greater optimism, both rural and city dwellers regarded long waiting times, difficulties communicating with medical staff, and insufficient time spent with physicians as problems that would persist into the future.

About 80 percent in the city and 60 percent in the countryside have had no health insurance coverage since legalization. Of those who did carry a policy, only 11 percent of Los Angeles respondents and 21 percent in the Imperial Valley cover themselves. Twelve percent of the city dwellers and 20 percent of respondents in rural towns provide coverage for their spouses, and only 10 percent of the urban parents and 18 percent of rural parents covered their children, even though two-thirds of the immigrants reported that children were living in their households. Over 85 percent of the urbanites had taken their U.S.-born child or children for preventive health care, before they were legalized, as did 56 percent of those in the rural area. After legalization and permanent residency, 78 percent of parents in the city and 64 percent of rural parents indicated that they would seek preventive services for their children.

One-third of the respondents at the border and nearly one-quarter of those in the city indicated having experienced one or more major life events, such as job loss, separation, death of a loved one, disability, or a jail term, since legalization. However, only half of them had sought professional counseling for these problems; the other half indicated that they had thought of seeking such help, but had not done so. For the most part, two-thirds of the Los Angeles respondents and nearly three-quarters of those at the border reported that they could almost always mobilize their social networks in the event of major life crises. Twenty percent of the individuals in each locale said that they could only sometimes depend upon these social networks for help; 13 percent in the city and 5 percent at the border lacked the ties necessary to mobilize any support during crises.

TAKING REFUGE IN THE CITY

The many legal immigrants and the large number of undocumented aliens from Mexico and war-torn Central America account for the recent growth of the Latino, Spanish-speaking population and its supporting culture in the Los Angeles area. Latino Los Angeles is more a civil society built upon traditions carried along with recent immigrants as they resettled areas of the city. Unlike other groups who chose to assimilate to Anglo-American life, recent Latino immigrants have created "an independent cultural Other," which is reinvented with each crossing of the fluid Mexico-U.S. border. In the words of Rubén Martínez, "Latin culture, as well as people, travel across the border daily. Unlike other U.S. immigrants, Latinos can touch their roots with ease."[22] The proximity of recent immigrants to their homelands may, in part, explain why the rate of citizenship among eligible Latino immigrants is only 16 percent, compared with about 60 percent of Chinese and Filipino immigrants. Many recent Latino immigrants are reluctant to apply for citizenship because they someday wish to return home. Then there are the procedural complexities of filling out a four-page form, which asks many personal questions in English, providing the requisite set of fingerprints and photographs, and registering for English and civics classes.

The government extended the deadlines to apply for amnesty and increased its role in financing immigrant health services, but the newcomers' transnational status has clearly affected their ability to seek certain kinds of help. Transmigrants know how to access acute care services, but they have limited knowledge of preventive health services, including immunization for contagious childhood illnesses such as whooping cough and measles. Because of limited English-language skills, jobs that provide no medical insurance, and limited knowledge of how to mobilize health care resources, recent immigrants remain medically unevaluated and untreated. Many public and private agencies of potential help to immigrants do not know how to find, reach, and work effectively with at-risk immigrant populations.

After a decade of massive immigration, health officials in Los Angeles are faced with a steady rise in untreated tuberculosis cases and of high rates of measles, hepatitis, and HIV infection in the undocumented population.[23] A measles epidemic, attributable in part to inadequate preventive care for illegal immigrants, killed seventy-two children in California between 1988 and 1991, thirty-four of them in Los Angeles County. The majority of the county's new TB cases over this period of intensive transnational migration have involved foreign-born patients. This goes along with a statewide trend in the incidence of the disease. California reports the highest number of TB cases of any state. California also has the largest number of immigrants of any state, and most of these immigrants are from countries with high endemic rates of TB. The following case profiles Pico-Union, an area of Los Angeles transformed by major demographic shifts after the massive emigration from Mexico and Central America since the early 1980s. The case focuses on the demands placed upon each community's publicly financed health service network as a result of the influx of foreign-born residents from war-torn Central America.

In 1980, there were 30,000 Salvadorans living in Los Angeles; by 1990, the Salvadoran population had increased to 300,000, with 52 percent of these newcomers fleeing the civil war in their homeland. Many began their stay in this country in the Pico-Union/Westlake District, a five-square-mile neighborhood of approximately 120,000 residents living in apartment hotels and overcrowded households in the heart of Los Angeles. The predominantly Central American neighborhood is one of the most densely populated areas in the United States, with 147 people per square acre—four times that of New York City. The Salvadoran refugees had fled the repression and genocide that characterized daily life in their homeland. In the 1970s, peasant communities in the countryside were systematically slaughtered by paramilitary and National Guard troops because they favored land reform and had organized farmers' federations and agricultural workers unions to fight for better wages. In 1980, the violence spread to the cities as students, teachers, trade unionists, and others joined forces to form the Farabundo Marti National Liberation Front. By the end of that year, 13,000 Salvadorans, mostly poor farmers and workers, had been killed by government troops. The government was carrying out this campaign with planes, guns, ammunition, and night-sighting devices provided by the United States. The American government also increased its aid to El Salvador from $65 million in 1979 to $570 million in 1985. After a decade, an estimated 70,000 lives were lost during El Salvador's brutal civil war. Living standards within the country had plunged, and unemployment had reached 58 percent. Nearly a quarter of the country's 5 million people had been displaced. Thousands were forced into refugee camps in Honduras or on the outskirts of San Salvador, the nation's capital. Many Salvadorans fled their country and took refuge as illegal aliens in North American cities.[24]

The Pico-Union area is also home to refugees who have fled similar civil strife and deteriorating economic conditions in Nicaragua and Guatemala. A high degree of community disorganization and unemployment, and a lack of health and social services, has characterized this area since the early 1980s. In response to the growing health care crisis in Pico-Union, community leaders, health care workers, and members of the Santana Chirino Amaya Refugee Committee organized the Clinica Msr. Oscar A. Romero, named for the Salvadoran archbishop who was gunned down as he said mass on March 24, 1980. Founded in 1983 as a nonprofit corporation, the Clinica had its beginnings in the grassroots efforts of those determined to provide primary health care and education to the newly arrived "voiceless poor" of Central America who resettle in this country. Later in the decade, these same concerns would be expressed by the Coalition for Humane Immigrant Rights of Los Angeles, with its mix of religious, political, business, and professional leaders who advocated for a wider range of issues on behalf of diverse immigrant and refugee groups. The Clinica Romero was able to reach thousands of refugees in its first year through a grant from the Ford Foundation. After four years, the Clinica moved into the Edificio Romero together with other refugee service agencies, including El Rescate, providing legal and social services, and Community Counseling Service/Amanecer, offering outpatient mental health services. Central American refugees are thus able to take advantage of targeted bilingual and bicultural services at a single multiservice center located on a major bus line. The Clinica then became licensed and eligible for certain types of state and county funding, and for third-party billing programs. The Clinica extends public health and related services to the indigent, the homeless, and the undocumented in the Pico-Union community. Most area clinics charge service fees, which members of these groups cannot afford to pay. Many also avoid going to county health services when they are sick because they fear being exposed as illegal aliens and thus deported to their homelands. Throughout the 1980s, a refugee's application for public medical assistance would be sent automatically to the INS.

Salvadorans and other Central American refugees clearly have limited access to public health care because of their inability to obtain official refugee status. Most refugees in Pico-Union also have limited financial resources and low levels of both literacy and formal education. However, many teachers and college students from war-torn Central America also fled to Los Angeles after they were targeted for political persecution. All have confronted barriers when they sought emergency and acute care services in county health facilities. These included misunderstandings because of language and cultural differences, which only reinforced their beliefs that health and other service providers were insensitive to their needs. Interviews with sixty recent Salvadoran immigrants residing in Pico-Union have confirmed the visibility of the Clinica and its sister organizations.[25] Most had sought medical care services in the community when they were sick. They were referred to medical care by friends or neighbors and reported that they were satisfied with the services they received. However, a closer look at their domestic situations and at their work lives reveals a troubling picture of these new immigrants' unmet needs not only for health care, but also for familial support and economic security.

The majority (80 percent) of the group had been living in the United States for less than five years. As a result of limited formal education, only half were working in unskilled or semiskilled jobs; the other half were unemployed. Most were either young adults (38 percent) or in their middle years (57 percent). Almost 40 percent were married or had steady partners, but only 20 percent were living within a nuclear family, that is, with a spouse and children. The rest lived with members of their extended families, or with friends and acquaintances; and one person was homeless. Although their domestic arrangements varied widely, they reported having a total of 139 dependent children. Given this large number of children and their diverse living arrangements, it is apparent that many of these recent immigrants were not living together with their dependents.

Over 80 percent of these recent immigrants knew where health care services were located and expressed confidence that they would receive medical care when needed. However, a third had never received medical care in the United States, even though over two-thirds of the respondents stated that they or a family member had been either ill or seriously ill since entering the United States. Those who had sought medical care services in the community were referred by friends or neighbors or an indigenous organization and indicated that they would return again when ill. While two-thirds were not willing to seek preventive services for themselves, a few indicated that they would seek such services for their partners, and half stated that they would seek them for their children. To increase new immigrants' utilization of preventive services, the Clinica developed the *Promotores de Salud* program that trained community health workers to promote health and disease prevention within its catchment area. This cadre is responsible for implementing community-wide health campaigns, often going door-to-door, to increase residents' awareness of prevention and self-care. Their task would be a substantial one, for refugees residing in Pico-Union confront structural factors in the social environment that clearly threaten their health and well-being. These include unemployment, nonnuclear

family structure, and lack of training for skilled work, each of which increases
their risks of stress-related physical and emotional disorders.

A study of the mental health of Salvadoran refugees in Pico-Union found
that 70 percent claimed to have experienced stress-related symptoms such as
anxiety, depression, and nervousness, and that over three-quarters had observed similar symptoms within their network of friends and acquaintances.[26]
In another study, key health-related concerns of one hundred Salvadorans in
Pico-Union were such community-scale stressors as robbery, assault, and
drug-dealing.[27] It is not surprising that half of the reported health concerns for
these refugees were stress-related symptoms such as depression, headaches,
and nervousness. For many Central American refugees in Pico-Union, free
mental health treatment is located at the *Clinica Para las Americas* (Clinic for
the Americas).[28] Founded in 1990, the clinic was staffed by mostly Latino immigrants, along with countless volunteers. Patients sit on benches in the Clinica's overcrowded reception area awaiting medical and mental health services. The Central American clientele has been scarred by the psychological
traumas of displacement, immigration, and resettlement. Many witnessed the
murders of loved ones and sustained countless physical and sexual abuses
while escaping political violence in their homelands. Most have been terror-
ized by the violent gang warfare that is a continuous presence in Pico-Union
neighborhoods. A sizable number of the Clinica's patients regularly consulted
the Clinica's therapists seeking cures for their posttraumatic stress and depressive reactions. In an interview study of 200 immigrant women who had
recently crossed the U.S.-Mexican border in San Diego, 20 percent of the
Latinas were suffering from posttraumatic stress disorder.[29] During individual
and group therapy sessions at the Clinica, patients recounted the seemingly
endless assaults on their psyches, from robbery to rape in the city's refugee
enclave to the 1994 Northridge Earthquake. Such events act as "reminders"
that will often retraumatize these survivors of social and political repression.
These recalled stresses many times manifest as psychosomatic symptoms,
such as rashes, ulcers, body aches, and insomnia, and can also lead to a
widening circle of trauma, including physical and sexual abuse within the
family, and school and community violence.

Traumatic stress symptoms were also found among the 150,000 Cambodian refugees who have resettled in the United States, including the port city
of Long Beach in Los Angeles County—the largest Cambodian community
in the nation with over 17,000 members according to the 2000 census—since
the Khmer Rouge insurgency in their country in the late 1970s. Many had survived some form of brutality under the harsh Pol Pot and his regime. The
Khmer Rouge's reign of terror destabilized civil society in Cambodia, abol-
ishing the nation's religious institutions and its currency, and forcing millions

of city dwellers into the countryside. Between 1975 and 1979, nearly 3 million of Cambodia's 7 million people died of starvation, disease, or torture on the country's killing fields. Many others underwent years of forced labor in camps where they were beaten, deprived of food, and both physically and emotionally tortured by soldiers. These survivors will experience long-term depression, disorientation, psychosomatic complaints, recurrent hallucinations, and intrusive memories of friends and loved ones who were tortured to death before their eyes. At the Asian Pacific Mental Health Program in Long Beach, clinicians used both medication and diverse therapeutic methods to treat refugees whose suppressed feelings of grief, anger, and resentment have resurfaced a decade or more after resettlement.[30] They have tried to reach many of the lower-functioning patients, especially those with limited verbal skills, through art and other expressive techniques. For patients with greater self-awareness, there were weekly therapy groups facilitated by a Chinese-born clinical psychologist and by a Cambodian Buddhist monk. Together, these two practitioners offered traditional and modern modes of cultivating insight and behavioral control for the traumatized refugees. The group run by the Western-trained clinician, assisted by Cambodian community workers who acted as interpreters, used verbal techniques to help patients express their suppressed emotions. At the more traditional gathering, patients greeted the Buddhist monk with bows, as this figure is afforded great respect and authority by Cambodians. The monk encouraged them to use meditation, visualization and relaxation techniques to control their emotions. Cambodian society has no tradition of mental health, and its people do not openly share their emotions. The clinic thus required the support of a practitioner of traditional Cambodian healing arts to both enlist trust and to help care for its clients. Hence, many Salvadorans and Cambodian exiles who found refuge in Los Angeles neighborhoods in the 1980s were able to access appropriate health and mental health services through programs crafted in a more sensitive manner, using familiar elements of each group's "ethnic culture." However, to understand the organizational framework of mutual aid and social support in recent refugee and immigrant communities, it will be necessary to examine the networks and associations established by earlier groups of newcomers to the United States.

TRANSMIGRANT SOCIAL FORMATIONS

The more settled immigrants established mutual assistance networks to aid newcomers who swelled their ethnic neighborhoods in Victorian America's manufacturing cities. Many immigrant self-help networks formalized their procedures in response to a progressive municipal reform agenda and a nationwide organizational revolution. However, they remained independent of the established social service and charitable organizations, which often lacked the understanding or financial means to help southern and eastern European immigrant groups. In many cities, the established Jewish charities frequently limited their support to the Sephardic-Portuguese and German-Jewish communities. Russian and Polish Jews organized relatives and neighbors who had emigrated from the same region or town into *landsmannschafften* organizations. Members of these mutual-benefit societies in New York, Chicago, and Philadelphia provided one another with temporary housing, help finding work, sickness and death benefits, burial assistance, and even interest-free loans to start small businesses. These ethnically based organizations later established wayfarers' lodges, educational societies, and social agencies in cities with high concentrations of eastern and central European Jewish immigrants.

Other immigrant groups first organized their mutual benefit societies on local or regional affiliation. In Utica, New York, emigrants from the southern Italian province of Calabria founded the *Societa Calabria* in 1903. These lodges tended to perpetuate the kinds of attitudes and social interactions that members experienced under the feudal arrangements that characterized life in the southern Italian countryside. Italian immigrant enclaves within the larger cities contained numerous families from diverse towns and provinces of *Il Mezzogiorno*, meaning midday in Italian because of the strength of the midday sun in southern Italy. *Il Mezzogiorno*, as an underdeveloped agricultural area where large-scale land reforms only began after the Second World War, is also referred to as "the land that time forgot." Many big-city lodges would accept only members who had emigrated from a particular locale in the old country. Often, progressive community leaders in a "Little Italy" would try to develop a political base by building a coalition among members of the diverse regional associations. These reform-oriented urban politicians frequently became frustrated with the deep-rooted suspiciousness and competitiveness among an enclave's fraternal organizations. The membership of diverse lodges would even reference archaic rivalries between their ancestral towns as a reason for not cooperating with one another in the United States. This divisiveness had inhibited peasant cooperation in nineteenth-century political movements to reform the poverty and backwardness of *Il Mezzogiorno*'s agrarian order. Similar attitudes prevented many southern Italian immigrants to the United States from establishing the cooperative ventures that would have allowed them to generate economic assistance among themselves for capital accumulation and economic mobility. To remedy this sense of territorial exclusiveness, later immigrant mutual aid organizations were federated on the basis of nationality, such as the Order of the Sons of Italy, L'Association Canada-Américaine, the Polish National Alliance, and the Pan Hellenic Union.

Since the turn of the century, many immigrant groups developed entrepreneurial networks and cooperative associations to help ensure their economic survival within American cities. By 1914, thirty-one consumer cooperatives for buying food and other products had been organized by non-English-speaking Lithuanian, Finnish, Italian, Polish, French, German, Jewish, Swedish, and Belgian immigrants in Massachusetts. Many immigrant groups established ethnic banks to make small loans and to facilitate the transfer of newcomers' remittance payments to those in the home country. In San Francisco, Amadeo Pietro Giannini's Bank of Italy aided immigrant laborers, fishermen, and ranchers who had previously borrowed from usurious moneylenders in the city. Giannini also encouraged Italian immigrant families to open interest-bearing savings accounts in his bank. He provided capital to enterprises that profited from the city's rebuilding campaign after the 1906 earthquake and fire. These and other wise investment strategies led to the incorporation of his immigrant bank, which, later renamed the Bank of America, became one of the world's largest and most diverse financial institutions.

Japanese and Chinese immigrants organized paternalistic mutual assistance associations to provide business capital and advice on how to manage company finances. Japanese *kenjinkai* organizations provided émigrés from the same province with social aid, legal services, and recreational activities. They served as guilds to place *kenjin*, or fellow members, in certain trades and to regulate economic competition within the community. Japanese immigrants also founded rotating credit associations to help members start their own businesses. Chinese immigrant groups formed *hui*, or rotating credit associations. A fellow émigré needing money would organize a group of friends who would each initially pay that individual a lump sum and then contribute the same amount of money to a monthly pool. In lieu of repayment, the organizer of the *hui* would hold a dinner each month at his home where there would be a lottery. At each feast, a different member of the *hui* would win the month's lottery until every participant received back their cumulative outlay of funds. The system provided an interest-free loan to the originator who, in turn, reciprocated with a number of celebratory meals for members of the *hui*.

Mutual Aid Associations (MAAs) have helped to promote the economic and social survival of immigrants during the current wave of transnational immigration from Asian countries. As transitional social formations, they have reoriented their perception, understanding, and acceptance of the constraints and opportunities of the host society. These smaller-scale networks have encouraged their participation in both the private service sector, which employs immigrant labor, and the state social services sector, which distributes benefits and subsidies that, in part, support their lives.[31] Organizations of this kind began to develop in the United States about 1975, at first among the wave of Southeast Asian immigrants and refugees and then among some other groups. The MAAs took on a number of different roles, including promoting cultural preservation and religious observance, providing leisure-time activities and social support to individuals, and encouraging the use of social and health services, and in some cases, political advocacy. Most had grassroots beginnings, with a few people of like ethnicity organizing themselves to improve their adaptation to the new culture, its unfamiliar language, customs, and social institutions. Aggregate natural networks, from the mutual benefit societies of the Progressive Era to the MAAs in recent times, have provided mutual aid between members of an ethnic association, and between the association and the broader community, through groups based upon either informal membership or a formal charter. By contrast, dyadic forms of support— ties based upon linkages between individuals rather than between group members—prevail in contemporary urban Latino immigrant communities, and these networks based upon reciprocity and exchange behaviors have a long history in Latin American societies.

WEBS OF SOLIDARITY

A comparative analysis of *tejido*, or "linkperson," natural support networks, usually based upon friendship, as they evolved in Latin American homelands, may throw light on the current structures of trust among transnational Latino migrants in North American cities.[32] Dyadic ties, based upon southern European peasant customs, have regulated social behavior in certain Latin American peasant communities since the sixteenth-century conquest of Mexico.[33] This neofeudal form of kinship was imposed upon traditional communities through the clergy and officials of the Spanish Empire. By combining elements of both the pre-Columbian and southern European kin structures, a Creole society with distinctly New World social relations was created. In Medieval Europe, the peasant family was extended by vertical bonds formed through unequal exchange in a feudal land tenure system. Tenant families would ask higher-ranking persons to become baptismal sponsors to their children. Ceremonial sponsorship sustained bonds of patronage and obligation, and residential stability on the manor.

The web of ritual kinship extended to include most village families. Since the Church prohibited unions with either kin or ritual kin, there were pressures to marry off the manor. Such out-migration would undermine the system of land tenure and the supply of labor on the estate. At first, feudal lords established local agreements to forestall marriage off the manor and levied indemnity payments to compensate for their loss of property rights. By the fourteenth century, feudal land tenures broke down as peasants won more rights, including the freedom to marry without interference. As peasants united in their protests for more of their rights, they derived a sense of neighborhood solidarity. In their struggles against the feudal system, they used the ritual kin, or *compadre*, relations of the manor to unite peasant neighborhoods. After the Protestant Reformation, the compadre form of extended kinship broke down. Ritual kin ties were incompatible with an emerging industrial capitalism where the individual, rather than the domestic group, was the primary unit of production. In the end, extended kin ties were incongruent with the norm of individualism associated with the rise of the middle class during this period.

Ritual kin ties were retained in parts of Europe where industrial capitalism and the middle classes were slower to transform the feudal order. These were the areas where peasants had not yet become farmers and thus still participated in a domestic mode of production. In sixteenth-century Italy and Spain, the peasant family was still extended by ritual ties established during Catholic rites of passage, including baptism, first communion, confirmation, and marriage. S. N. Eisenstadt and L. Roniger explain how a child became surrounded by spiritual or "fictive" kin, first through godparenthood (*compadrazgo*) at baptism and later by ceremonial sponsors at other life crisis ceremonies:

> Thus, patrons were asked by a dependent or a "friend" . . . to agree to sponsor the baptism of the client's son, which symbolized the entrance of the child's soul into the Church. By acting as godparent, the *padrino* endorsed responsibility for the spiritual and social welfare of the *ahijado*. This imposed on him the obligation to give presents at ritual occasions as, for instance, at the First Communion, to care for and guide the child through the school years, to help him to enter a career or a job, to give him advice when he contemplated marriage, etc. These deeds were considered as an act of grace, adding to the social prestige of the patron. At the same time, spiritual and natural parents became *compadres*—that is, ritual kin committed to helping each other, being joined in an unalienable relationship of absolute trust.[34]

As a result of the custom, a number of individuals were ceremonially bound together to guide an individual throughout life. The practice created a support "network of ritual kin folk through ceremonial sponsorship" that extended to economic and political clientship, including the granting of loans and building power domains.[35] These ties were reinforced and ritually sustained during ceremonies linked to significant feast days in the Church's ritual cycle.

George Foster observed firsthand the system of ritualized ties that existed up to a generation ago in Tzintzuntzan, a peasant community in Michoacán state.[36] Social relations are organized in a manner that resembles sixteenth-century southern Europe. Tzintzuntzan's economy is based upon pottery making, farming, and some fishing. The artisans make up almost half of the village population. They are known for moss green- and cream-colored pottery decorated with fish and bird motifs from nearby Lake Pátzcuaro and with scenes of village life. This occupational group is the most conservative and steadfast in its social relations. The potters maintain dyadic ties that are pragmatic both in village affairs and in the market town where they sell their handiwork. In fact, most Tzintzuntzeños organize their social relations through such informal contracts with others in the community. Three styles of two-person ties exist in Tzintzuntzan; all are based upon some form of need and implied mutual obligations and expectations. Colleague ties are symmetrical, as they were formed by persons of equal status. Patron-client ties are asymmetrical, as they are made between two people of unequal status. These latter contracts are formed primarily between villager and nonvillager, for example between local artisans and merchants in Michoacán's sixteenth-century colonial capital of Pátzcuaro, the market town some distance away. More formal ties are built around the Catholic sacraments of baptism and marriage, and in this way the Tzintzuntzeño family is extended by bonds of friendship and of patronage. Saint's day fiestas and other ceremonial activities based upon the Catholic liturgical calendar sustain the ritual of social relations in Tzintzuntzan. Ceremonial meals and gift giving during these times provide opportunities to reinforce these reciprocal ties and obligations. Such exchange transactions take on a symbolic meaning, since they imply that both parties are willing to continue the dyadic contract.

Tzintzuntzeños embrace an image of the "limited good," a cognitive orientation that maintains that natural and social resources in their environment are finite and in short supply. Furthermore, they do not perceive that it is possible to increase the available quantities of these resources. The community works together to regulate these scarce resources and organized individual and collective behaviors to conform to this belief. Tzintzuntzeños are thus steadfast and conservative in the face of change, and until recently, have discouraged modernization through a belief in a closed world and a fixed social order, similar to the prevalent conception of "the great chain of being" in Medieval and early modern Europe. Tzintzuntzeños believe that a zero-sum principle regulates status change, namely "that an individual or a family can improve a position only at the expense of others."[37] Those who challenged the status quo by seeking political leadership were held in suspicion. While active in traditional rituals, most villagers have not been motivated to participate in community development programs. This collective distrust of change rendered Tzintzuntzan marginal to national political processes up to the last few decades.

Despite their political conservatism, the villagers are economically bound to regional, national, and international organizations that regulate taxation, prices, markets, and economic development. Tzintzuntzeños form patron-client ties outside the village in recognition of these realities. Merchants in Pátzcuaro develop compadre relations with villagers, especially the artisans, and reinforce these ties through participation in the patron saint fiesta. The artisans sell their crafts at the town's weekly market day and gather with hundreds of other folk artists in the Plaza Vasco de Quiroga during the Day of the Dead festival each November in Pátzcuaro. The ensuing nexus of power-dependent ties is organized around the needs of the villagers who depend upon the town's goods, services, and central market. Since World War II, technology and economic development programs have transformed Tzinzuntzan. By 1970, its population had more than doubled to 2,200 after two decades of state-supported modernization efforts, including public health and sanitation campaigns. In the 1950s and 1960s, a guest-worker program sent Tzintzuntzeños, along with hundreds of thousands of other Mexicans, to work in the fields of California's Central Valley. Since the 1970s, there has also been illegal migration across the U.S. border to find work in farms and factories. However, for most Tzintzuntzeños, Mexico City, only hours away by bus, is the key destination. It is mostly younger men from more prosperous village families who migrate to the capital to *buscar la vida*, or to search for life, as factory workers but also as urban professionals.

When a Tzintzuntzan migrant arrives in the capital, according to Robert Kemper, he lives *arrimado*, or "up close," with friends and family members in the city.[38] Most often, these relations were established in the village before migration. However, a new pattern of relations will develop as recent arrivals and longer-term residents become linked in an urban migrant network. "Senior" migrants serve as patrons, providing temporary housing and transportation for their newly arrived "clients." New migrants quickly accrue social debts to seniors who serve as *palancas*, or "levers," to help them find their first jobs. However, this initial dependency will abate as the new migrant gains job security and establishes his own household. Social ties for urban Tzintzuntzeños tend to dissipate as they become longer-term residents of the city. Families will relocate to other areas of the twenty-five-square-mile city for better jobs and housing. They will maintain only a few close ties, usually through visiting close friends and relatives over the year.

Working-class migrants make up two-thirds of all Tzintzuntzeño urbanites. However they have resisted efforts to preserve village ties through social clubs and regional associations, choosing instead to seek new contacts beyond the migrant group. Such village-based organizations often encourage social drinking to sustain reciprocity networks and male authoritarianism in the capital's immigrant enclaves. *Cautismo* is a fictive kin relation based on male bonds of friendship that often serves as the basis of network formation in village life. After migration, men use these ties in their search for housing, work, loans, and other forms of self-help. Getting drunk together creates a bond based on mutual trust and provides "time out" from the formality of customary social relations. Cliques based on cautismo are developed and maintained through joint drinking, and the ensuing bonds serve as an economic leveler because the *caute* in possession of a cash surplus is expected to buy drinks for his companions.[39]

Working-class Tzintzuntzeños, unlike other migrant laborers in the capital, quickly abandoned the constraining two-party ties and traditional *machismo* of the village in exchange for the promise of upward mobility and urbanity. Ironically, middle-class Tzintzuntzeños in Mexico City required a regional association that celebrated village values to sustain their cultural identities after migration. In 1975, they chartered the *Agrupación* of Tzintzuntzeño migrants to provide social assistance to the newcomers in the capital. The mutual aid association founded by a school principal supports an annual pilgrimage to the village for the patron saint festival and fund-raising campaigns for the village's church and secondary school. Even after a wide-ranging membership campaign to involve all urban Tzintzuntzeños in its activities, few working-class migrants affiliated with the *Agrupación*, opting instead for broader-based groups like labor unions, neighborhood organizations, and parish associations.

THE IMPACT OF TRANSNATIONALISM

Latino communities in the United States are not homogeneous, as immigrants or first generation families come from various Latin American nations. These families bring with them cultural traditions and views of the larger society and of the family, health and illness, child rearing and schooling, personal and community responsibility, and of their *barrio*, or neighborhood. While many in-migrating families arrive from Latin American cities, others come to the United States directly from small, rural communities as individuals, not as families, and their perceptions and lifeways tend to be prescribed by their rural experiences, including raising farm animals such as chickens, ducks, and game hens in their backyards. The newcomers from both city and countryside will often arrive with little understanding of environmental concerns. Many initially live with strangers in substandard housing without proper sanitation.

Diseases prevalent in third-world countries, such as shigellosis, are now found in states along the border. Often cut off from their natural support networks, they are easily victimized by gangs and by illegal business practices, such as "notario" fraud. The latter takes place when unlicensed legal and financial consultants mask as licensed attorneys and charge exorbitant fees to unwitting newcomers; in fact, immigrants may often lose many of their rights as a result of this nonprofessional legal advice. Hence, lacking traditional forms of cultural support, they are overcome by the unfamiliarity of both the dominant culture and the barrio.

Furthermore, there may be a difference between persons who immigrated to the United States after they were seventeen years of age and those who grew up in this country. It seems that arriving in this country as an adult makes it more difficult to access health, legal, and social services, which may be related to unfamiliarity with or perhaps a sense of discomfort when accessing public entitlements. Related to this is the fact that those who immigrated to this country at an older age are more likely to be undocumented, and therefore less willing to enroll in public programs. This situation may be compounded by other competing needs, such as family and work responsibilities, and various personal demands. Therefore, accessing health care and other public services may be a secondary concern. Despite these discontinuities of transnational migration, many Latino families share traditional cultural norms that have organized personal life and social relations in Latin American communities for centuries. Based upon this assumption, Renato Rosaldo has used the term "cultural citizenship" to indicate a more vernacular notion of citizenship within Latino communities in the United States, one that is pluralist and inclusive in the face of exclusionary and marginalizing practices, such as the notions of "illegality" as defined by federal and state policies and practices.[40] In the face of the exclusionary processes of elite and state power, members of Latino communities, especially in metropolitan areas, have begun to negotiate citizenship, and its attendant rights and obligations, on sources of identity formation based upon cultural inheritance, including familism, dyadic ties, and religious faith.

In light of these ethnic cultural, situational, and political concerns, increasing access to health and social services for recent immigrants has emerged as an arena for the negotiation of cultural citizenship in Latino communities. Strategic activities have focused on outreach and health promotion, using culturally appropriate messages and familiar styles of communication.[41] Faith-based outreach is one way to gain access to Latino immigrant families frequently "overlooked" by traditional health and social services safety net providers. Latino members of Protestant churches tend to be poorer and have a lower level of acculturation than their Catholic counterparts, suggesting greater resource deficits and a relatively higher need for outreach services for members of the smaller Protestant congregations.[42] A lay approach trains indigenous community residents, who have been selected because they are charismatic and able to communicate and display leadership qualities, to engage in health education as *Promotores de Salud*.[43] They typically conduct outreach for neighborhood medical clinics, welcome families at the clinic sites, and assist with paperwork. *Promotores* trained in the new regulations around health care eligibility have informed families and facilitated their enrollment in health insurance programs. Through these indigenous arbiters and mediators, recent immigrants have been able to understand socially marginalizing legal and administrative barriers to accessing public services, and have begun to negotiate services for themselves and their families. Despite confusing information about health and welfare reform, and the sense of distrust of state power within immigrant communities, many more legal immigrants have become eligible for a variety of social programs. In the past, recent immigrants believed that accepting these benefits could affect their immigration status, and, until recently, a consistently large number of their children have remained uninsured. While not a panacea for overcoming barriers of knowledge, experience, and worldview, culturally appropriate outreach and educational activities appear to be helpful in enrolling eligible members of immigrant populations. Accessible care and social safety net services clearly impact the quality of life within immigrant communities. Furthermore, to set out to achieve the often-illusive "American Dream" and its promise of upward mobility, recent immigrant groups will require accessible health and social services so that members can optimize their role in both the pubic sphere and the global economy.

NOTES

1. Nina Glick Schiller, Linda Basch, and Christina Blanc-Szanton, eds., "Towards a Transnational Perspective on Migration: Race, Class, Ethnicity, and Nationalism Reconsidered," *Annals of the New York Academy of Sciences*, vol. 645, 1992.

2. Saskia Sassen, *The Global City: New York, London, Tokyo*, 2nd ed. (Princeton, NJ: Princeton University Press, 2001).

3. Josiah McC. Heyman, *Finding a Moral Heart For U.S. Immigration Policy: An Anthropological Perspective* (Arlington, VA: American Anthropological Association, 1998).

4. Patrick J. McDonnell and Paul Jacobs, "FAIR at the Forefront of Push to Reduce Immigration," *Los Angeles Times*, November 24, 1993, sec. A.

5. Robert Reinhold, "Reinventing California: A Welcome for Immigrants Turns to Resentment," *New York Times*, August 25, 1993, national edition, sec. 1.

6. John Higham, *Strangers in the Land: Patterns of American Nativism, 1860–1925* (New Brunswick, NJ: Rutgers University Press, 1963); John Higham, *Send These To Me: Immigrants in Urban America* (Baltimore: Johns Hopkins University Press, 1984).

7. Richard Hofstadter, *Social Darwinism in American Thought* (Boston: Beacon, 1955); Stephen Jay Gould, *The Mismeasure of Man* (New York: Norton, 1981); George W. Stocking Jr., *Race, Culture and Evolution: Essays in the History of Anthropology* (Chicago: University of Chicago Press, 1982); Daniel J. Kevles, *In the Name of Eugenics: Genetics and the Uses of Human Heredity* (Berkeley: University of California Press, 1986).

8. Randolph Bourne, "Trans-national America" (1916), quoted in Casey Nelson Blake, *Beloved Community: The Cultural Criticism of Randolph Bourne, Van Wyck Brooks, Waldo Frank and Lewis Mumford* (Chapel Hill: University of North Carolina Press, 1990), 115.

9. Blake, *Beloved Community*, 119.

10. Louis Uchitelle, "The New Faces of U.S. Manufacturing," *New York Times*, July 3, 1994, national edition, sec 3.

11. Anna Kondratas, Alan Weil, and Naomi Goldstein, "Assessing the New Federalism: An Introduction," *Health Affairs* 17 (1998): 17–24.

12. A. E. Benjamin, Steven P. Wallace, Valentine Villa, and Kathy McCarthy, *California Immigrants Have Mostly Lower Rates of Disability and Use of Disability Services than State's U.S.-Born Residents*. Policy brief (Los Angeles: UCLA Center for Health Policy Research, 2000).

13. Paul W. Newacheck, Jeffrey J. Stoddard, Dana C. Hughes, and Michelle Pearl, "Children's Access to Health Care: The Role of Social and Economic Factors," in *Health Care for Children: What's Right, What's Wrong, What's Next*, edited by Ruth E. K. Stein (New York: United Hospital Fund of New York, 1997), 53–76.

14. Marilyn R. Ellwood and Leighton Ku, "Welfare and Immigration Reforms: Unintended Side Effects for Medicaid," *Health Affairs* 17 (1998): 137–51.

15. Leighton Ku and Alyse Freilich, *Caring for Immigrants: Health Care Safety Nets in Los Angeles, New York, Miami and Houston* (Washington, DC: Henry F. Kaiser Foundation, 2001).

16. California Policy Research Center, *Children in Immigrant Families: Issues of California's Future* (Berkeley: California Program on Access to Care and UCLA Center for Health Policy Research, 2000).

17. Neal Halfon and Miles Hochstein, "Developing a System of Care for All: What the Needs of Vulnerable Children Tell Us," in *Health Care for Children: What's Right, What's Wrong, What's Next*, edited by Ruth E. K. Stein (New York: United Hospital Fund of New York, 1997), 303–30.

18. Neal Halfon, David L. Wood, R. Burciaga Valdez, Margaret Pereya, and Naihua Duan, "Medicaid Enrollment and Health Services Access by Latino Children in Inner-City Los Angeles," *Journal of the American Medical Association* 277 (1997): 636–41.

19. Glenn Flores and Luis R. Vega, "Barriers to Health Care Access for Latino Children: A Review," *Family Medicine* 30 (1998): 196–205.

20. State of California Health and Welfare Agency, *A Survey of Newly Legalized Persons in California* (Sacramento: State of California Health and Welfare Agency, 1989).

21. Alfred H. Katz, Carl A. Maida, and Roberto Belloso, *Utilization of Health Services by Legalized Immigrants* (Sacramento: State of California Department of Health Services, 1990).

22. Rubén Martínez, "The Shock of the New," *Los Angeles Times Magazine*, January 30, 1994, 12.

23. California Tuberculosis Elimination Task Force, *Strategic Plan for Tuberculosis Control and Elimination, Implementation Priorities, Year I* (Berkeley: State of California Department of Health Services, 1994); Sheryl Stolberg, "Taking It to the Streets: A Small Cadre of Community Workers and Nurses Struggle to Contain an Outbreak of TB," *Los Angeles Times Magazine*, October 24, 1993, 14–20, 44–46.

24. Kathy McAfee, *Update: El Salvador: The Ordeal of a Nation* (Boston: Oxfam America, 1990); Tommie Sue Montgomery, *Revolution in El Salvador: From Civil Strife to Civil Peace*, 2nd ed. (Boulder, CO: Westview Press, 1994); Elisabeth Jean Wood, *Insurgent Collective Action and Civil War in El Salvador* (Cambridge: Cambridge University Press, 2003).

25. Roberto Belloso, Carl A. Maida, and Alfred H. Katz, "Health Care and the Adaptation of Salvadoran Immigrants in Los Angeles," *Abstracts* (Davis, CA: American Association for the Advancement of Science Pacific Division) 1990; Roberto Belloso, Alfred H. Katz, and Carl A. Maida, "Work and Health Status of Salvadoran Immigrants in Los Angeles," *Abstracts* (Chicago: American Anthropological Association, 1991.

26. Roberto Belloso, *A Study of the Mental Health among Central American Refugees Living at the Pico-Union District of Los Angeles*. Unpublished paper. Department of Health Sciences, California State University, Northridge, 1989.

27. Roberto Belloso, *Health Concerns of a Salvadoran Refugee Population*. Masters thesis, California State University, Northridge, 1992.

28. Dave Gardetta, "Class Unconsciousness: Immigration and Mental Health at Clinica Para Las Americas," *Los Angeles Weekly*, July 8, 1994, 16–18.

29. Nora Zamichow, "Latina Immigrants Suffer Post-Traumatic Disorders," *Los Angeles Times*, February 18, 1992, sec. A.

30. David Haldane, "Cambodians Struggle to Leave Nightmare Behind," *Los Angeles Times*, June 6, 1987, sec. A.

31. N. V. Hien, D. Bui, and L. X. Khoa, *Ethnic Self-Help Organizations* (Washington, DC: U.S. Department of Health and Human Services, 1983); Peter W. Van Arsdale, "Assessing Human Services: Ethnographic Perspectives on Refugee Communities and Mutual Assistance Associations," *Information and Referral* 9 (1987): 1–25.

32. Ramón Valle and William Vega, eds., *Hispanic Natural Support Systems: Mental Health Promotion Perspectives* (Sacramento, CA: State of California Department of Mental Health, 1980).

33. George M. Foster, "The Dyadic Contract: A Model for the Social Structure of a Mexican Peasant Village," in *Peasant Society: A Reader*, edited by Jack M. Potter, May N. Diaz, and George M. Foster (Boston: Little, Brown, 1967), 213–30.

34. Shmuel N. Eisenstadt and Louis Roniger, *Patrons, Clients and Friends: Interpersonal Relations and the Structure of Trust in Society* (Cambridge: Cambridge University Press, 1984), 76–77.

35. Sidney W. Mintz and Eric R. Wolf, "An Analysis of Ritual Co-Parenthood (Compadrazgo)," in *Peasant Society: A Reader*, edited by Jack M. Potter, May N. Diaz, and George M. Foster (Boston: Little, Brown, 1967), 174–99.

36. George M. Foster, *Tzintzuntzan: Mexican Peasants in a Changing World* (Boston: Little, Brown, 1967).

37. George M. Foster, "Peasant Society and the Image of Limited Good," in *Peasant Society: A Reader*, edited by Jack M. Potter, May N. Diaz, and George M. Foster (Boston: Little, Brown, 1967), 305.

38. Robert V. Kemper, "Tzintzuntzeños in Mexico City: The Anthropologist Among Peasant Migrants," in *Anthropologists in Cities*, edited by George M. Foster and Robert V. Kemper (Boston: Little, Brown, 1974), 63–69.

39. Larissa A. Lomnitz, *Networks and Marginality* (New York: Academic Press, 1977).

40. Renato Rosaldo, "Cultural Citizenship, Inequality, and Multiculturalism," in *Latino Cultural Citizenship: Claiming Identity, Space, and Rights*, edited by William V. Flores and Rina Benmayor (Boston: Beacon Press, 1997), 27–38.

41. Arthur Kleinman, *Patients and Healers in the Context of Culture: An Exploration of the Borderland between Anthropology, Medicine, and Psychiatry* (Berkeley: University of California Press, 1980).

42. Felipe G. Castro, John P. Elder, Kathryn Coe, Helen M. Tafoya-Barraza, Santiago Moratto, Nadia Campbell, and Gregory Talavera, "Mobilizing Churches for Health Promotion in Latino Communities—*Companeros en la Salud*," *Journal of the National Cancer Institute Monographs* 18 (1995): 127–35.

43. Irma N. Ramos, Marlynn May, and Kenneth S. Ramos, "Environmental Health Training of *Promotoras* in *Colonias* Along the Texas-Mexico Border," *American Journal of Public Health* 91 (2001): 568–70; Darryl M. Williams, "*La Promotora*: Linking Disenfranchised Residents Along the Border to the U.S. Health Care System," *Health Affairs* 20 (2001): 212–18.

Chapter Six

Worlds Turned Upside Down

When disaster strikes, the contours of a city take on a new shape to its people. Buildings and streets, power lines and water mains, bureaucracies and businesses, charities, landmarks, and civic pride—all are redefined by the disaster. A city's geography, and its history—features of everyday life that are so taken for granted that they are virtually invisible—suddenly acquire a new reality. Recognized anew as the foundations of urban living, a disaster reveals their strengths, weaknesses, and interconnections. Community-scale crises, such as natural disasters, reveal the degree and kind of civic engagement among individual citizens, policy makers, and other influentials within a city's public and private sectors. The return to equilibrium after a disaster provides residents with opportunities to reassess their attitudes about survival within vulnerable cityscapes, adaptability within an unpredictable environment, and reliance upon place-focused culture and community.[1]

Natural disasters are community-scale crises. Fires, floods, earthquakes, hurricanes, and tornadoes are inevitable, and are usually unpredictable. Disasters affect diverse populations in a metropolitan region: suburban and urban, wealthy and poor, culturally assimilated and recently immigrated. They disrupt the lives of individuals from every social class and ethnic group. When there is no loss of life, the loss of residence, with its attendant displacement, is the central crisis for survivors of a disaster. Those displaced from their homes often feel suddenly rootless, an emotion marked by depression, despair, and longing for a secure base. Even when there is only minor residential damage, a disaster has a major impact. Transportation, water, electricity, and other municipal networks are affected, and schools and worksites are damaged. Working adults and school children may be forced to stay at home or be relocated to temporary workplaces and schools.

Survivors describe how their perception of the world as coherent has changed after a disaster renders their surroundings uninhabitable, even unidentifiable. The perception of the community as a "place" is eroded in direct relationship to the extent of destruction. The impact of the event is multiplied manifold when loved ones are killed or maimed and with the loss of pets and familiar objects in the home and of landmarks in the environment. Children are especially place oriented, as locales convey a concrete sense of security and familiarity to their lives. This was apparent as wildfires burned about 200,000 acres in Southern California's wildland-urban interface in 1993, damaging or destroying over 1,200 homes and structures. The firestorms disrupted the lives of residents in the fire-devastated communities bordering Los Angeles, as more than 30,000 were evacuated from their homes. One *Los Angeles Times* reporter described the scene from the vantage point of a news helicopter:

> As gusts of wind periodically poured into the chopper the view from 600 feet was spectacular, and spectacularly grim. Aside from occasional hot-spot bursts of flame that looked like bonfires, the landscape was an expanse of ashen peaks and canyons that recalled poet Siegfried Sassoon's works about the killing fields of World War I: "Death's gray land, drawing no dividends from time's tomorrows." Ahead, the Pacific was a smoky blur.[2]

The aerial perspective conveys both an objective spectacle of elemental change and a fear-inspiring scene of destructiveness. This paradoxical and strikingly modern image of disaster has haunted Americans since the outbreak of World War I. This form of imagery was first realized in the landscapes of France, which for many Americans represented aristocratic splendor, but especially after the fin de siècle, the decadence of European civilization; the latter condition was even considered by some to be responsible for the war. Landscape and memory, together, contributed to reinforce the horror and the consequences of modern warfare, both in the visual images of widespread devastation to France's cities and in remembrance of the hundreds of thousands of American youths who were maimed or killed in the French countryside.

THE GREAT WAR AND THE MODERN IMAGE OF DISASTER

During World War I, the medieval and Renaissance cityscapes of Ypres, Arras, Reims, and Lille were so devastated by continuous battles that their residents were left to find shelter "in caves, cellars, attics, and shacks."[3] The Great War both disrupted and transformed these battle-torn cities and their surrounding countrysides, as armies moved through them en route to battle, only to return as casualties requiring treatment in hospitals and rehabilitation facilities, or as war dead to be buried in newly created cemeteries and monuments, and thereafter honored in war memorials.[4] The war led to dramatic population increases elsewhere in France: Paris and its suburbs absorbed some 300,000 industrial workers and their families; port cities, such as Rouen and Bordeaux, grew as thousands of British and American soldiers and tons of supplies passed through them each day; and Bourges more than doubled in size, as refugees, workers, and Americans increased the city's population from 46,000 to over 110,000.[5] After the armistice, the infrastructure of war-damaged cities needed to be rebuilt, and this called for massive redevelopment projects that provided steady work not only for the manufacturers of building materials and those in construction trades, but also for practitioners of the nascent field of city planning.

The early decades of the twentieth century witnessed the expansion of diverse institutions in the United States that focused public attention on modern warfare, but also dealt with its tragic consequences.[6] These included the political use of mass communications and propaganda techniques to instill a sense of patriotism on the home front, the mass mobilization of fighting men through the draft, and a global-scale relief effort organized by the Red Cross to help mitigate the suffering of both soldiers and civilians. The expanding American metropolis, itself, became a central arena for the celebration of both nationalism and patriotism, as evidenced by the numerous Liberty Bond campaigns and parades on behalf of the war effort that passed along its main thoroughfares. Childe Hassam, an American painter, portrayed these nationalistic sentiments writ large on the urban landscape in a series of "Flag Paintings" depicting New York's Fifth Avenue draped in Allied flags for diverse patriotic celebrations between 1916 and 1919.[7]

In the summer of 1914, war broke out in Europe after a century of peace. Industry and empire had transformed modern Europe during the nineteenth century. A growing militarism also spread throughout the continent as nations increased their purchases of arms. A series of political crises, combined with the massive stores of weapons, led to war among them. Many Americans were horrified by the destructive scale of modern technological warfare, with its immense mortars, machine guns, and poison gases. However, many others saw the war as an indicator of the success of the new form of corporate capitalism that had developed in Germany, America, and other Western economies since the late nineteenth century. For this arsenal was amassed through global financial capital but also the inventiveness and industrial acumen of the newer corporate enterprises.

Victorian America still retained a sense of optimism and faith in industrial progress even in the face of these disastrous conditions of modern warfare.

Convinced that the very destructiveness of the new artillery would actually shorten the war, they predicted a speedy end to the conflict. This worldview would require five more years to shatter and eventually fade into the disillusionment that characterized the 1920s. By the end of that decade, war veteran Erich Maria Remarque would write about this general sense of malaise in a passage from *All Quiet on the Western Front* describing a visit to a hospital of wounded soldiers:

> How senseless is everything that can ever be written, done, or thought, when such things are possible. It must be all lies and of no account when the culture of a thousand years could not prevent this stream of blood being poured out, these torture-chambers in their hundreds of thousands. A hospital alone shows what war is.[8]

However, in 1914, American elites suggested that the Great War could contribute to a national sense of "moral uplift." The word *preparedness* was forged in the vocabulary of ordinary Americans with the outbreak of hostilities in Europe. Theodore Roosevelt and other advocates of the martial spirit called for universal military training of young men and increased military spending. The tone of the new rhetoric of militarism recalled Roosevelt's previous urging that Americans adopt "the strenuous life" as a form of inner discipline and cultural renewal. For Roosevelt believed that military training would hasten the "Americanization" of the sons of immigrants, stating "The military tent where they all sleep side by side will rank next to the public school among the great agents of democratization." Industrial giant Henry Ford fully opposed these calls for preparedness and, in November 1915, even chartered a "peace ship" and invited 115 other prominent Americans to sail to Europe to set up a permanent peace conference. Many progressive reformers, including people as different in style as Jane Addams and William Jennings Bryan, mobilized in a different manner. They established channels of aid for the civilian survivors of the carnage. Their fund-raising efforts resulted in dispatches of food, clothing, and medical supplies to European victims of war. This coalition of social reformers and woman suffragists, including Lillian Wald and Charlotte Perkins Gilman, also built a peace movement and, in August 1914, organized the first modern antiwar march down New York's Fifth Avenue.

The print media played a prominent role in shaping American perceptions of the horrors of modern warfare. Pictures of wide-scale destruction photographed from the air brought the European war into their parlors, and into their consciousness. Images of war landscapes along the western front of France and Belgium and of the sinking of the British passenger liner *Lusitania* off the coast of Ireland in 1915 were widely circulated in the American press. The German submarine attack, which killed 1,198 passengers, including 128 Americans, shattered the sense of security that most Americans felt at the time. It also challenged their isolationism in international matters outside of the Western Hemisphere. Most Americans regarded the Atlantic as a buffer from the ravages of war. The *Lusitania* incident reduced the distance between the war and the home front. It forced Americans to accept that the European tragedy was a disaster for them as well. They had to relinquish an obsolete collective self-image of the United States as a "new nation" that had developed independently of the "Old World" of monarchies and empires. The war made it obvious that the country, as a result of its economic expansion during the late nineteenth century, had thrust itself into a global economy and had emerged as a world power.

Americans sought to understand the war's destructiveness through both secular and religious imagery. At first, the war in Europe inspired the secular imagination. Upon its outbreak, many compared it to a natural disaster, like "lightening out of the clear sky," because of its rapid onset and spread. Theodore Roosevelt compared its scale to that of "the disaster on the *Titanic*." Writer Henry James referred to the European War as "this plunge into an abyss of blood and darkness." Wars and other disasters have always inspired the religious imagination. Catastrophes have been viewed either as forms of divine retribution or as signs of the millennium, and World War I was no exception. John Milton Cooper Jr. points out that the predominantly Protestant Bible-reading public seized upon eschatological images from the New Testament to comprehend the European disaster, especially that of "Armageddon" or "the vision from the book of Revelation of the kingdom-shattering miracle that would precede the Day of Judgment."[9] These supernatural images of divine retribution and ultimate triumph over evil captured the imaginations of Victorian America. It is no wonder that over 24 million Americans had registered for the draft, and over 2 million had enlisted in the armed services in 1917 and 1918. George M. Cohan's song "Over There" became the anthem for a nation embarking on a secular crusade in a global arena.

TRAUMAS OF WAR

By 1918, Americans had mobilized a massive war effort, sending more than 2 million troops to Europe along with airplanes and motorized vehicles. How youth were conditioned to fight abroad was another indicator of modernity's influences on a tradition-bound American institution. The military had always used the services of the freestanding professions, namely physicians, clergymen, and attorneys. The war effort also enlisted the expertise of emergent middle-class occupations of industrial America, such as social work, recreation, journalism, psychology, nursing, and public health, to carry out the military's policies of moral uplift. The Army camp was now the site of organized sports, entertainment, and news coverage. The troops were also subjected to experimental indoctrination programs, psychometric testing, and public health campaigns.[10]

Along with these military-sponsored programs, many thousands of Americans, especially women, ventured overseas by joining in organized voluntary efforts on behalf of war victims. Their sense of public activism was matched by the many voluntary agencies that had organized relief efforts in Europe, including the YWCA, the American Society of Friends, the American Ambulance Corps in Nueilly, and the Smith College Relief Unit. None, however, could surpass the resources and organizational acumen that the American Red Cross brought to relief work during World War I. A quasi-official agency whose top executive was appointed by the president, the Red Cross was a public-private partnership. Geoffrey Perrett observes that managers from private enterprise, such as Herbert Hoover, considered the Red Cross's "High Victorian" relief work to be "the fairest, most enlightened approach to a free people, in which citizens helped each other and brotherhood not bureaucracy flourished."[11]

The American Red Cross had the financial means and the sanction to mobilize an array of relief services throughout the world. It served civilians through diverse public health campaigns for children and the tubercular. Red Cross workers cared for hospitalized soldiers, manufactured their prosthetic devices, and rehabilitated those blinded and crippled in battle. They sheltered refugees displaced by the war until they were able to return to their homes. Even before the United States declared war in 1917, the American Red Cross worked behind the scenes to finance the efforts of other relief organizations. By June 1917, the French and American governments charged the agency with primary responsibilities for providing civilian war relief. The other private relief efforts were invited to "cooperate" with the lead agency and found they had very little choice if they wanted to move supplies and personnel, since the Red Cross controlled virtually all of the available shipping space. Given its massive financial resources and political clout, other agencies could at best "negotiate to retain some control, some autonomy, and some identity. Private enterprise gave way to systematization, with all the benefits and all the faults of one huge overarching organization."[12]

The Red Cross expanded its base in Europe, from 20 workers at the start of the war, to 6,000 workers in January 1919. Both skilled professionals and newcomers to the task worked on behalf of orphaned and abandoned children.

In Marseilles, where almost 50 percent of the city's population perished, the Red Cross worked jointly with fifty French organizations to establish a child-welfare program. In Italy, the Red Cross operated in much the same way. In 1914, before America entered the war, it financially assisted the American expatriate community in its efforts to form an Italian branch of the American Relief Clearing House. In the fall of 1917, after the defeat of the Italian Army at Caparetto, the War Council of the American Red Cross in Washington provided $250,000 to the American Embassy in Italy to set up canteens for soldiers and civilians alike through its various consulates. By December 1917, the Permanent Commission of the Red Cross arrived in Italy, increasing the number of American relief workers from 31 to 949. This cadre operated schools and rest houses, workshops and sewing rooms, and even constructed a refugee settlement near Pisa. The Red Cross established a Children's Health Bureau and ran two hospitals staffed with American nurses. Red Cross volunteers and numerous other relief workers perished or were disabled from bombardments and air raids. However, their greatest suffering came from blood poisoning, meningitis, pneumonia, tuberculosis, typhus, and the flu epidemic. The Women's Overseas Service League estimated that at least 348 American women died overseas during the Great War.

Those facing combat discovered the squalid conditions of trench warfare. The trenches were always filled with pools of standing water, infested with vermin and lice, and shattered under the constant bombardment of artillery shells. The mobilization cost over $24 billion and left 300,000 Americans dead or wounded. Over 7,000 soldiers returned home suffering from "shell shock," a diagnosis created by the recently established field of psychiatric medicine. In 1917, the British Army psychiatrist C. S. Myers reported that troops diagnosed with shell shock were being referred to special receiving centers for mental treatment. At Craiglockhart War Hospital in Scotland, one of these centers treating the "war neuroses" of British soldiers, the psychiatrist and anthropologist W. H. R. Rivers observed that "the neuroses of war depend upon a conflict between the instinct of self-preservation and certain social standards of thought and conduct, according to which fear and its expression are regarded as reprehensible."[13]

Rivers made early contributions to the nascent field of traumatic stress studies. He was one of the first to recognize the primacy of the emotional stresses of modern warfare in the etiology of these symptoms. Rejecting a strictly organic interpretation of the war neuroses, Rivers instead claimed that they resulted from the mental strains associated with trench and air warfare. He found that the symptoms observed in combat troops differed from those seen in civilians. He also saw differences between the symptoms of enlisted men and those of their officers, observing that "the men were trained to obey,

and their neurotic responses to strain were those—paralysis, mutism, anaes-
thesia—that removed them altogether from further participation in the war;
officers, who were trained to take responsibility, responded with anxiety neuroses—nightmares, obsessions, hysteria."[14]

A new "forward psychiatry" developed out of the British experience of
treating combat stress during the first years of the Great War. Its first principle was the reclassification of war neuroses as mental conditions, rather
than as physical injuries resulting from blasts and other noises. Upon observing these changes in the diagnosis and treatment of British soldiers, Dr.
T. W. Salmon of the National Committee for Mental Hygiene's War Work
Committee wrote to the U.S. Surgeon General. The insights contained in
Salmon's 1917 report enabled the U.S. Army to profit from British treatment experiences of the previous three years as it mobilized its own war
effort. Rivers's patients would now be diagnosed as suffering from some
form of posttraumatic stress syndrome. War combat experiences are the
kinds of life-threatening situations likely to result in severe posttraumatic
reactions. In fact, clinicians have developed a better understanding of this
syndrome because of reports of persistent psychological symptoms occurring among Vietnam veterans. In 1980, the American Psychiatric Association recognized the growing scientific evidence of the immediate and long-
term consequences of extraordinarily stressful situations, such as disasters,
terrorist attacks, school shootings, and other mass casualty events, that
are likely to have an intense emotional impact on those who experience
them.[15]

UNFAMILIAR LANDSCAPES

During World War I, psychologist Kurt Lewin spent several years in the army,
most of it on the battlefield, where he had been wounded in combat. In "War
Landscape," he described how the perceived reality of the landscape changes
as one moves nearer to the front.[16] What first appears as a peaceful landscape
of farmhouses, fields, and wooded areas is gradually transformed. The
forested hillside becomes an observation post; its sheltered side the location
for a gun emplacement. An unexpected hollow is seen as a probable battalion
aid station. Aspects of the natural landscape that were attractive only a few
kilometers back are now viewed as ominous. Features of the war landscape
that threaten, beckon, reassure, and steer one's course across the terrain are
objectively indistinguishable from scenes just a short distance behind the
front lines. Paul Fussell sees this dichotomy between safety and danger in the
war landscape as one of the central tenets of the experience of war, stating

that "the sharp dividing of landscape into known and unknown, safe and unsafe, is a habit no one who has fought ever entirely loses. . . . One of the legacies of the war is just this habit of simple distinction, simplification, and opposition."[17]

Renowned for his field theories of human behavior, Lewin viewed behavior as a function of the interplay between the person and the environment.[18] For Lewin, the crucial factor in understanding an individual's psychological field is that person's own interpretation of it. This phenomenological conception of the environment focuses on the way that an individual perceives his "life space." Lewin established a topological psychology of how regions, boundaries, pathways, and barriers in this space direct human action. A person's behavior is not merely steered from within but is motivated by the environment. For Lewin, objects, activities, and other people in the psychological field also direct a person's behavior. Combat behavior, or any other form of human action, cannot be understood solely from the objective properties of an environment without reference to its meaning for the people in the setting. As a soldier, Lewin experienced the primacy of the phenomenological over the real environment in steering behavior. He was compelled to recognize the motivational character of events and objects of the war landscape. The war zone had to be surveyed as a "total situation" with each region contributing to the soldier's sense of safety based upon its proximity to danger. Lewin also recognized the value of the unreal and the imagined in steering behavior in combat, including the sense of fear and apprehension over an unseen enemy, and the imagined prospect of a safe return to camp with its promise of a warm meal and another night of sleep or restlessness.

The circumstances that accompany a major disaster are, for the most part, also unfamiliar to most people. These include witnessing death and injuries, wide-scale damage to property, disruption of transportation and communication systems, and, in some instances, looting and violence. The resulting "mazeway disintegration," stems from perceiving the familiar environment as disorganized and feeling displaced from it. A reporter for the *Miami Herald*, observing how the force of Hurricane Andrew leveled and reshaped both the built environment and the natural landscape of shade and ornamental trees in South Florida, writes:

> Where once there were lush tropical canopies, rich with color and shade, now stand rows of naked banyans, uprooted, with bent and broken limbs. Where there were stately royal palms, sprouting symmetric fronds of green, now stand topless cylinders of dead wood. Where once there were neighborhoods defined by fertile greenery . . . now are neighborhoods imprisoned by chaos, defined by tons of tangled flora, torn street signs, shattered roof tiles, shards of glass.[19]

The disaster-shaped environment, like Lewin's war landscape, steers individuals' behavior and profoundly influences their general sense of well-being. Disaster-affected communities are challenged to find ways to restore the sense of safety and of coherence that residents derive from the familiarity and predictability of the environment. In the words of a *Los Angeles Times* reporter after the 1994 Northridge Earthquake in Los Angeles:

> Surveying the damage, you are left with the feeling that the quake has done far more than was visible to the eye. Also left in the ruins was our shared belief in the complexity and well-ordered nature of modern cities. Environmental impact reports, City Council meetings seismic studies—all the fine bureaucratic machinery that was supposed to tame the natural world was ground into dust.[20]

The raging inferno of a fast-moving firestorm will equally effectively destroy the sense of familiarity and security people associate with home and neighborhood. In fact, the loss of a home, possessions, and the familiarity of everyday life increases both anxiety and depression. New routines supportive of reconstruction come to replace the familiar ones destroyed by the disaster. Those forced to relocate must look for temporary housing and then spend countless hours seeking assistance at the one-stop Disaster Application Center run by the Federal Emergency Management Agency (FEMA). Many recovery tasks require individuals to stand in line or to wait on the phone to register for various assistance programs. Survivors will often become frustrated with the length of time it takes to process these applications and actually receive the promised benefits. Sometimes a local homeowner association will serve as a clearinghouse for recovery information. Meetings will be scheduled at a school or church to help residents manage their rebuilding efforts and apply for insurance and federal entitlements. In the first weeks, these informational meetings will likely serve as support groups for survivors to express their anger and frustration.

Many survivors report an increase in psychosomatic and physical health problems during the recovery period. In fact, a wide range of emotional reactions to disaster has been reported in studies of disaster victims since World War II. Sleep disturbances, such as insomnia, nightmares, and dreams about the event, are common reactions. Survivors also report jumpiness, loss of appetite, difficulty concentrating, and general lethargy. Many continue to experience intrusive thoughts, feelings, and imagery regarding the event well after the immediate crisis has passed. The following cases illustrate how fires causing wide-scale property damage seriously disrupted the lives of residents of two upscale Los Angeles neighborhoods: Baldwin Hills—an urban African American hillside community that overlooks the entire Los Angeles basin—

and Altadena—a predominantly white community in the foothills of the San Gabriel Mountains high above Los Angeles.

In 1985, a major fire in the Baldwin Hills community of Los Angeles burned fifty-three homes and killed three people. The Red Cross provided overnight shelter and other forms of assistance to 108 families. FEMA's one-stop center provided assistance to 147 families. In an interview study, twenty-five victims of the disaster reported an array of emotional, psychosomatic, and physical health problems following the event, including posttraumatic stress and depressive symptoms.[21] Many experienced intrusive thoughts, feelings, and imagery regarding the event up to three to four months after the fire. Those who were present in the area during the fire reported posttraumatic stress symptoms, predominantly sleep disorders, nightmares, and dreams about the event. They also sought help from doctors for adverse health effects and used medication after the event to a greater extent than those who did not witness the fire. Those who lost their homes and possessions reported widespread depressive symptoms. They also sought help from doctors or mental health professionals and used prescribed medications to a greater extent than those whose homes sustained only limited damage.

In the months after the fire, Baldwin Hills residents attempted to reconstruct their lives. Many expressed difficulties coping with the transition. Those who had intended to rebuild had to cope with, among other problems, the effects of inflation on replacement costs. One couple did not return to the site of the event. The two had lost their home in the fire in addition to the wife suffering burns to over 60 percent of her body. The pair decided to leave the community and live elsewhere. A recently widowed woman reported both depressive and anxiety symptoms after her home burned down and she lost the last reminders of her marriage along with important business and personal documents. This caused additional stress because her husband had always assumed full responsibility for family affairs and she lacked the skills to deal with these matters.

Those witnessing the fire reported having persistent invasive thoughts about the destructiveness and the deaths caused by the fire. The bodies of two neighbors and of pets were in the street and were seen by residents. One woman arrived home while the fire was in progress to see the house beside hers in flames from gas explosions and burning debris. She was a helpless witness to this destruction and still suffers intrusive recollections of the devastation, despite the minimal damage to her home. In another family, each spouse's postdisaster reactions can be attributed, in part, to whether they were present during the fire. The husband was home and witnessed the fire; he is still experiencing posttraumatic stress reactions. His young wife was at work during the fire and reports that she is still blaming herself for not doing more to assist her husband and prevent the devastation of the fire.

After the fire, only charred lots with chimneys left standing could be seen when looking at the hill where homes had once stood. Several weeks passed before street lighting was restored. One resident reported that these became daily reminders of the fire. She had acquired "her dream house" after many years of hard work and had lived in there for only one year. The destruction around her made her too anxious, and she decided to leave the community. Other residents witnessed the dispossession of their neighbors and experienced survivor guilt. One woman whose property was not affected by the fire reported feeling guilty and self-conscious about her attire. Her neighbors had only the clothing they were wearing when the fire occurred; all their other clothes were destroyed by the fire. She reported that she deliberately changed into simpler attire so as not to feel conspicuous among her neighbors. Residents had to wait for hours to learn of the status of their homes, since the fire and safety officials had closed off the street to cars and pedestrians. The home of one resident was the lone house on the street that survived the fire. She reported experiencing stress exacerbated by not knowing for several hours that her house had been saved. Another woman reported such severe anxiety symptoms during this waiting period that she felt she might have a heart attack. A fireman checked for her and she learned that her home was in fact destroyed. She demanded to see this for herself, and because of her husband's political influence, she was flown by helicopter over her destroyed home. She was still unable to understand why the knowledge of the status of her home, despite its destruction, resulted in the abatement of her symptoms.

The experiences of Baldwin Hills residents shed light on coping in disasters and other extreme situations. Being present in the area and witnessing the terror and destructiveness of a disaster caused posttraumatic symptoms. The loss of a residence or possessions appears to have resulted in depressive symptoms. The actions one took to confront the danger clearly affected survivors' subsequent psychological resilience and overall well-being. Those survivors who were paralyzed by the fire and its aftermath reported increased symptoms of distress. By contrast, residents who were able to extinguish even smaller fires on their properties or on those of their neighbors reported feeling good about their efforts. Exercising some means of control over one's personal survival and contributing in a helpful manner thus seemed to produce more positive psychological consequences, as was the case among survivors of the Altadena fire. For two weeks in the fall of 1993, wildfires devastated numerous Southern California hillside and canyon communities. The worst of the fires were in the rural foothills of the San Gabriel Mountains northeast of Los Angeles, where homes are built amid brush lands with a history of fire. By the autumn, these areas were dense with dry foliage. The brush had flourished thanks to heavy spring rains and then dried out through months of summer drought. More than 2,100 firefighters were mobilized to subdue the firestorm in record-breaking, ninety-degree temperatures. They tried dropping water and fire retardant from helicopters to halt the fire's spread but lost control of the blaze, which was being fanned by sixty-mile-per-hour Santa Ana winds from the northeast. Residents stood on their roofs with garden hoses and even pumped water from their swimming pools, but all eventually fled their neighborhoods. The fires destroyed 5,700 acres and 121 homes in the communities of Altadena and Sierra Madre. Twenty-nine firefighters and nine residents sustained minor injuries. Over 2,500 residents from 500 homes were evacuated to four shelters in the Greater Pasadena area. When they returned to their neighborhoods, they found only "the blackened pile of ash and melted, twisted rubble that was their home and possessions."[22] They faced the task of reconstruction without the security of homes and cherished personal objects and lacking the familiar routines that comprised their everyday lives. One survivor described the resulting sense of disorientation:

> We look and sound like whole people. . . . But we're really shells. We're brain-dead from all the trauma and disassociation from familiar routines, habits and accoutrements of life. There's so many disorienting things.[23]

An interview study of twenty-four individuals residing in the Altadena area found that three-quarters had lost their homes; the remainder sustained considerable damage to their homes, but not total destruction, as a result of the fire.[24] To begin with, the study interviews in-depth only a few of the more than 2,500 residents who were forced to evacuate their homes and take shelter elsewhere. The sample is made up of residents who went out of their way to volunteer their time and who went to some trouble to arrange their interviews. In fact, most respondents were "help seekers," for they indicated that they had obtained assistance from disaster services, especially the Red Cross and the Disaster Assistance Center. Nearly all reported talking about their feelings about the fire. Their confidants were family members, friends, neighbors, coworkers, church members, ministers, and even news reporters. Thus, they were highly motivated, highly outgoing, and highly cooperative. The sociodemographic data indicate that the sample is relatively upper middle class and above, with almost 80 percent earning $50,000 and up, and educationally with over three-quarters indicating at least some college and half reporting completing college and beyond. Also, most of the residents owned their own homes.

One striking difference is in the relatively low level of emotional and stress reactions in the Altadena sample compared with the levels reported in other similar studies. The average score of less than one (.54) on the Beck Depression

Scale means that the respondents in this study in general reported most of the symptoms as absent or infrequently experienced.[25] The range of the mean scores for each item extends only to 2.32, which indicates that relatively few respondents felt a recognizable amount of some of the individual symptoms that make up the syndrome of depression. A glance at those items with the highest mean scores indicates the most commonly reported feelings were of excitement, sadness, and loss, feelings that are quite normal and to be expected in reacting to a catastrophe. Further supporting the conclusion that emotional distress was limited among the Altadena respondents is the fact that the lowest mean scores on any of the individual items of the Beck scale were those indicating possible psychopathology or severe depressive feelings, such as thoughts of suicide, spells of terror, or vague bodily feelings of numbness or tingling. These results of the Altadena study are in marked contrast with those reported by other investigators who have described increased levels of sleep disturbances, jumpiness, loss of appetite, and general lethargy in their sample studies. Similarly, minimal stress reactions are reported by the Altadena sample. The Impact of Event Scale (which measures subjective stress due to a catastrophic event) mean score of 1.90 indicates that, on the average, the respondents reported "rarely" being disturbed by memories or feelings about the event or of trying to avoid recollections of it.[26] The rankings of individual reactions indicate that while intrusive thoughts and feelings were most commonly experienced, they still occurred only infrequently on average, while the least common reactions were avoidance maneuvers, such as trying not to talk about the fire, trying to remove it from their memories, or trying to stay away from reminders of the event. Many of the items in the Impact of Event Scale are similar to symptoms describing PTSD. Other studies of disasters have reported that PTSD was common in victims of disasters. The Altadena respondents did not report such reactions as jumpiness, loss of appetite, general lethargy, or trouble concentrating. One specific symptom illustrates clearly the difference in reaction of the different populations studied. In a study of the reactions of victims of the Baldwin Hills fire, the dominant symptoms reported were sleep disturbances. In the Altadena study, sleep disturbances were rarely reported, on average, and were ranked ninth (out of fifteen) on the list of reactions on the Impact of Event Scale.

Another difference worth noting between the results of the Altadena study and those of the Baldwin Hills fire is that no significant differences in emotional distress and feelings of stress were found between those who had been exposed or were present for the fire versus those who had not, and for those who had suffered major loss or damage compared with those who had suffered only minor or no damage. The victims in the Baldwin Hills fire who had been present for the fire reported persistent intrusive thoughts. In the Altadena sample, no significant differences between the two groups were found. The Baldwin Hills fire victims who had suffered complete or severe damage also reported many more depressive reactions and symptomatology than those who did not. Again, the Altadena study showed no significant differences between the two groups.

Reasons for the differences between the results of the two studies of victims of devastating fires, namely the Altadena fire and the Baldwin Hills fire, are difficult to find. Among the efforts in looking for an explanation was an examination of the sociodemographic characteristics of the two sample populations. For example, they were similar in mean age, gender, education, household members, mean length of residence, and employment status. The major difference was ethnicity, with all the respondents being African American homeowners in the Baldwin Hills sample, and twenty-one of the twenty-four respondents in the Altadena sample being white, along with two Asian/Pacific Islander respondents and only one African American. However, both populations were considerably stable, longtime homeowners, and middle class.

One major difference does lie in the location of the fires. Baldwin Hills is located within the city, where streets and pavements have been long established, street lamps lighted the area, and the typically suburban development was of rows of moderately expensive homes. Altadena is one of the border suburban areas of Los Angeles, with many of its homes built into the hills and canyons that encircle the city in the north. The surroundings are rugged and the terrain mountainous, filled with trees and brush. The residents in these hillside communities in the Altadena area knew from experience and disseminated information that they were living in a high-risk fire area. The people in the Altadena study had taken measures to protect their house and property prior to the fire: most had installed fire-resistant or noncombustible roofing materials, used stucco or brick exterior or installed fire-retarding undersiding for wood exterior, and kept thirty feet around the home clear of highly flammable vegetation. At the time of the fire, a little over half reported they used garden hoses, sprinklers, and pool water in an attempt to prevent loss or damage to their homes, and a few raked and removed dry leaves near their homes. Although the homes are separate and nestled into strategic spots in the hills, the sense of community is strong in the Altadena sample. The residents were longtime homeowners who, for the most part, loved their isolated locations in the rugged hills. If they had to leave, they stated, they would be unhappy and would miss their surroundings. Even after suffering such major losses, the number who said they might consider leaving the area increased by only one among those who said they had at one time considered leaving. A sense of community was also evident from their responses that most had been friendly with their neighbors, and that they had found their neighbors helpful, both materially, and emotionally. Even though they felt somewhat critical of their neighbors' efforts at preparedness for a possible fire, with only a quarter estimating that their neighbors were well prepared, there were practically no expressions of anger or recriminations voiced against their neighbors. They also felt that the government and community officials had been well aware of their needs in the case of fire, with over half of the respondents rating them either well or somewhat prepared, while the rest rated them either fairly or very unprepared. While the possibility of a connection between the degree of psychological distress and emotional problems and the level of community spirit seems rational and makes good clinical sense in terms of the feeling of concern and mutual sharing of a traumatic experience, the evidence for it is only suggested in the Altadena fire study.

DISASTER AS A COMMUNITY CRISIS

A large-scale disaster will activate the formal organizational units that constitute the emergency response system.[27] These are established organizations like the police, firefighters, and general hospitals and "expanding" relief organizations like the Red Cross and Salvation Army. When there is a major disaster, public systems are predictably unpredictable. Loosely structured communities in the metropolis often deal with catastrophes more through the nongovernmental organizations, rather than with governmental agencies. These emergent organizations work with and are often integrated into the functioning state and local government agencies that form the emergency services system. This system usually does not activate after smaller-scale events, like an apartment house fire or a plane crash. The Red Cross will provide emergency services in such events; however, survivors will depend more on their personal resources to recover. A major disaster will often incapacitate regional systems and require local communities to rely more upon their existing resources. When service demands exceed the capacity of local resources, assistance becomes available through federal funds. Federally funded efforts are strengthened when local government and community leaders get involved in advocacy and oversight in the recovery period. These leaders will see to it that residents apply for and receive benefits from the government-funded programs that become available in the immediate aftermath of a disaster. The following case study illustrates how the organizational resources of an urban community, including public and nonprofit agencies, the schools, and citizen volunteers, responded to both the material and emotional needs of residents in the wake of the 1994 Northridge Earthquake.

On January 17, 1994, at 4:31 a.m., a major earthquake measuring 6.8 on the Richter scale shook Los Angeles. The temblor, centered one mile south of the San Fernando Valley community of Northridge, was the largest and most violent to hit an urban area in the United States since the 1906 San Francisco Earthquake. It left 25,000 people homeless, 1.2 million without electricity, 150,000 without water, and 40,000 without natural gas. The initial earthquake was followed by over 3,000 aftershocks. The Northridge Earthquake, perhaps the nation's most destructive disaster at the time, caused at least $20 billion in damages. Communities hardest hit were in the San Fernando and Santa Clarita Valleys, Santa Monica, and West Los Angeles. Over 55,000 structures were deemed uninhabitable. There were 61 earthquake-related deaths; 18,480 people were treated for injuries at local hospitals; and 1,533 were admitted for care.

Thousands of residents were evacuated and remained homeless for extended periods of time. Over 13,000 people were housed at forty-seven emergency shelters. Many survivors lived in their automobiles or camped outdoors in makeshift shelters and tents. Almost 2,000 individuals were housed in Army tents at five San Fernando Valley parks. Two area hospitals were closed due to extensive structural damage, and thirty-five other medical facilities were damaged. Residents of nursing and convalescent homes and patients from damaged hospitals also needed to be evacuated and relocated. After the earthquake, tens of thousands of low-income residents fled in panic as the walls of their homes collapsed. They sought refuge in the local parks and open areas of the San Fernando Valley. Despite the fact that enclosed Red Cross shelters in local schools and recreation centers were made available almost immediately, many residents rejected the use of still-standing buildings because of their fears that the frequent aftershocks would cause further collapses. Many of the victims in these temporary encampments were immigrants from Central American countries, such as El Salvador, Guatemala, and Nicaragua. Their prior experiences with earthquakes in their homelands where buildings continued to collapse after the initial quake were the basis for their rejection of offers of enclosed shelter. Instead, they set up pup tents or their own makeshift shelters of cloth and cardboard under the trees. They gathered with their families and neighbors to cook meals on the public grills of city parks.

Once they set up camp, the quake victims sought drinking water, which was in short supply because the municipal water district was not functioning. During the first two days, adults spent a considerable amount of time seeking basic necessities. They were usually able to obtain supplies in other neighborhoods less severely affected; however, there were some reports of price gouging by local merchants. Certain areas of the camp were designated as communal, where food, water, clothes, diapers, blankets, and medical supplies were distributed from Red Cross and Salvation Army trucks. By the end of the first week, many of the families had moved into canvas army tents erected by the National Guard. They were issued cots, blankets, and a Red Cross comfort kit containing personal items such as toothpaste and shampoo. The tent cities served as disaster communities for residents waiting to return to their damaged homes and neighborhoods. However, many others who had moved into the encampments had no home to go to or were reluctant to return to their damaged houses. They were fearful of returning to buildings that they perceived to be hazardous.

The Los Angeles Unified School District, the nation's second largest school district, was severely affected by the earthquake. All 800 campuses, with an enrollment of more than 100,000, were closed for a week after the quake. Approximately 300 district schools suffered structural damage. An estimated 1,000 classrooms were lost to quake destruction, and upon returning to school eight days later, thousands of children found themselves in makeshift classrooms, such as offices and auditoriums. Approximately 400 portable classrooms were deployed, with only 200 in place by early February. About forty-four teachers assigned to San Fernando Valley area campuses were themselves left homeless, and some faculty members exhibited serious enough emotional responses to warrant crisis counseling.

School crisis teams, comprised of school counselors, nurses, psychologists, and teaching and administrative personnel, helped organize parent and children groups in the weeks following the earthquake. These teams facilitated discussions in schools that were damaged but still could be used for meeting with parents and school children, and they also conducted debriefing sessions for school administrators prior to reopening of schools. The initial debriefing activities were targeted to administrators and key personnel to provide them with an opportunity to talk about their own experiences and to express their own reactions to the disaster. Dr. Robert Pynoos, a disaster expert from the University of California, Los Angeles (UCLA) Neuropsychiatric Institute's Trauma Psychiatry Service, conducted training sessions for the staff. Each session included a psycho-educational component to discuss the stress response and the grief process as normal ways of coping with disaster. The goal was to assist school personnel to understand and to learn to cope with their own psychological reactions so they could understand better the children's grief and fears. Many of the teachers were residents of the community and were themselves disaster victims. The interventions helped them work through their own reactions so that they could to return to the classroom and more effectively carry out their teaching roles. The earthquake resulted in a great deal of news coverage that included many announcements regarding public services, psychological counseling, and specific advice about coping with the disaster. A classroom intervention where the teacher debriefed students during their first week back to school was shown on the local public television station. This program not only showed the procedure used in the debriefing, but also illustrated the school's awareness of the presence of children's emotional distress as a result of the earthquake and the value of providing this type of classroom intervention. The schools also began to offer counseling to students, teachers, and staff through Los Angeles County's Project Rebound Crisis Counseling Program with FEMA funding.[28] Project Rebound, which was created after the civil disturbances in Los Angeles in 1992 and continued its operations during the 1993 wildfires in the area hillsides and canyons, had trained a cadre of disaster counselors and stationed them in schools and other community settings. Because of those recent disasters, the schools also had staff members who had participated in Red Cross crisis training and who were also trained in debriefing techniques. With the earthquake and its aftershocks, the demand for counseling was great, requiring over 300 trained clinicians to provide onsite services during the recovery period. Within a month after the initial quake, parents were reporting that their children were experiencing sleep disturbances. Bed-wetting was reported among some sixth-grade students.

The Valley Community Clinic, a privately funded nonprofit agency, received funding from Project Rebound and developed teams of therapists to provide crisis counseling in the San Fernando Valley public schools. Students were referred to therapy when acting-out behaviors interfered with classroom performance. Teachers in the elementary school reported that some students could not be controlled in the classroom. Fights broke out daily as aggression and oppositional behavior made lesson plans impossible to carry out. A "round 'em up and rope 'em in" policy was implemented, but it did little to bring order. Repeated aftershocks upset both the teachers and many of the children. Counseling revealed that many of the students with marked distress from the earthquake had also suffered prior to the earthquake from battering, molestation, abandonment, and, as the area was gang turf, witnessing of violence and death. Counselors working in two elementary schools in the northeast San Fernando Valley with a largely Latino student body, whose homes were hard-hit by the quake, reported that the teachers had suffered their own losses and panic and that they were increasingly concerned and upset as the aftershocks continued. Some schoolchildren had lost their homes; some had been trapped or injured or had seen parents in stark terror or injured. The loss of cars, plumbing, heat, water, electricity, telephone service, and familiar roads took its toll. Many families were forced to move in with relatives in already overcrowded houses or apartments. The children suffered classic symptoms of traumatic stress: irritability, hypervigilance, sleep and eating disturbances, nightmares, flashbacks, and regression to infantile behaviors such as thumb-sucking, nocturnal and diurnal enuresis, and baby talk. Almost all refused to sleep alone, and many were sleeping again with one or both parents. Counseling for the children depended on consent for therapy and the cooperation of the parents. This was a problem, for many parents had a cultural distrust of "outsiders meddling in family business." Many already had been given advice by friends, teachers, school counselors, and school psychologists, as well as children's protective services workers. For the most part, the children proved eager to talk to the counselors. The concern of their schools and the dependability and compassionate interest of the therapists enabled them to talk to the Valley Community Clinic's disaster counselors about their experiences, and this helped them to harness their acting-out behavior. Reports from the clinic's counselors doing school-based interviewing have indicated that, through drawings, journals, or stories, prior child abuse experiences were revealed among the so-called "earthquake groups."

As this case demonstrates, schools have become an essential part of the community's disaster response because they are used as shelters, disaster assistance centers, and community meeting places. Since schools are essential to the functioning of the community, municipalities make a conscious effort to restore them to their normal activities. The school also operates as a smaller community that includes administrators, teachers, health personnel, support staff, parents, and children, so it is desirable to reestablish this functional community as soon as possible after a catastrophe. Hence, school districts have been required to develop an emergency plan that includes activities in response to community-scale disasters and to more localized occurrences such as schoolyard shootings, construction accidents, and transportation accidents. School crisis teams play a significant role in major disaster planning efforts. Many schools have now included debriefings and counseling services as part of their immediate disaster response plan. Teachers and administrative and nonteaching personnel also receive training in postdisaster counseling interventions to supplement the often-limited mental health services.

Most schools now consider crisis-response services as their own responsibility and have developed crisis plans as part of their crisis team development and training activities, including critical incident stress debriefing. Planning has focused on the roles of their various professionals, the circumstances under which outside crisis teams would be mobilized, the linkages to be made with local emergency personnel, and when involvement with other agencies in the community was to be sought. As a result, schools are no longer isolated from the services of the community at large.

RESOURCE LOSS AND SOLIDARITY

A disaster exposes the physical and social conditions of a community. The more stable communities are characterized by high-quality infrastructure, an array of municipal services, and strong social networks that link individuals sharing common concerns. These qualities attract people to a community and contribute to their ongoing sense of residential attachment. Residents in these communities often form ad hoc networks and coalitions to address reconstruction efforts. Such "emergent" structures are sources of anchorage amid disorganization.[29] As new forms of collective behavior, they provide a facilitating social context for reestablishing normalcy. They often carry out postdisaster tasks not routinely handled by already-established groups and organizations. Less stable and less affluent communities, by contrast, are frequently less politically organized and often lack the advocates or spokespersons to identify service needs, set priorities, or request funding after a disaster. As a result, they are deprived of many of the services obtained by the higher-income communities. Economically disadvantaged residents also have to spend more time attending to their immediate needs than those in affluent areas, and because their frequently substandard housing is more likely to sustain greater damage, they are more likely to be displaced from their homes and neighborhoods for longer periods of time and to need shelters and other Red Cross services.

A major disaster alters not only the landscape but also the status of its victims. The ensuing loss of resources can thus limit an individual's potential, materially and psychologically. The loss of valued resources after a disaster has a direct and lasting impact on a person's ability to function and to cope. The kinds of resources that are jeopardized include necessary or cherished possessions; everyday routines and responsibilities; personal self-image and worldview; and a general dissipation of energy in the form of time, money, and information. Individuals use these personal and social resources as tools to maximize their well-being. Major disasters may affect, reduce, and even eliminate one or more of the resources, producing stress in direct relationship to the extent of personal or community loss. Centrifugal disasters like a major air crash generally scatter their survivors away from the locus of the event. They thus create multiple disaster communities widespread across time and space.[30] Centripetal disasters like a flood, hurricane, fire, or earthquake, by comparison, affect a community by disrupting families and social networks that continue to share the same physical environment after the event. The survivors who experience this type of disaster most often stay in place and continue on as part of the recovery environment. Disaster victims frequently become involved in collective endeavors out of the shared experience of catastrophe and a sense of communal loss.[31] The disaster community may crosscut boundaries of social class and ethnicity.

People working together in disaster communities also reduce their own sense of isolation and powerlessness. Such action often fills gaps left when community leaders are unable to fully mobilize emergency resources from the top down. This may result from insufficient emergency planning and coordination or a breakdown of administrative authority and of community organizations that routinely support residents' resource needs. All of these factors contribute to the perception of a community as an unsafe place. In fact, residents will often spearhead collective efforts because of their persistent sense of insecurity and their disillusionment and distrust of community elites. They will usually create networks, from the bottom up, to restore lost resources in the disaster environment. People, material, but also ideas contribute to the efficacy of these emergent social movement organizations. Popular movements succeed or fail based on how well they respond to loss, or threatened loss of material or organizational resources. However, ideas and expressive factors also explain both the efficacy of crisis movements and the reasons for their failure. Strong interpersonal ties are required to support individuals in what is often a harrowing effort to mobilize lost personal and communal resources after a disaster. Without the cultivation of a sense of solidarity, organizations forged in a crisis are incapable of motivating members to take direct action. These bonds appear to be the principal condition for the effectiveness of crisis organizations as transitional resources. One such crisis organization, the North Hills Phoenix Association, arose from the ashes of the 1991 East Bay Hills firestorm in Oakland and Berkeley, California, that killed 25 people, injured 150 others, and destroyed over 3,800 structures. Nearly 10,000 people were left homeless for a period of time, and damage estimates exceeded $1.5 billion.[32] The "phoenix organization" provided a supportive context to confront issues, determine actions, and interpret outcomes in a manner that is personally meaningful to disaster survivors. The emergent group developed into a nonprofit organization of neighbors in the 1,500-home area "in order to help residents rebuild and to ensure that fire safety would serve as a guiding principle in rebuilding," according to the mission statement. Beyond working toward emergency preparedness, committees of neighbors deal with common concerns, such as vegetation management, drainage, parkland, and "design review" of proposed development in the hillside area. The disaster communities that arise when survivors unite to mobilize resources after a natural hazard share similar features with the oppositional "cultures of solidarity" that emerge from workers' efforts to organize and to strike. Both striking workers and disaster survivors maintain a moral economy in the face of threats to their well-being, such as residential displacement or job loss. These ad hoc communities establish norms through a negotiated order—an interpersonal, cognitive practice whereby core values, sensibilities, and interpretive strategies are reframed to define a crisis situation. The routine and the ordinary are renegotiated within communities forged in the wake of crisis so that their members can make sense of the dramatic and extraordinary events reshaping the immediate environment and their lives.

"Holistic Disaster Recovery" is a social practice that uses a consensus-building, participatory process to apply sustainability principles in the recovery community.[33] The process ensures that members of a locality systematically consider sustainability principles in each decision about reconstruction and redevelopment; this process requires ecological design practices.[34] A holistic recovery framework, combining quality of life, economic vitality, social and intergenerational equity, environmental quality, disaster resilience and mitigation, and participatory processes, allows a community to adopt a course of action that will both identify concerns and issues and disseminate information to all constituents. This framework is useful to either predisaster planning for recovery or during the recovery period itself. The goal is to promote both inclusion of all stakeholders in recovery decision making, and conceptual and operational linkages among community interests and representative constituent groups. The community has the opportunity to build disaster resilience into its recovery strategies using regulatory tools, such as zoning, and nonregulatory tools, such as preservation and public awareness. The emphasis throughout is a community-centered process for both measuring and ongoing monitoring of disaster resilience. Holistic recovery principles, when enacted in the aftermath of a disaster, may propel a community toward achieving a state of recovery that surpasses the predisaster state, or the "phoenix effect."[35] The nascent state may create new social, economic, and cultural capital beyond what existed before the disaster. Should the recovery effort succeed, and a reframed mazeway emerge to accommodate all elements of the local community, most constituents would then begin to reorganize their lives within the changed environment. Mazeway revitalization is a radical resynthesis of existing beliefs and values, in essence the abrupt creation of a new culture—a "culture of response" in the aftermath of a disaster. Without a successful crisis response to facilitate social reorganization, a locality faces large-scale disruption of the social and cultural norms that both guide everyday behavior and help restore a sense of normalcy.

NOTES

1. Kai T. Erikson, *Everything in Its Path: Destruction of Community in the Buffalo Creek Flood* (New York: Simon and Schuster, 1976); Kai T. Erikson, *A New Species*

of Trouble: The Modern Experience of Disasters (New York: Norton, 1994); Anthony Oliver-Smith, *The Martyred City: Death and Rebirth in the Andes*, 2nd ed. (Prospect Heights, IL: Waveland Press, 1992); Anthony Oliver-Smith and Susanna M. Hoffman, eds., *The Angry Earth: Disaster in Anthropological Perspective* (New York: Routledge, 1999).

2. Howard Rosenberg, "High Above the Calm after the Firestorm," *Los Angeles Times*, November 6, 1993, sec. F.

3. Josef W. Konvitz, *The Urban Millennium: The City-Building Process from the Early Middle Ages to the Present* (Carbondale: Southern Illinois University Press, 1985), 169.

4. George L. Mosse, *Fallen Soldiers: Reshaping the Memory of the World Wars* (New York: Oxford University Press, 1990); Jay Winter, *Sites of Memory, Sites of Mourning: The Great War in European Cultural History* (Cambridge: Cambridge University Press, 1995); see also John Keegan, "The Somme, July 1st, 1916," in *The Face of Battle* (New York: Viking, 1976), 204–84; Robert Wohl, *The Generation of 1914* (Cambridge, MA: Harvard University Press, 1979); Stephen Kern, "Temporality of the July Crisis and The Cubist War," in *The Culture of Time and Space, 1880–1918* (Cambridge, MA: Harvard University Press, 1983), 259–312; Modris Eksteins, *Rites of Spring: The Great War and the Birth of the Modern Age* (New York: Houghton Mifflin, 1989); Peter Gay, "Epilogue: August 4, 1914," in *The Bourgeois Experience, Victoria to Freud*, vol. 3, *The Cultivation of Hatred* (New York: Norton, 1993), 514–27.

5. Konvitz, *The Urban Millennium*, 170–71.

6. Ellis W. Hawley, *The Great War and the Search for a Modern Order: A History of the American People and their Institutions, 1917–1933*, 2nd ed. (New York: St. Martin's, 1992); David M. Kennedy, *Over Here: The First World War and American Society* (New York: Oxford University Press, 1980); Alfred W. Crosby Jr., *America's Forgotten Pandemic: The Influenza of 1918*, 2nd ed. (Cambridge: Cambridge University Press, 2003).

7. H. Barbara Weinberg, Doreen Bolger, and David Park Curry, *American Impressionism and Realism: The Painting of Modern Life, 1885–1915* (New York: Abrams, 1994), 196–99.

8. Erich Maria Remarque, *All Quiet on the Western Front* (Boston: Little, Brown, 1929), 224.

9. John Milton Cooper Jr., *Pivotal Decades: The United States, 1900–1920* (New York: Norton, 1990), 221.

10. Ronald Schaffer, "The Great War, Prohibition, and the Campaign for Social Purity," in *America in the Great War: The Rise of War Welfare State* (New York: Oxford University Press, 1991), 96–108.

11. Geoffrey Perrett, *America in the Twenties: A History* (New York: Simon & Schuster, 1982), 446.

12. Dorothy Schneider and Carl J. Schneider, *Into the Breach: American Women Overseas in World War I* (New York: Viking, 1991), 56.

13. W. H. R. Rivers, "War Neurosis and Military Training," in *Instinct and the Unconscious*, 208. Originally a report to the Medical Research Committee, London, and

published in *Mental Hygiene* 2 (1918): 531–33. Quoted in Samuel Hynes, *A War Imagined: The First World War and English Culture* (New York: Atheneum, 1990), 177.

14. Hynes, *A War Imagined*, 177.

15. American Psychiatric Association, *Diagnostic and Statistical Manual of Mental Disorders*, 3rd ed, DSM III (Washington, DC: American Psychiatric Association, 1980); Robert S. Laufer, Mark S. Gallops, and Ellen Frey-Wouters, "War Stress and Trauma: The Vietnam Veteran Experience," *Journal of Health and Social Behavior* 25 (1984): 65–85; Rick Mayes and Allan V. Horwitz, "DSM-III and the Revolution in the Classification of Mental Illness," *Journal of the History of the Behavioral Sciences*, 41 (2005): 249–67.

16. Kurt Lewin, "Kriegslandschaft," *Zeitschrift für angewandte Psychologie* 12 (1917): 440–47, cited in Stephen Kern, *The Culture of Time and Space, 1890–1918* (Cambridge, MA: Harvard University Press, 1983), 361n38.

17. Paul Fussell, *The Great War and Modern Memory* (New York: Oxford University Press, 1975), 79.

18. Kurt Lewin, *A Dynamic Theory of Personality* (New York: McGraw-Hill, 1935); Kurt Lewin, *Field Theory in Social Science* (New York: Harper & Row, 1951).

19. Patty Shillington and Curtis Morgan, "Paradise Lost? South Florida Discovers a Changed Landscape," *Miami Herald*, August 30, 1992, sec. J.

20. John Johnson, "Searing Images Depict Pieces of a Disaster," *Los Angeles Times*, January 21, 1994, sec. A.

21. Carl A. Maida, Norma S. Gordon, Alan Steinberg, and Gail Gordon, "Psychosocial Impact of Disasters: Victims of the Baldwin Hills Fire," *Journal of Traumatic Stress* 2 (1989): 37–48.

22. Stephanie O'Neill, "Out of the Ashes," *Los Angeles Times*, January 2, 1994, sec. K.

23. O'Neill, "Out of the Ashes."

24. Norma S. Gordon, Carl A. Maida, Norman L. Farberow, and Linda Fidell, *Residential Loss and Displacement among Survivors of the 1993 Altadena Fire*, Report No. QR 73 (Boulder, CO: Natural Hazards Research and Applications Information Center, 1995).

25. Aaron T. Beck, Robert A. Steer, and Margery G. Carbin, "Psychometric Properties of the Beck Depression Inventory: Twenty-Five Years of Evaluation," *Clinical Psychology Review* 8 (1988): 77–100.

26. Mardi J. Horowitz, Nancy Wilner, and William Alvarez, "Impact of Event Scale: A Measure of Subjective Stress," *Psychosomatic Medicine* 41 (1979): 209–18.

27. Robert A. Stallings, "The Structural Patterns of Four Types of Organizations in Disaster," in *Disasters: Theory and Research*, edited by Enrico L. Quarantelli (Beverly Hills, CA: Sage, 1978), 87–104.

28. State of California Department of Mental Health, *Final Report: January 17, 1994 Northridge Earthquake Crisis Counseling Assistance and Training Program. FEMA 1008-DR-CA Regular Services Program, May 18, 1994–August 17, 1995* (Sacramento, CA: State of California Department of Mental Health, 1995).

29. Thomas E. Drabek, "Emergent Structures," in *Sociology of Disasters: Contributions of Sociology to Disaster Research*, edited by Russell R. Dynes, Bruna De Marchi,

and Carlo Pelanda (Milan, Italy: Franco Angelli, 1987), 260–90; Enrico Quarentelli, *Emergency Behavior at the Emergency Time Periods of Disasters, Final Report* (Columbus, OH: Ohio State University Disaster Research Center, 1984); Enrico Quarentelli, "Emergent Accommodation Groups: Beyond the Current Collective Behavior Typology," in *Human Nature and Collective Behavior*, edited by Tamotsu Shibutani (Englewood Cliffs, NJ: Prentice-Hall, 1970), 111–23.

30. John D. Lindy, Mary C. Grace, and Bonnie L. Green, "Survivors: Outreach to a Reluctant Population," *American Journal of Orthopsychiatry* 51 (1981): 468–78; Suzanne Michael, Ellen Lurie, Noreen Russell, and Larry Unger, "Rapid Response Mutual Aid Groups: A New Response to Social Crises and Natural Disasters," *Social Work* 30 (1985): 245–52.

31. Kathleen M. Wright, Robert J. Ursano, Paul T. Bartone, and Larry H. Ingraham, "The Shared Experience of Catastrophe: An Expanded Classification of the Disaster Community," *American Journal of Orthopsychiatry* 60 (1990): 35–42.

32. Norma S. Gordon, Carl A. Maida, and Norman L. Farberow, *The Immediate Community Response to Disaster: The East Bay Hills Fire*, Report No. QR51 (Boulder, CO: Natural Hazards Center, 1992); J. Gordon Routley, *The East Bay Hills Fire, Oakland-Berkeley, California*, U.S. Fire Administration/Technical Report Series USFA-TR-060/October 1991 (Washington, DC: Federal Emergency Management Agency).

33. Natural Hazards Research and Applications Information Center, *Holistic Disaster Recovery: Ideas for Building Local Sustainability after a Natural Disaster* (Boulder: University of Colorado, 2001); Jacquelyn L. Monday, "Building Back Better: Creating a Sustainable Community After Disaster," *Natural Hazards Informer* 3 (January 2002).

34. Sim Van der Ryn and Stuart Cowan, *Ecological Design* (Washington, DC: Island Press, 1996).

35. Christopher L. Dyer, "The Phoenix Effect in Post-Disaster Recovery: An Analysis of the Economic Development Administration's Culture of Response after Hurricane Andrew," in *The Angry Earth: Disaster in Anthropological Perspective*, edited by Anthony Oliver-Smith and Susanna M. Hoffman (New York: Routledge, 1999), 278–300.

Chapter Seven

The City Is the Frontier

At the interface of expert and lay knowledge is the prospect of comprehensive community building through neighborhood-based initiatives that can bridge efforts between the socioeconomic, cultural, and physical development of poor communities. As a resident-driven process, community building values local knowledge and broad participation in efforts to revitalize the physical and social infrastructures of low-income neighborhoods. An example of this is the work that was done in Pacoima, California, a community of 101,000 persons in the northeast San Fernando Valley in the City of Los Angeles. A largely African American community until the mid-1990s, Pacoima is now over 85 percent Latino. Pacoima has endured multiple crises, including deindustrialization, transnational migration, and environmental degradation, compounded by natural hazards, as the community was near the epicenter of the 1994 Northridge earthquake. In many ways the trauma of the earthquake forced residents to acknowledge that their community's built and natural environments had become progressively degraded well before the earthquake. The shared experience of the disaster helped to establish a place-centered community identity among neighbors, many of whom had recently migrated into the area, as they began to reconstruct after the tembler. As neighbors set out to repair their homes and to clean up their blocks, they also extended their helping resources to people in adjacent neighborhoods. Out of these often small efforts grew a number of community-based initiatives to improve Pacoima, including one that will be the focus of much attention in this chapter, a grassroots organization called Pacoima Beautiful, which was initially formed to help residents clean up but then grew to promote environmental education, leadership development, and advocacy skills to residents, with an agenda of civic engagement on behalf of environmental awareness and community building.

PACOIMA: A COMMUNITY IN TRANSITION

Pacoima is a low-income, working-class community located in the northeast San Fernando Valley in the City of Los Angeles. It covers six square miles at the base of the San Gabriel Mountains and is bounded by three major freeways. The community contains a small-plane airport, with over 300 flights per day, around the clock, and is bisected by railroad tracks. About 20 percent of the residents live in garages or rental rooms in single-family homes; many live in extremely overcrowded conditions. In several areas in the community, residences are adjacent to commercial or industrial facilities. According to UCLA environmental health sciences professor John Froines, "while Pacoima does not have the worst conditions in the city of Los Angeles, no other community has as many conflicting types of land uses."

Pacoima was established as a railside stop for Southern Pacific Railroad passengers in 1887.[1] Its proximity to the "grapevine" passage through the mountains to the north made the area a desirable assembly site for livestock and goods moving north to the Central Valley of California. From its beginnings the area was home to European Americans, *Californios*, and Mexican nationals. The community was originally planned to conform to the newly laid railroad, with a large brick passenger station, a hotel, concrete sidewalks and curbs, a two-story school building, commercial buildings, and many large, two-story homes. However, extensive flooding very soon after this early boom erased the commercial landscape and led to Pacoima's subsequent development as a farming area dotted with olive groves, peach and apricot orchards, orange and lemon groves, alfalfa fields, and chicken ranches. From the beginning of the twentieth century to World War II, the area remained a community of small farms, vineyards, and orchards. During and following World War II, aircraft and other assembly plants turned mostly inexpensive property into land valuable both for residential and commercial purposes. During the war, restrictions were relaxed to permit African Americans to purchase homes in Pacoima in order to provide a workforce for the industry in the Northeast San Fernando Valley. After the war, the area became a blue-collar community of mostly single-family homes with a predominately African American population. In 1946, other African American families began to move into Pacoima when the Basilone Homes, 800 units of temporary public housing, were built. In the early 1950s, the African American middle-class population grew with the development of the Joe Louis Homes, a large tract of private homes for African American families, and later with the development of a community called Hansen Hills. Low-income black families also began moving to Pacoima in the early 1950s, with the completion of public housing called the San Fernando Gardens. This trend continued into the 1960s with the construction of two federally subsidized (Section 8) apartment complexes, the Van Nuys-Pierce Park Apartments.

Jobs were plentiful for both low-income factory workers and more middle-class working families; however, change came during the 1980s and 1990s in Southern California's economy as aerospace-related and automobile manu-facturing, and consumer product light manufacturing left the northeast San Fernando Valley. These changes had an enormous impact on local employ-ment in Pacoima and surrounding communities. It is estimated that half of the minimum-wage and lower-wage manufacturing and warehousing jobs have moved from the area since the signing of the 1994 North American Free Trade Agreement (NAFTA), which removed most barriers to trade and in-vestment among the United States, Canada, and Mexico. A large number of good-paying jobs with benefits left the area with the closure of the General Motors assembly plant in Van Nuys, Lockheed's aircraft plant in Burbank, and the Price Pfister plumbing fixture plant in Pacoima. Lack of jobs eventu-ally led to the displacement of African American families from Pacoima. Be-cause of newly available inexpensive housing, Pacoima attracted recent Latino immigrants, many of whom pooled their earnings to rent or buy a house.

Pacoima sits at the edge of the San Fernando Valley, where it rises to-ward the San Gabriel Mountains. Pacoima, which means "rushing waters," was a name given to the area by the San Gabrielino Indians, who helped farm the extensive mission gardens after the founding of Mission San Fer-nando Rey in 1771. A stream of water flows into the area from the nearby mountain canyons. True to its name, Pacoima twice experienced extensive flooding: during the Great Flood of 1891 and again in 1938 when twenty-nine inches of rainfall swept away homes and took the lives of some resi-dents. Flooding has been controlled somewhat by an extensive flood plain managed by the Army Corps of Engineers at nearby Hansen Dam. How-ever, inadequate storm drainage causes water to back up on many streets during light rains.

The area's natural environment, particularly the brush- and grass-covered foothills to the north and east, block and modify winds. They "capture" Los Angeles–basin smog and other air pollutants during most of the spring, sum-mer, and early autumn. In the late autumn and winter months the winds re-verse, blowing dust, plant particulates, and manmade pollutants off of the hills and onto the neighborhoods below. A flood basin, nearly three miles in cir-cumference, is much of the area. Fall and winter winds blow across the flat ter-rain of mostly dirt and rocks, bringing dust and sand into residential neigh-borhoods. Several large operating and abandoned open-pit gravel processing/cement works proximate to the flood basin also contribute airborne particulates.

The foothills are a natural barrier to residential building; however, the visual screening of the hills also make the small valleys and gullies behind them ideal locations for landfills. Their proximity to greater Los Angeles makes these sites, immediately above Pacoima neighborhoods, locations of choice for lower-cost industrial, residential, and petrochemical waste disposal. Over the years, millions of tons have been dumped. Two of the largest urban landfills in the nation were located near Pacoima, as are thirty smaller dump sites. In addition, one of the city of Los Angeles' primary asphalt recycling centers is located at the edge of a residential area. Hundreds of diesel-powered dump and disposal trucks thread their way twenty-four hours a day through Pacoima's neighborhoods.

ORGANIZING PACOIMA'S NEIGHBORHOODS

Community organizing in Pacoima began in 1986, when the United Way–North Angeles Region initiated community building in Pacoima after its "Underserved Geographic Areas Project" identified the community as underserved, and formed a "Northeast Communities Action Project" with a local steering committee to determine how to invest foundation resources. The steering committee invested in parenting seminars, recreation for children and youth, alcohol and drug prevention, and employment studies. A year later, the regional agency formed the United Way Community Analysis and Problem-Solving Council to oversee a more comprehensive funding strategy. The council cited the lack of education as underlying residents' health and human service needs and adopted "Youth at Risk of Education Failure" as the first priority area. The council's educational subcommittee identified Vaughn Street Elementary School as its first demonstration site to address noneducational barriers to educational success through integrating services.[2]

In 1989, the United Way partnered with Los Angeles Educational Partnership (LAEP), a Los Angeles–based nonprofit education reform agency, to help create the Vaughn Family Center to support the school community. Operating out of a converted bungalow on the school grounds, the Vaughn Family Center served as the demonstration site for a one-stop resource and referral center that would assist children's transition from preschool and promote parental involvement in the school community. The Vaughn Family Center was intended to meet the needs of the residents as identified by the residents themselves. Two residents were hired to serve as community advocates. These advocates helped other residents to articulate community needs and served as recruiters for resident involvement. More than 200 parents, teachers, and residents participated in crafting center activities and helped to implement them. At its height, the Vaughn Family Center integrated the services of more than thirty providers through "public-private partnerships." At the same time the Vaughn Family Center was being created, Vaughn School's principal was moving toward instructional reform, namely obtaining "charter school" status that would give the school both budgetary control and the freedom to redesign curriculum. The success of the Vaughn Family Center led to the expansion of the concept to five other schools in Pacoima, as well as schools in other parts of the city of Los Angeles.

In 1993, the United Way and LAEP developed the FamilyCare Healthy Kids (FCHK) program to manage a five-school Healthy Start Grant, a state-funded initiative to provide comprehensive, school-linked services through collaborations with community agencies to improve student learning and support families.[3] Through the grant, FCHK was established at five Pacoima schools, with the goal of starting a parent center at each of these schools. Parents participating in activities at the five schools were provided with the opportunity to define their needs and to help develop the programs to implement those needs. The parents identified the following needs: English as a second language, citizenship and parenting classes, workshops on how to help your child with homework, cooking and nutrition, literacy, "New Woman," and computer literacy. Early on, parent-center leaders learned that child care was crucial and brought in BASE, a community-based agency to train mothers in child care, including cardiopulmonary resuscitation and first aid. The model that emerged from the Vaughn Family Center and FCHK Initiatives was that of community residents working side by side with professionals and paraprofessionals linked through collaboration.

In January 1994, the Vaughn Family Center served as the hub of recovery efforts after the 1994 Northridge earthquake. Center staff, parents, and friends distributed food and clothing, and provided shelter, emergency medical assistance, and counseling to families during the first two weeks after the earthquake. FEMA-funded Project Rebound programs in Pacoima were coordinated through the center. The federal dollars for crisis counseling provided a significant portion of the center's 1994–1995 budget. Buoyed by the success of its broad-based disaster recovery efforts, the Family Center's staff and volunteers devised a community "empowerment" strategy to "unleash the human capital" within the disadvantaged neighborhoods that it serves. The strategy was called the "Pacoima Urban Village," and its aims were to improve quality of life for all residents by improving the work skills and competitive know-how of "village" residents, to retain employers and employment, and to encourage residents and businesses to invest resources and energy into the community. The village was conceived as a network of residents in six contiguous neighborhoods who have a commitment to the socioeconomic development of their community.[4] From late 1994 through 1996, hundreds of residents were mobilized in focused activities at the five FCHK schools and at Vaughn School. These activities attempted to link members of these communities to a set of goals worked out by the center activists: financial self-sufficiency, community self-governance, and a model for the organization of surrounding neighborhoods. Through these activities the village became an identifiable "place" to residents and professionals alike. Programs were initiated to address quality-of-life issues, including health care, environmental stewardship, child and teen academic success, and employment. The Pacoima Urban Village was short-lived because it was too ambitious in its scope and lost focus; however, out of the Pacoima Urban Village grew the Pacoima Model.

THE PACOIMA MODEL: SYSTEMS INTEGRATION AND COMMUNITY CHANGE

Following the 1992 Civil Unrest, the Los Angeles Urban Funders (LAUF), a "foundation collaborative" project of the Southern California Association of Philanthropy, through its relationship with LAEP, selected Pacoima and South Central Los Angeles, as target communities for comprehensive, systemic change.[5] At the time, there were two dominant models for community organization: the Chicago Model of political activism[6] and the Cleveland Model of collaborative systems reform.[7] These models parallel LAUF's original criteria for selecting the two target communities: South Central's tradition of political activism and civil rights, and Pacoima's emerging community organizing model of integrating the community through school-based health and human services at Vaughn School. In the wake of the Los Angeles riots, Pacoima was designated as an Empowerment Zone by the Los Angeles City Community Development Department, as an Enterprise Zone by the State of California, and as a site for a Targeted Neighborhood Initiative by the Los Angeles Mayor's Office. As a funding collaborative representing a diverse mix of thirty-three foundations, LAUF developed a coherent strategy of capacity building, comprehensive planning, and collaborative implementation to support school-based programs in Pacoima.[8] Initially, LAUF's involvement supported the efforts of United Way and LAEP to assess community assets, health services provision, housing, businesses, and jobs. The assessment reinforced the previous findings of the United Way, which found Pacoima to be severely lacking in services and resources.[9]

LAUF later assisted selected nonprofit organizations in Pacoima to build their organizational and financial capacity. The nonprofit organizations included Pacoima Beautiful, San Fernando Valley Neighborhood Legal Services, LAEP and its FCHK network of school-based parent centers, and Valley Economic Development Center, which established a network to link the parents at these centers to jobs and employment opportunities through LAUF's Workforce Development Initiative. Project GRAD Los Angeles, a nonprofit affiliated with a national educational reform effort with funding from the Ford Foundation, initiated an early college outreach program in Pacoima. The synergies among foundations, the nonprofit sector, and school-centered reform activities brought about and supported by LAUF also produced useful knowledge to guide philanthropic investment and an effective evaluation strategy on behalf of community change in Pacoima.[10] The power of collaboration became central to the evolution of the model that was developed to bring about systemic change within Pacoima. The "Pacoima Model" underlies an evolving partnership between professionals, paraprofessionals, and community volunteers working together toward common school and youth-centered programmatic goals.[11] The model has proven effective in working within the existing educational system and local political structure, as it promotes change from within the system and not from outside. As a collaborative model, it advances efforts to bring together those who want to help engaged community residents address their needs and achieve their goals.

The involvement of LAUF was critical in the development of the model: as the residents defined their needs and developed programs, many foundation collaborative members provided direct funding to the programs. In addition, LAUF funded surveys to verify needs and provided resources to test theories and concepts and to expand the knowledge base of the program participants. The Pacoima Steering Committee was made up of representatives from agencies whose programs had received funding from foundations that were a part of LAUF. The original purpose of the committee was to oversee the LAUF-sponsored Workforce Development Initiative. The committee did not act autonomously, nor was it intended to be a policy board; rather, it served as a sounding board, an opportunity for collaborating organizations to meet and share ideas. Over the years, the committee evolved into a broader-based "think tank" through which program representatives from school-centered agencies and organizations working in Pacoima could discuss ideas, collaborate on projects, and support each other's efforts to help community members to improve Pacoima. The committee explored ways to better serve the residents either within existing programs or by helping develop new ones. Committee members brainstormed ways to address the needs expressed by the residents themselves, and then worked together as a collaborative to help residents define and develop concepts for programs that would meet the needs of the wider community. The committee did not develop the programs;

rather, it served as a conduit so that residents' ideas and recommendations could be introduced to their respective agencies for program development. The members of the committee thus served as a network linking engaged community residents to nonprofit agencies and local organizations.

INVOLVING RESIDENTS IN COMMUNITY BUILDING

Historically, most residents in Pacoima believed that they could have no impact on their community. The community, they believed, was destined to have children who did poorly in school and could not get decent jobs, neighborhoods filled with trash, and inadequate health facilities. According to surveys, the residents had little or no understanding of entitlements within public service systems or avenues through which they could change the community, and, specifically, had little understanding of their role in the their children's education. In less than ten years, many residents had changed their thinking about their community and its impact on their own quality of life and that of their children. Since 1997, hundreds of residents developed the skills needed to become community advocates for grassroots and school-based initiatives. More specifically, as parents have become actively involved in the schools, they are helping to impact the way their children learn, and the schools are improving. Residents have been hired as parent center leaders, *Promotores*, job coaches, outreach workers, and survey interviewers through LAUF's Workforce Development Initiative. Parents in the parent centers developed skills to work side by side with professionals as a team to provide services; parents also conduct classes at school parent centers. Many residents are taking advantage of educational classes at community colleges, workshops, and skill-building opportunities inside and outside the community. As community members continue to develop skills, they have assumed greater leadership roles within the programs and within the community.

Adopting the systems integration model, a number of community-based and grassroots organizations have been active in areawide health and environmental advocacy, education reform, family strengthening, and neighborhood revitalization. The FCHK collaborative, LAEP (now Urban Education Partnership), Pacoima Beautiful, and Project GRAD Los Angeles have actively partnered to sponsor education, child health and development, community environment, and health promotion projects over the years. As a result of these synergies, other partners were brought on board. The "culture of advocacy" promoted among Healthy Start and LAUF collaborative partners stimulated public agencies and foundations to fund community-based health initiatives focused on Pacoima, where residents, school personnel, local health

providers, public officials, and county agencies had identified health education, disease prevention, and primary care as community needs.[12] These alliances across diverse constituencies, including health and early childhood
advocates, human rights and environmental justice organizers, and school reformers, represent an emerging trend of mobilizing to ameliorate conditions
resulting from patterns of uneven and inequitable development in metropolitan areas.[13]

Following the 1992 civil unrest and the 1994 Northridge earthquake, service agencies used a crisis intervention model to disseminate knowledge as
well as to guide helping strategies to meet residents' immediate needs and to
reconstruct community infrastructure, including schools, health care, and human services. The model used by FEMA after an emergency declaration is
top-down and short term, with the goal of returning control to civic and organizational leaders as quickly as possible. In communities such as Pacoima,
where the schools had become the centers of crisis response and rebuilding activities, and a locale for the reestablishing of trust between professionals and
residents as well, a "school-based systems integration" approach evolved. The
incorporation of FEMA-funded activities within the existing network of the
United Way–integrated services on behalf of community building in Pacoima
only increased localized trust in outside helping efforts.[14]

As the systems integration approach gradually replaced the crisis-driven
model, residents began to work side by side with professionals, including university professors and their students engaged in school-based activities, and
paraprofessionals linked through collaborative activities in school-based parent centers and Healthy Start programs. Within this "bridging network," all
parties worked together toward common school and youth-centered programmatic goals within the existing educational system and local political structure, with the overarching goal of bringing about change from within the system.[15] However, the school-based service settings, where collaborative
partnerships had taken place in the years following the multiple urban disasters, were facing severe budget cuts as the economic downturn of 2000–2001
began to affect public funding in California.

In the ensuing years, the trend shifted to "academic community-focused
partnering." With publicly funded education, health care, and urban services facing severe budgetary cutbacks, a local university would contribute
technical assistance, research, and professional personnel, but no direct
funds, to high-need communities. The idea being that such synergies would
afford opportunities for training, service, and research to help disadvantaged
populations with political will, but very limited resources, to confront their
economic, educational, health, and other disparities. As a result, university-
based initiatives rapidly devolved, from broad-based collaborative support

of building community assets to funding specific projects linked to individual faculty or staff members. Rather than working together with colleagues in multidisciplinary projects on behalf of a particular community, individual faculty and staff members would now have to compete for funds and recognition as a "community partner" aligned with a specific community-based project. In the end, this shift away from collaboration toward competition for scarce university funds, between "faculty-partnered" projects and between communities, created a sense of distrust in the nascent university-community partnerships that had just begun to emerge in places like Pacoima. This lack of trust of academe's shifting commitments to community-building efforts was highest among the many nonacademic professionals who had worked hard to sustain ties to local schools and agencies throughout a decade of civic crisis. The following case of Pacoima Beautiful demonstrates how a resident-driven organization founded in the wake of deindustrialization, civil unrest, and natural disaster came to embody the features and goals of the Pacoima model, and was able to take advantage of the many different resources that became available to it.

PLANTING GARDENS AMID THE WORKSHOPS

Pacoima Beautiful is a grassroots organization promoting environmental justice that has brought residents together to confront diverse environmental challenges. These green activists have established an agenda of civic engagement on behalf of environmental justice, and are taking on issues of toxic dumping and pollution prevention through both needs-assessment surveys and block-by-block education, monitoring, and cleanup efforts. Since 1997, Pacoima Beautiful activists have increasingly become stakeholders in the community revitalization process and have been identified throughout the community as positive change agents. Pacoima Beautiful began in February 1995, when parents who were participating in activities at the Vaughn Family Center formed the Pacoima Urban Village "Beautification Committee." The committee was formed by Tamara Cohen, a pro bono UCLA-trained urban planner, who had been a volunteer at Vaughn since 1993. Cohen brought a world of nonprofit-sector leadership experience to the task, as she had served on the boards of TreePeople, an urban tree-planting, water-management, and beautification organization, and Coro Southern California, a nonprofit training organization. She was a founding board member of the Los Angeles Neighborhood Initiative, through which she worked with nine different Los Angeles neighborhoods to help community groups to access resources to improve degraded transportation corridors. She served as an appointee to the

Los Angeles City Board of Zoning Appeal, where she gained valuable insight into how the city works. In the collaborative spirit of what was later to be the Pacoima Model, Cohen partnered with a young Pacoima resident, Martha Flores, who was then working for the Pacoima Urban Village as an administrative assistant assigned to work with the Beautification Committee. Flores moved to the United States at age fourteen from Jocoro, El Salvador. The civil war there had ravaged her hometown; as a child, Martha had moved from town to town to escape the terror, and was separated from her family for six years. Once reunited with her family in Los Angeles, Flores entered Le Conte Middle School in Hollywood, graduated from Hollywood High School, and earned a bachelor's degree in health science from California State University, Los Angeles. While in college, she moved with her family to Pacoima, where she noticed the widespread dumping of trash, including old mattresses and sofas, and the general disrepair of the streets and neighborhoods. An American citizen since her early twenties, Flores was the "pied piper," in Cohen's words, who mobilized Pacoima's residents early on to take action, by first cleaning up their neighborhoods and then planting grass and trees in their neighborhoods.[16]

As a project of the Urban Village that focused on "enhancing the physical infrastructure," the committee helped residents to organize and to become proactive to effectively deal with the environmental problems on their block and in their neighborhood. The initial work of the committee was to conduct a needs assessment in order to determine what could be done to beautify the community in the short and long term. The committee organized cleanup days, conducted a community engagement survey, and arranged to have graffiti removed from the area around Vaughn School. When the committee received 200 fruit trees from TreePeople, participating residents organized a beautification weekend to distribute the trees and to clean up neighborhood streets. The committee also provided an ongoing forum for discussions on the physical conditions of the area. The residents discussed community issues including gang activity, abandoned houses, illegal dumping, graffiti, lack of streetlights and of trees, and unpaved streets and sidewalks. The committee helped residents develop relationships with the police, public works agencies, and the City Councilman's office. These relationships resulted in strategies to get rid of two crack houses, scores of abandoned vehicles, and graffiti. It also resulted in the credibility of the committee as a positive effort to improve the community.

With the support of the Beautification Committee, a number of residents initiated activities on behalf of greening the community. A group of neighbors bordering Vaughn School organized cleaning of the streets every weekend in 1996. Every Monday, students arrived at school to find the street facing the school clean. A Latina organized her neighbors to clean up their block after receiving and planting fruit trees from TreePeople. Another Latina organized her neighbors through cleanup projects. By establishing a sense of community through these cleanup activities, neighbors began to trust one another. An African American resident shared his passion for gardening with a family in trouble as a way to reach out to them. In the fall of 1996, at the request of LAUF, Beautification Committee members developed a work plan to assure longer-term sustainability of their greening efforts. Through the planning process, the Beautification Committee became "Pacoima Beautiful, Pride of the San Fernando Valley," named in the spirit of the Progressive City Beautiful Movement. Later shortened to Pacoima Beautiful, the group developed a mission, a specific focus, goals, and projects and engaged residents in more cleanup activities. In June 1997, LAUF helped identify a funding source so that Pacoima Beautiful could open an office and pay the salary of Martha Flores. At LAUF's urging, LAEP become Pacoima Beautiful's fiscal agent and helped the fledgling organization to develop relationships with the local schools.

The first activities of Pacoima Beautiful were to collaborate with the FCHK collaborative in the writing and implementation of a "community engagement" survey in order to identify key environmental and health problems, and to conduct a cleanup day at which more than 250 people participated. The survey of more than 300 Pacoima residents revealed the problems that residents had with the degraded physical infrastructure in the community. Residents identified concerns about a lack of trees and ground cover, leaking septic tanks, and flooding of streets even during light rains. Also identified was widespread illegal dumping by residents, businesses, and others from outside the community. The survey revealed the extent of the problem, especially that of illegal car repair facilities operating in residential neighborhoods and dumping oil into catch basins and onto streets. Residents said that they did not know how to adequately dispose of trash; many were unaware of the danger of some of their household products and how or where to properly dispose of them. Residents were unaware that dumping into the storm drains results in the pollution of the ocean twenty-five miles away. A lack of street and sidewalk paving throughout Pacoima caused residents to walk to school or to shops on muddy paths when it rained and in dust storms when the wind was blowing. Those surveyed viewed Pacoima's physical infrastructure as contributing to the high incidence of asthma and other respiratory ailments in the area, falling property values, and a perception of decline that causes businesses to leave the area.

When Pacoima Beautiful and FCHK shared the findings of the survey with Los Angeles city officials, the officials acknowledged that there were many problems in the community that could not be addressed because, in part, the city's enforcement budget was continuously being cut. There were no promises of help. As a result, Pacoima Beautiful activists concluded that they must find the solutions for themselves. A key solution was the creation of the Community Inspectors Program late in 1997. Community inspectors were, and continue to be, a rotating group of twelve or more Pacoima residents who volunteer their time to identify, record, and report unhealthful conditions and hazardous materials in Pacoima to the appropriate city and county agencies for removal. Community Inspectors have at various times worked with the Senior Lead Officers from the Foothill Division of the Los Angeles Police Department, the Building and Safety Department, the Sanitation Department, and the Code Watch program operating through the mayor's office. Community inspectors look for things such as illegally dumped trash, oil, car parts — including tires and other types of hazardous waste — and illegally operating businesses, particularly auto repair operations. All community inspectors volunteer for a finite period of time, usually six months. Groups of residents have been working with Pacoima Beautiful consistently since 1997 to develop, test, and improve the program. Community inspectors meet regularly, often with representatives of the regulatory agencies, to discuss recurring problems and to resolve specific issues. They provide information on environmental problems and solutions to residents and serve as guides to fellow residents who wish to become proactive in the community. The case of Violet Lopez illustrates the benefit of community-based leadership development through the Community Inspectors program.

Violet is a young Pacoima resident who was affiliated with Pacoima Beautiful at this time. At the age of twenty, and a single mother of a one-year-old, Violet became a summer youth employee for the City of Los Angeles. Her assignment was to work as a receptionist at the Pacoima Youth and Family Center, the offices of Pacoima Beautiful. On August 16, 1997, Violet with her child volunteered for the first major cleanup day that Pacoima Beautiful held, when over 250 people participated. Violet took charge of the preschoolers and did a wonderful job of engaging little children in the cleanup process. The following Monday, Tamara Cohen and Martha Flores asked Violet if she would come to work with them. Although she viewed herself as shy and having little self-confidence, in fact she exhibited great phone skills and had a wonderful way of engaging people. Violet was born and raised in Pacoima and lived in San Fernando Gardens, a low-income public housing complex, until she was fifteen, when her parents purchased a home. She became involved in the community after the Northridge earthquake when she was seventeen years old. Her older brother, Thomas, asked her to go with him to help neighbors turn off their water and gas. The neighbors were panicky, but Violet and

Thomas helped to calm them down. In her job at Pacoima Beautiful, Violet spent a great deal of time getting to know the residents who came into the office to voice their problems and concerns. She often found it difficult to complete her daily tasks because, of necessity, she always stopped to chat and listen to the stories; however, it is this quality that brought people to the organization. Violet did much of the emotional work and "the face work" of Pacoima Beautiful in the early years. Over the years, Violet participated in many workshops and trainings, including Coro Southern California Neighborhood Leadership programs, Liberty Hill Foundation's environmental justice workshops, and all of the Pacoima Beautiful workshops and trainings. She organized cleanup days, participated in tree and grass plantings, and helped many people to produce flyers and materials for distribution. Violet came to find her voice as a positive, constructive advocate for Pacoima. In November 1999—two years after she volunteered in her first community cleanup—Violet attended a Los Angeles City Public Works meeting at a local park. For the first time, she made an impassioned and convincing plea on behalf of adequate child care facilities at the park. In an effort to revitalize Pacoima's blighted commercial zone, Violet organized the "Adopt-A-Spot" and "Adopt-A-Basket" programs through which merchants agreed to use a broom on a regular basis to keep the area in front of their business clean and to empty a trashcan. In her advocacy efforts on behalf of residents and merchants, Violet has shown herself as a person who not only talks but also acts.

DESIGNING A SUSTAINABLE SCHOOL

Pacoima Beautiful has organized various community-building development projects to incorporate an environmental "voice" in social and land-use planning. Residents of all ages, including teens and young adults, have become involved in initiating plans and identifying needed resources to tackle the identified problems. Community-based planning serves as a focused resource for training residents and assisting them in accessing funding from state and federal agencies to improve their quality of life; it also serves as a way to enhance the learning opportunities available to residents. The case of the Broadous-Humphrey Park Project is an example of this form of collaborative planning. When academic scores were released in the summer of 1997, it was found that Hillary Broadous Elementary School had among the lowest scores in the state of California. Representatives from LAEP initiated discussions with the Broadous principal and Pacoima Beautiful to determine if hands-on beautification projects could serve as a vehicle to improve learning, and therefore test scores. All parties agreed that it was possible, and a broad-based community forum brought together parents, teachers, Healthy Start and Parent Center leaders, TreePeople, Los Angeles Conservation Corps, and the leadership training organization Coro Southern California to develop a work plan. Pacoima Beautiful began working with the fifth-grade teacher to develop curriculum for the "Cheetos Bag Project," inspired by the City of Los Angeles Stormwater Program's campaign, "The Ocean Begins in Your Neighborhood," using the following story created by the teacher: "A Cheetos bag not thrown in the trash wound up in the Pacoima Wash, which wound up in the ocean being eaten by a fish; the fish was caught by a boy and his father when fishing; the boy got sick after eating the fish, and it all could have been prevented if the Cheetos bag was disposed of properly."

At the same time, during the summer of 1997, Hubert M. Humphrey Memorial Park, which is directly across the street from Broadous Elementary School, was under siege by gangs and drive-by shootings. On August 16, 1997, Pacoima Beautiful organized a cleanup day and lunch at Humphrey Park and around the school. The cleanup day was intended to make a statement that the community cared about the school and the park and were willing to expend efforts to protect them. The police and park maintenance staff assisted in the effort, as did a local trash disposal company. Unfortunately, the next day, August 17, a young African American boy, riding his bike on the street next to the park was shot and killed by Latino gang members; young children witnessed the death. This was a devastating blow to those who were so hopeful just the previous day. However, some hopeful residents who lived across the street from the park and the school invited Pacoima Beautiful to help establish the Mercer Street Block Club, which served as both a neighborhood watch group and the pilot program for community-based inspection to monitor and clear the Mercer Street area of factors contributing to urban blight, such as graffiti and illegal dumping. The club sponsored three cleanup days and a grass-planting project and developed plans to turn an empty lot into a community garden. For its efforts, Pacoima Beautiful was able to help residents gain a better understanding of the community and the park environs, and to help residents become more involved in both the school and the park.

In October 1997, a group of public and nonprofit agencies including Pacoima Beautiful applied for and received county funds to engage idle youth to paint murals on park walls and to improve the landscaping. All the groups helped to recruit the youth, who ranged in age from seven through eighteen. In addition to painting murals, the youth were invited to participate in a community mapping project to determine the locations where children live and the routes they take to get to school. The youth teamed up with experienced surveyors to interview residents living around the park and the school. One of the findings from the survey was that there were not enough constructive things for children to do after school and on weekends. Pacoima Beautiful spent nearly two years helping Broadous Elementary School and Humphrey Park staff to address the needs identified in the survey. The results led to the improvements in both the school and the park. Together with a landscape designer, Broadous students have created a tot lot and garden to be used by children while their parents are attending parenting and caregiver classes. The garden has edible and touchable plants, moveable equipment, and an educational mural designed by a former tagger. The students have also designed a community garden on a lot adjacent to the school. Through surveys and discussions with parents and teachers, Pacoima Beautiful learned that the Broadous campus flooded during the rainy season. After years of work Broadous is now one of the "sustainable schools" in the Los Angeles Unified School District. Pacoima Beautiful, working with TreePeople and Los Angeles Conservation Corps, redesigned the campus to channel the rainwater into an underground retention system beneath a new soccer field. TreePeople's Campus Forestry staff recruited a "Green Team" of students, parents, teachers, and administrators who created a plan to "green" the Broadous campus with 170 trees and a water filtration system. Working together with a local engineering firm, TreePeople also developed a plan to solve flooding problems on the school grounds and adjacent streets. A system was installed underground on the school campus to capture and treat polluted storm water before returning it to the groundwater.

Pacoima Beautiful also created an effort to link Broadous Elementary School with the park across the street. The school did not use the park, and the park was not part of the school. There were a number of good programs at the school and at the park, but there was little collaboration or cooperation between the two. With the support of the school principal and the park supervisor, Pacoima Beautiful spearheaded a two-day intergenerational community problem-solving forum that brought together adults, youth, the school district, and park personnel to discuss the types of after-school environmental activities that would link the school and the park. A skilled facilitator from the National 4-H Council moderated the forum. The results of those discussions have led to improvements that made the park safer and resulted in closer relations between the school and the park that are still going on to this day. A key contributor in the Broadous-Humphrey project was Francine Schwartz, a University of Oregon graduate with a degree in Landscape Architecture. In 1997, she was working for a landscape contractor and wanted hands-on, community-based design and community-organizing experience. Hoping that she would find it at Pacoima Beautiful, Francine approached the executive director just at the time a project was emerging. Residents needed help for the design of a median strip, which they hoped would serve as a "gateway" to Pacoima. Francine was able to receive the hands-on experience she was seeking, and the residents received their design. Francine's next assignment was to assist with the CASE program. She assisted forty children aged five to eleven in the design and construction of a garden outside the Pacoima Beautiful offices. Most of the children, all residents of San Fernando Gardens, had never held gardening tools or planted a plant. It was a special experience for them. Francine learned from this experience that she preferred working with children rather than adults.

Francine also helped elementary and high school students to design and paint murals and to plant vines, shrubs, and trees at Humphrey Park. Francine's job was, in part, to encourage residents to allow their children to go to the park to work on the jobs. A noteworthy event occurred one day when she was walking the children from San Fernando Gardens to the Pacoima Beautiful offices—a two-block walk. As the group was walking past a building in San Fernando Gardens, a drive-by shooting occurred. Francine, and the parents accompanying her, herded the children behind a building. While Francine was frightened, the others, children and adults alike, registered no reaction, as it was simply part of life at San Fernando Gardens.

Fortunately, as the mural/planting project evolved there were no incidents that involved the elementary or high school students. However, gang members offered Francine another challenge. Three of the gang members in the "Humphrey Boys" who hung out at the park wanted to participate in the project. They were welcome to do so as long as they were sober, came to the job site without weapons, and did their best to be part of the team. As the project progressed, it was apparent that the gang members were very bright, talented artists and were inquisitive about plant materials. Their work on the project lasted for one tumultuous month. Grand promises had been made about possible employment opportunities by a partnering organization that never came to pass, demoralizing the gang members. The gang members did not remain sober; when they came to work drunk or high, they became aggressive. The police would then "hassle" them for being aggressive or for no reason at all, making working conditions for the rest of the youth very difficult. Ultimately, all three wound up in jail; two had "three strikes" against them. Francine learned from this experience that she did not have the specific skills to work with gang members. Her experiences helped Pacoima Beautiful staff to learn the importance of early intervention. The experience at San Fernando Gardens showed her that children become hardened at a very early age.

The next activity that Francine engaged in was to help families, teachers, and school administration to design a "tot lot" on the grounds of Broadous Elementary School. Francine organized many of the same faculty and families who designed the tot lot to start to plan for the tree planting on and around the school campus. Francine's efforts have resulted in opportunities for her own personal and professional growth and for the betterment of Pacoima.

In the end, the community-organizing efforts of Pacoima Beautiful resulted in a new environmental voice for the community's youth. These intergenerational efforts on behalf of Broadous Elementary School and Humphrey Park demonstrated the competency of youth to participate in the community-planning process. As a result, Pacoima Beautiful developed more comprehensive programs so that children and youth could become involved in its partnership efforts with local government, including public housing and planning agencies, on behalf of community building.

CULTIVATING ENVIRONMENTAL AWARENESS

At the time of the Broadous-Humphrey Park project, Pacoima Beautiful developed another intergenerational initiative to inform community residents, this time children and their parents, on how and why to respect and protect the physical environment of Pacoima. CASE (Children are Saving the Environment), an after-school environmental education program led by the residents themselves, provided hands-on activities, information, and education to children, their parents, and senior citizens living in San Fernando Gardens. Beginning in January 1998 and continuing every week for two hours a week for four months, forty children, their parents, and seniors from the local senior center participated in the pilot intergenerational program. During the first month, students explored the environment of Pacoima, including the problems (oil dumped onto the streets, trash, lack of trees), who was responsible and why, and possible solutions. The children and their parents participated together in a cleanup day and identified locations for tree plantings and gardens. In the second month, students explored the ecology of Pacoima, taking a look at the vegetation, water, and soil; the impact of abuse and pollution on the immediate environment; and the consequences of local actions downstream, including pollution of the ocean twenty-five miles away. The second month culminated in the planting of a garden. In the third month, students explored principles of source reduction, including how to prevent pollution from occurring and how to set up a recycling station at San Fernando Gardens. They collected bottles and cans for recycling, took them to the local recycling station, and used the funds received for crafts projects. In the last month, they covered the environment and health-related problems, including contaminants in the air, the accumulation of hazardous household materials, and lack of trees and ground cover, and discussed solutions such as safe substitutes for cleaning products, efficient disposal of household waste, and tree and grass planting campaigns.

The CASE initiative extended well beyond the forty children and their parents who participated in the pilot project, to reach the hundreds of families living in the public housing community. The management of San Fernando Gardens supported the four-month pilot project by offering its community room for classes, its grounds for outdoor activities, and the use of its buses for field trips; it also permitted a recycling station on the premises. In addition, housing managers assisted residents in helping to find ways to make San Fernando Gardens more environmentally responsive to source reduction and pollution prevention. Through discussions, arts and crafts programs, and activities, the participants became responsible environmental citizens. They learned how to prevent pollution by using existing resources more efficiently; they set up a recycling station and taught fellow residents how and why to use it, and they worked with the local councilperson to establish relationships with city regulatory agencies to prevent pollution before it occurs.

Another Pacoima Beautiful initiative that grew out of the Broadous-Humphrey Park project was to provide environmental work activities for the older youth of the community. By way of background, in fall 1999, Pacoima Beautiful, FCHKs, and LAUF organized a celebration event to mark the decade-long work done in Pacoima by many agencies and organizations. The event was held at Charles Maclay Middle School and more than fifty agencies and organizations were represented. During the event, those present were divided into small groups and asked to identify the needs of the community. The number one issue identified was the need for activities for youth. Out of that celebration event, many of the organizations indicated that they would work on developing ongoing youth activities. Pacoima Beautiful was one of the first to actually implement such a program. The opportunity that presented itself was linked to a planning initiative that had been mounted to confront the emerging threat to the viability of Pacoima's commercial areas as a result of the redevelopment along Van Nuys Boulevard, a major north-south spine that runs the length of the San Fernando Valley. A former General Motors plant located just south of Pacoima was recently transformed into a shopping district with big-box retailers and outlet stores. Further south, the City of Los Angeles was funding efforts to improve the streetscape around the Van Nuys Civic Center. The stretch of Van Nuys Boulevard had become a favorite shopping district for Latino consumers. While both projects would have the beneficial effect of upgrading run-down areas of the East Valley, a side effect of concern to the Pacoima merchants was the loss of local business. Revitalizing the northern segment of Van Nuys Boulevard in Pacoima would help the area maintain a competitive hold on local consumers.

In 1997, Los Angeles Mayor Richard Riordan initiated the Targeted Neighborhood Initiative (TNI) program to focus public and private sector resources to revitalize communities throughout the city. The program provided $3 million to develop, implement, and sustain public improvements in a neighborhood over a three-year period. The initiative was intended to assure that the local community was fully mobilized and invested in the effort. The decisions about how, when, and on what to spend money were to be made by the people who lived and worked in the community, and not the bureaucracy. Van Nuys Boulevard in Pacoima was selected to be a TNI neighborhood. The Community Redevelopment Agency (CRA) was charged by the local city council member to spearhead the efforts. The efforts were unsuccessful because they failed to get any public participation. In 1998, the CRA invited Pacoima Beautiful and two other organizations to help design and implement a successful process. Out of the process came Pacoima Partners—a group of residents, merchants, and heads of community-based organizations—to serve as a committee to implement the TNI project and to help guide the revitalization of a 1.5-mile stretch of Van Nuys Boulevard. The commercial strip included storefronts, industrial parks, offices, vacant lots, residential homes, apartments, and three miles of sidewalk. The area had run-down buildings, some totally abandoned, and many with boarded-up windows. Other buildings showed visible cracks from the 1994 Northridge earthquake. With few exceptions, the area was barren; telephone poles dominated the skyline. There were seventy-eight trees on the three miles of sidewalk, but they were small and thin with few leaves, and many trees were dead or damaged. There were fewer than a half dozen bus stops with benches in the corridor, and only three that were covered, though most of the community used the bus system. The types and quality of services found on other parts of Van Nuys Boulevard were not found in Pacoima, and residents did not patronize the shops that were there.

Pacoima Partners used the approach developed by the National Main Street Center, a program of the National Trust for Historic Preservation, to encourage public participation in preservation efforts.[17] This team approach involved a network of community members, who worked to transform Van Nuys Boulevard in Pacoima into an economically viable commercial district. Pacoima Partners served as a liaison to community groups, businesses, and public officials, as they were responsible for introducing the commercial revitalization concept to the rest of the community and for representing the community's interest to governmental agencies and private investors. The project developed three program components. First, the commercial rehabilitation program would provide loans to business and property owners interested in expanding, improving, or relocating in the area, and would promote the image of the Pacoima Town Center to prospective businesses and investors. Second, the commercial facade improvement program provided a target area for the renovation, repair, and improvement of approximately thirty storefronts along the boulevard. Third, the streetscape program would develop an urban design plan to provide for an entry gateway, coordinated street signs and banners, street trees, planters, decorative sidewalks, coordinated signage, bus shelters, improved bus information, and pedestrian lighting. The program also would implement a streetscape design by installing street furniture and managing a cleanup campaign that would place trash cans along the boulevard, steam clean the sidewalks, and repair broken curbs and sidewalks.

In the first months of Pacoima's TNI, Pacoima Partners held two focus groups and a series of meetings to agree upon an organizational plan and how the plan would be presented to the wider community. Pacoima residents conducted over 950 interviews to determine residents' shopping needs and to learn about the concerns of the business owners. Pacoima Beautiful staff held meetings with more than a hundred Pacoima residents and business owners to ascertain needs and desires for Van Nuys Boulevard. Pacoima Beautiful volunteers met with most business owners in order to inventory the types of enterprise along the boulevard. They placed this information on a database and a map. The partners then held a community meeting to explain the proposed organizational plan; present the findings from the survey, interviews, and meetings with residents; and invite broader participation in the initiative. At the same time that Pacoima Partners was in its development phase, the Los Angeles County Parks and Recreation Department awarded a "Proposition A" grant to the CRA to plant trees along Van Nuys Boulevard in Pacoima. The CRA asked Pacoima Beautiful to manage the grant. There were two requirements of the grants: one was for Pacoima Beautiful to recruit, hire, and support fifteen Pacoima youth, ages fifteen to sixteen, in the planning and implementation of the tree plantings, and the other was for Pacoima Beautiful to be a nonprofit organization. At the time of the awarding of the grant, Pacoima Beautiful still had Los Angeles Educational Partnership as its fiscal agent. The grant from CRA provided the needed spark for Pacoima Beautiful to become an independent nonprofit (501c3) organization. The grant also provided Pacoima Beautiful with the skills to provide administrative support for the grant project, including coordination with the L.A. City Council and mayor's offices, CRA, Los Angeles City Bureau of Street Services (BoSS), and TreePeople.

Another initiative began in the spring of 2000 when the City of Los Angeles allocated $3 million to improve Van Nuys Boulevard, through the existing TNI. The goal was to make improvements to the streetscape and facades on Van Nuys Boulevard in Pacoima to begin a revitalization process. Pacoima

Beautiful helped to link the streetscape and tree-planting initiatives by volunteering the youth hired under the CRA grant to work on the TNI project. The project served as a way to link the tree-planting project to the streetscape improvements and provide the youth with meaningful, relevant work. Fifteen youth were recruited; for most, this was their first job. The youth met after school at least two days a week and as needed on Saturdays. Pacoima Beautiful hired additional staff to make sure the youth were well trained and safe on the job. It was difficult to maintain a cadre of fifteen youth throughout the program for various reasons, including that of parents who did not want their children out on the streets, particularly after dark. The first assignment was for the youth to set rules for themselves. Through consensus-building activities, the youth decided on a group name, "Pacoima Beautiful Youth Environmentalists," or PB YES. They designed a logo and business cards. They also wrote the following mission statement: "Pacoima Beautiful Youth Environmentalists are educated to provide the community with the tools needed in order to have a cleaner and safer environment here in Pacoima." The youth concluded, on their own, that only those youth who complied with the rules would be able to participate in the project. Some youth were asked to leave because they did not follow the rules. The second assignment was to develop a scope of work and a set of tasks with the TNI architects and landscape architects. With architects and landscape architects, the PB YES inventoried and mapped Van Nuys Boulevard. They learned how to do street surveying and to read and interpret architectural drawings. They photographed all of the boulevard's streetscape and mounted and labeled photos on presentation boards. The youth learned how to use a digital camera, how to prepare photos for a presentation, and how to read maps. Throughout, they were expected to perform at a professional level, including setting and meeting deadlines. The photo boards presented Van Nuys Boulevard in 2000 at the beginning of the revitalization process. The architects and landscape architects have continued to use the boards in their design work. Upon the completion of the project, the boards were presented to the new Pacoima library for their archives. An additional task was for the youth to conduct interviews with residents of Pacoima. The interviews further helped the youth develop communication and writing skills and provided them with a historical perspective of Pacoima, specifically Van Nuys Boulevard. The architects, landscape architects, and youth incorporated what was learned from the interviews into the designs for Van Nuys Boulevard.

Pacoima Beautiful staff invited a number of adults working in Pacoima to team with the youth. The teams met merchants on Van Nuys Boulevard to explain the improvement project and to invite them to the community workshop, which they helped to organize. As the youth met residents and merchants, they developed skills in communication and self-confidence. This phase culminated in a community workshop in October 2000 designed to inform and engage the community in the improvements to take place on the boulevard. To prepare for the community meeting, the youth were teamed with adults and went out to meet all merchants and residents on Van Nuys Boulevard to inform them about the scope of the project. Through these conversations, the community had a chance to see the involvement of its youth. The youth then helped set the agenda, planned the food to be served, set up the meeting space, helped the architects and landscape architects to arrange the presentation boards, and served as greeters at the meeting. Several of the adults who walked with the youth to meet the merchants became mentors to the youth, offering guidance on issues ranging from the value of a college education and courses of study to ways of coping with interpersonal relationships and family conflicts. The mentors included a staff member from the mayor's district office; a local merchant whose family has owned a business in Pacoima since the 1960s; a former army staff sergeant who was operating a local travel agency; a state senator's chief of staff; a single mother of two who lives and works in Pacoima, attended school at night, and was applying to law school; the founder of local nonprofit health clinic in Pacoima; and the director of the local nonprofit workforce development program. The adult mentors were supportive and consistent and took their role very seriously. For example, one youth who wanted to become a midwife was invited by her mentor to meet his wife, an obstetrics nurse at a local hospital, and to spend some time at the maternity center. As many of the youth had poor reading and writing skills, considerable time was devoted to writing and then reading aloud what was written. Through mentoring, the youth gained self-confidence. At the beginning of the project it was difficult for the youth to speak to adults, let alone look them in the eye. However, this changed through constant exposure to adults. The youth had no confidence that their efforts could have an impact. One youth, who at the beginning of the project was cynical and unresponsive, stated after the October workshop, "I now understand that I can make a difference." He then became the first to volunteer and to offer assistance on any project.

Due to various city timelines and the grant deadlines, the CRA, Pacoima Beautiful, the County of Los Angeles, and Pacoima Partners agreed that the tree plantings would be completed by April 2001. That meant that the plans needed to be prepared by the landscape architects, the plans had to be accepted by the city, BoSS needed to complete the tree wells in time for each of the tree plantings, and the youth needed to go back to each merchant to explain the program, to seek permission to remove existing dead or dying trees, to hand out materials on how to plant and care for trees, and to get signatures from all merchants to agree to care for the trees. In preparation for the actual tree planting, the youth learned how to become tree-planting supervisors. With the assistance of the TreePeople's forestry staff, the youth received instructions on how to correctly plant trees and how to teach others to do the same. In October, the youth participated in a community tree-planting project, at which time the youth became tree-planting supervisors. As supervisors, the youth could then teach others to plant trees. Several tree-planting dates were set from January through May. The goal was to plant all 240 trees between those dates. The landscape architect selected the trees, which needed to meet all the city standards. However, it was then up to Pacoima Beautiful and TreePeople to locate the trees, and this proved to be a difficult task, as the trees selected proved to be popular and therefore were scarce. BoSS's Street Tree Division required that soil tests be conducted along Van Nuys Boulevard to determine the quality of soil and any needed amendments; the youth then collected the soil samples and sent them off to the lab for testing.

In February 2001, the first tree planting took place. In preparation for the plantings, the youth met with merchants on Van Nuys Boulevard to seek their permission to remove sick or damaged trees and explained how to plant new ones and to care for and maintain the trees. The planting took place on a cold and rainy February morning. With the coordination of Pacoima Beautiful staff and TreePeople, PB YES helped to supervise 250 people, mostly youth, to plant fifty-four trees. The participants in the event came back to hot chocolate and sandwiches donated by Burger King and listened to an inspirational talk by the local state assemblyman on why these youth should work hard in school so they can get into college. The youth were then involved in planting ten to twelve trees at a time until April, when Pacoima Beautiful, PB YES, and TreePeople organized a major Earth Day tree planting. Three hundred fifty participants from all over Los Angeles planted 94 trees. In preparation for each of the plantings, the youth contacted all merchants to get them to agree to care for the trees; every merchant agreed, without exception. In addition to tree planting, many of the youth have found other ways to get involved in the community. One youth helped to get his government class to become involved in Pacoima Beautiful activities. Another youth began to serve as a member of Pacoima Beautiful's board of directors. All youth assisted a group of college students in conducting a survey of residents living adjacent to Van Nuys Boulevard to determine their commercial-use patterns. When the youth were asked how they felt about working with the college students on the commercial-use survey, all agreed that it was a positive experience for them. The youth said that the training and experience they gained working with the mentors and merchants gave them the self-confidence they needed to meet with the residents. Through the efforts of a college student intern turned employee, the youth have been able to explore the world beyond Pacoima. PB YES youth took an overnight camping trip to a state park where they went on nature walks and learned to ride minibikes. Throughout the project, they were mentored in community organization, advocacy, grant writing, and environmental stewardship, and they were exposed to a number of job opportunities, including "greening professions," such as landscape design, landscape contracting, urban planning, waste management, and civil engineering. The youth continued to build skills within the PB YES program, and their mentors continued on to other successful collaborations, notably with Project GRAD Los Angeles on behalf of engaging college-bound youth in environmental restoration, urban recreation, and environmental justice activities.

ENGAGING YOUTH IN SCIENCE AND COMMUNITY SERVICE

Pacoima Beautiful has collaborated with Project GRAD LA to increase the number of youth entering and succeeding in college. Nationally, Project GRAD supports teacher training to improve student achievement in reading and math, guides students in developing self-management skills to succeed in school and at home, and connects them with counselors to help with academic and personal needs.[18] Youth who want to earn a Project GRAD college scholarship participate in two "College Institutes" during school breaks to increase their skills and experience in reading, critical thinking, communication, and problem solving; other factors toward the scholarship include a minimum GPA and satisfactory completion of a math curriculum. The Ford Foundation acknowledges Project GRAD nationwide as "an unusually successful systemic public-school-reform project with strong results in test scores, improved school atmosphere, high-school graduation rates, reduced teen pregnancy and higher college enrollment."[19]

To implement its programs, Project GRAD LA partners with thirteen schools, with over 18,000 students and 1,000 teachers, in the Los Angeles Unified School District in the northeast San Fernando Valley, including elementary and middle schools in Pacoima, as well as administrators, parents, community volunteers, business sponsors, and mentors. Area high schools have a graduation rate of 18 percent and only 10 percent of those who graduate continue their education. Fifty percent of the students are "limited English proficiency" and qualify for school-based lunches. Before the Project GRAD LA program, students consistently performed below state and district averages in standardized testing. In 1994, Pacoima's children were two to three grade levels behind in reading and mathematics. Since the inception of the comprehensive educational reform program in 1999, the number of students reading at grade level has quadrupled to 40 percent. The reform effort has led to outstanding performance on the California Department of Education's Academic Performance Index (API), an indictor of student academic progress and success, with scores ranging from a low of 200 to a high of 1,000. When comparing the six-year growth of API points, from 1999 to 2005, Project GRAD LA schools doubled that of California's statewide average growth for all levels. The unweighted average API score for the elementary schools grew from 419 to 668, middle schools grew from 441 to 612, and San Fernando High School grew from 476 to 585.

In 2003, the first group of 190 Project GRAD LA scholars to graduate from San Fernando High School completed the requirements for college scholarships. Nearly all of the scholars were Latino and the first in their families to go to college. By the time the fifth class of 180 scholars graduated in 2007, scholars from the previous four graduating classes, together, had surpassed the four-year college-going rates for California's Latino population. In California, 71 percent of Latino high school graduates attend community colleges and only 29 percent choose four-year universities. Of the 2003, 2004, 2005, and 2006 classes of scholars, 74 percent selected, gained admission, and were enrolled in four-year colleges and universities; only 26 percent of the scholars were attending community colleges. Parental involvement in the schools improved along with these successes; each year, there is an increased number of parents attending classes and volunteering in the schools.

Project GRAD LA has created College Institutes, month-long learning activities for "off-track" students, as a productive use of vacation time from school, as stimulation and enrichment activities are critical to academic and social development. The institutes engender a spirit of excitement, a passion about learning, and a way of seeing college as a pathway for quality of life. They also promote a sense of the "interactivity of learning" through a mix of cognitive, social, and affective activities that develop communicative and cultural competencies, successful learning and organizational skills, time management, and planning. As the main interface between Project GRAD LA and students, the Institutes are socializing experiences aimed at instilling a number of qualities. They cultivate an appreciation of the promise of college, support the development of higher personal academic standards, and help low-income students gain a better understanding of college enrollment issues. Their structure also supports leadership and intellectual development by cultivating the experience of a "learning community" outside the ordinary school environment. Institute activities develop interpersonal competencies, such as supportive peer groups, which upon their return to school would reinforce the "scholar" identity through studying together, sharing rides, supporting Advanced Placement coursework, and engaging in intergenerational discussions with parents and teachers. The institutes thus promote affective development, for example motivation, self-esteem, and self-efficacy, and they support emerging peer bonds through the successful completion of a common task in the humanities, the social sciences, and the sciences. Project GRAD LA began to focus on science as an institute modality in response to numerous national and regional studies that have documented the deplorable state of science education at the high school level, particularly for students of color. One noteworthy example is the "Nation's Report Card: Science 2000," which found that California's science scores declined for both eighth and twelfth graders between 1996 and 2000.[20]

In 2001, Project GRAD LA approached Pacoima Beautiful about putting together a College Institute for "Track B" students at San Fernando High School who received little if any opportunities to participate in enrichment activities. The goal was to engage as many students as possible in collaborative environmental research, stressing math and science. This was a very important opportunity for Pacoima Beautiful to begin to share what it had been learning about environmental health and to bring in experts who had been helpful in the past. In putting together the first of many College Institutes to follow, Pacoima Beautiful invited university faculty and students and community residents to participate in developing and implementing a curriculum. Faculty from five area universities, California State University, Northridge (CSUN), UCLA, University of Southern California (USC), University of California, Irvine (UCI), and the California Institute of Technology, designed the research questions and outcomes for each study. Agency staff and residents then created a platform of seven environmental science service projects, including hazardous waste, air quality, soil lead, watershed conservation, atmospheric science, environmental advocacy, and mural design, from which the students could choose. An action research approach informed the specific objectives, data collection methods, and the action plan for each project. Each addressed an environmental issue as framed and prioritized by Pacoima residents and provided a vehicle for students to improve their science, math, and language skills. The Institute brought together eighty-four San Fernando High School students, fourteen college students, and seven community residents for one month, beginning with a weekend leadership training session at UCLA. Students then worked on their service-learning projects in the community during the morning and attended classes at the local community college in the afternoon with high school science teachers. College students served as "near-peer" mentors for the high school students as they implemented the projects; cross-age mentoring also took place between students and adult volunteers from Pacoima Beautiful. The latter reinforced the notion that these projects were only the beginning of service, and that youth would need to step forward and continue in their efforts to address severe environmental issues in their home community. To this end, each project team included a Pacoima resident serving as a recorder, who brought a community perspective to project activities and then conveyed the information learned from the project to the community. The data gathered from these projects provided valuable information to help improve the quality of life in Pacoima. Reflective activities, including discussion of alternative paths of action based upon the research, took place among university and high school students and residents.

A nascent sense of self-efficacy also developed around students' ability to actively learn science concepts through service projects and then advocate for change. As the Institute was underway, various stakeholders became interested in having the students address a key environmental concern in Pacoima, Hansen Dam—a flood-control basin and mixed-use recreation area managed by the Army Corps of Engineers and the City of Los Angeles Department of Recreation and Parks—and they were willing to support them in that effort. The ten youth involved with this service project presented their findings at a "Town Hall" meeting attended by these two co-managing agencies as well as the Santa Monica Mountains Conservancy, a publicly funded parkland preservation organization; the Children's Museum of Los Angeles, which planned to build a facility at the site; the Audubon Society; local elected officials; homeowners; equestrian groups; school district personnel; and university faculty. The students also cited the need to teach the community the value and importance of the site; enlist cooperation to improve the park's appearance, significantly reducing the trash and graffiti problem; increase residents' use of the site; systematically remove invasive plants and replace them with natives; provide more facilities for individuals with disabilities; build a boardwalk and walkways for easier access to park destinations; increase the number of playgrounds; add wildlife information signs and viewing telescopes; expand water testing to determine safety for human consumption of fish caught in the area; and advocate to preserve the site as a wildlife habitat for the protection of over 260 species of birds found there. They also suggested that young and adult residents become more active in planning for both Hansen Dam and the proposed museum. The elected officials, representatives from the various constituency groups, and the Army Corps expressed their willingness to work with the students, albeit noting that addressing their concerns about the site would be complicated because of funding issues and overlapping jurisdictions. As a result of the meeting, the local congressman put in a request for additional federal funding for Hansen Dam; over $3 million was secured on its behalf. It was shortly after this meeting that the Army Corps started dumping construction wastes from the swimming pool at the top of Hansen Dam to the lower lake. This outraged residents, who had heard at the meeting that nothing major would be done without community input; they quickly mobilized to have the dumping stopped. The same group of stakeholders came together a few months later to set priorities for Hansen Dam, namely developing public awareness through needs assessments and media campaigns; monitoring water quality and the status of trees, birds, and endangered wildlife; exploring sustainable ways to link the natural and built environments; documenting the cultural heritage and historic preservation of the site; and demonstrating how the uses of the site impact the land and community and generate potential conflicts over land use issues. Following the meeting, agency staff and students from the original Institute consolidated these priority areas into four platforms for study at a second Institute that brought fifty-one students together to further investigate ecological issues at Hansen Dam. The students again shared their recommendations with decision makers, and two of them were selected by the Army Corps for possible implementation: natural trail creation and the construction of informational signage.

The activities developed for the Institute focused on introducing high school juniors and seniors to the promise of college through two pathways: (1) community-based service learning and (2) mentoring experiences in small learning settings outside of the school. These activities are viewed as ways to reorient students during the last eighteen months of high school toward the transition to young adulthood. Through them, youth begin to cultivate career confidence and competence through work with mentors, including university students and professionals. A sense of "knowing-in-action" comes from participation in practice-oriented learning experiences that include service learning and mentoring in various kinds of skilled work. These practice-oriented learning experiences are essential to the passage to young adulthood, which is characterized as a time for the assimilation of occupational and professional knowledge, skills, and values.

Such experiences are especially important for youth in transmigrant families, where the belief in the "American Dream" has driven adults to uproot for what they trust will be a better life. But it is often the case that the reality does not resemble this dream. Immigration and resettlement are intergenerational crises, with troubling life circumstances that include substandard housing, inadequate schooling, poor working conditions, language barriers, problematic legal status, and racism. For some, there is the additional burden of living within a split transnational family, with one spouse living in the home country, and the other in this country. For others, personal identity and worldview will differ between adults who immigrated to the United States after they were seventeen years of age, and their children who grew up in this country, as the majority of children living in immigrant households were American-born. These situations contribute to the sense of alienation and the emotional abandonment felt by many immigrant youth and children of immigrants.

Resilience is a key factor in the development of coping patterns that play a role in effective adaptation to challenging circumstances.[21] These include the dual challenges of young adulthood, namely emancipation from parental control concurrent with the transition to college and career paths. Resilience generally refers to manifested competence in the context of significant challenges to adaptation or development. Resilient youth have the capacity to "spring back," or to recover rapidly, from the disruptions that they experience. Resilience is, in part, related to the adolescent's disposition, familial strengths and resources, quality of parenting, and stability of the home environment. Three protective factors of resilient adolescents are dispositional and personality features, family cohesion, and the availability of external support systems.[22] A core quality of resilient adolescents is their ability to engage within an extrafamilial context by establishing bonds to prosocial adults outside the family, connecting to prosocial organizations, and attending effective schools.[23] The College Institutes' experiential activities supported and enriched the youth's extrafamilial world through the development of meaningful intergenerational bonds of mentoring, encounters with college faculty and students, and work practice activities in the community. As a result, high school students were exposed to a number of job opportunities in science and technology, including the health and environmental professions and cultural resource management. College students also mentored them in advocacy, community organization, and public communication skills. Once they acquired a repertoire of social and academic skills, the youth engaged with adult residents in support of public environmental issues identified by informed community residents.

Exposure to urban social knowledge, namely science and advocacy, served to increase the youth's environmental and community awareness and academic readiness. Collaboratively involving university faculty and students, high school students, and residents facilitated transmission of social knowledge in support of revitalizing this community. As these efforts focused on social development within a context of neighborhood resiliency, service learning projects not only improved educational outcomes but also served as a catalyst for community building.[24] Intergenerational efforts have demonstrated the capacity of youth to participate in the community-planning process and to become involved in public affairs through Pacoima Beautiful's partnership with local government and nonprofit agencies, such as Project GRAD LA. Together, these organizations are working to improve the chances of youth, encouraging them to move beyond outmoded class-reproduction practices, and embrace newer forms of learning that will help them to express their educational and occupational talents.[25] Their advocacy efforts for social equity and access to public goods, namely environmental and educational quality, compel young people to understand the broad structural contexts that affect their personal, educational, social, and political horizons. The College Institute activities inspired them to fully participate in local-level civic networks and organizations that have their basis in voluntarism, social trust, and reciprocity. In this case, recent immigrants and their children have begun to freely engage in a form of public culture that has until recently only been available to the more privileged families in American society. Enlarging these arenas to include youth issues has thus begun to expand the social capital of community social formations originally developed by transmigrant families in Pacoima to understand the host society and its unfamiliar language, customs, and social institutions and to accept its constraints and opportunities.

MONITORING POLLUTION

Beginning in 1998, Pacoima Beautiful has brought together residents, university environmental health scientists, environmental and other organizations, university service-learning classes, as well as representatives from governmental agencies to address environmental issues in the community. Being able to partner with experts in various fields served to expand the capacity of Pacoima Beautiful as well as build a valuable knowledge bank. As environmental health and environmental justice became a more prominent part of the work of Pacoima Beautiful, it was necessary to enlist the support of those who knew how to address the issues. Pacoima has long suffered from environmental neglect that can likely be blamed for the high rates of environmental health risks and the numerous sources of pollution throughout the area. In addition to freeways, the airport, and a railway line, there are more than 300 industrial sites that have left contaminants behind or continue to pollute the air, soil, and water. Pacoima is home to five U.S. EPA CERCLIS (toxic release) sites, two of which are currently being remediated. Community concerns are, in recent years, focusing on the cumulative impacts from contaminants, such as lead in paint and in the soil, emissions from freeways, commuter planes, diesel fuel from trucks and equipment, older "gross emitting" cars in the community, landfills, and the widespread use of toxic chemicals throughout the community.

Teaming scientists with community residents and youth, the organization created a network that has gathered data in order to understand the effects of environmental hazards on health. The data collection has been coupled with surveys of more than 2,000 residents and merchants. The approach is community-based and community-driven information gathering, following principles of community-based participatory action research.[26] Pacoima Beautiful has worked with UCLA nursing researchers using community-partnered participatory methods to reduce health disparities by training community members to function as lay health advisers to provide health education to other residents.[27] Much like Dutch "science shops," Pacoima Beautiful's research agenda on environmental quality of life is based upon concerns posed by community residents and carried out with local universities.[28] To remain operational, the organization has sought funding from foundations and public agencies with their own agendas and "narratives of legitimation,"[29] such as the U.S. Environmental Protection Agency's (EPA) "environmental justice" agenda, and the U.S. Department of Housing and Urban Development's (HUD) "healthy homes" initiative. However, at no time did Pacoima Beautiful deviate from its own agenda, and there was much foresight in planning well into the future so that, as opportunities came about, the organization was ready to take advantage of them. Strategic planning was an important part of the work of Pacoima Beautiful, dating back to its beginning in 1996. The prospect of partnerships with local nonprofit organizations, including universities, and patronage from public agencies and foundations has inspired dialogues around planning Pacoima Beautiful's future as a "sustainable" organization in a transmigrant community during its early years—a time when the American environmental movement was facing a national debate on issues of population and immigration.[30] The following case demonstrates how the organization initiated its commitment to addressing environmental justice and environmental health issues.

In 1998, the U.S. EPA Environmental Justice Office provided a grant to Pacoima Beautiful in partnership with university-based researchers that focused on increasing residents' awareness of the consequences of toxic dumping within their community and also moved Pacoima Beautiful's staff members and volunteers toward understanding their role in the environmental justice movement.[31] Specifically, the grant was used to expand the partners' efforts in monitoring pollution; to educate residents through a newsletter distributed through neighborhood schools; and to focus on the widespread illegal dumping practices of local residents, businesses, and others who view Pacoima as a dumping ground. The month before the start of the EPA initiative, Pacoima Beautiful worked together with Coro Southern California to train twelve Pacoima Beautiful community inspectors and eight local youth through a three-day intensive leadership program called "Pacoima Plunge." The participants learned how to access city services and developed ways to teach others how to request that illegally dumped items be picked up. Felicia is one of the twelve grassroots leaders to have emerged from the training. As a community inspector, she reports hazardous materials to the appropriate city agencies and has organized cleanup days, grass plantings, and tree plantings. Born and raised in Villanueva Zacatecas, Mexico, Felicia did not receive a formal education. She taught herself how to read and write in Spanish and English to about a third-grade level. She was married when she was nineteen. In 1974, she and her husband Jose came to Los Angeles. They lived in a number of different places, including a room in someone's home. Felicia and Jose saved their money and, with the help of her brother, bought a home. They have lived in their home since 1986. They have four children, ranging in age from five to twenty-four. Felicia became involved in Pacoima Beautiful when she became a volunteer at Pacoima Elementary School and later at Broadous Elementary School. She cared about Pacoima and found that she could make a difference through her participation in Pacoima Beautiful activities. Through Pacoima Beautiful, she participated in the Coro Southern California leadership-training program, TreePeople's "Citizen Forester" classes, the Los Angeles City Human Relations Commission conflict resolution series, a Workforce/Economic Development workshop series, and a prelicensing training program for child care. An especially demanding task was to help conduct surveys in over twenty-one neighborhoods and 240 households. Pacoima Beautiful hired Felicia part-time under its first EPA grant to distribute 3,000 newsletters per month. She distributed the newsletters to all the schools in Pacoima, most of the churches, and many local businesses. With the assistance of Pacoima Beautiful staff, Felicia applied for and received a Neighborhood Matching Grant offered through the City of Los Angeles Department of Public Works. With the small grant, she helped her neighbors to plant grass. Altogether she and her coworkers were responsible for planting thirty parkways. She spent much time following up to make sure that the grass was living and properly cared for. In one case, she helped an elderly woman in the neighborhood by mowing her lawn every two weeks, watering, and cleaning up her house. Felicia also took advantage of a loan program through the city of Los Angeles to get her house repaired. She did this in large part at the request of Pacoima Beautiful staff to see how the program worked so that the staff would know whether to recommend it to other residents. Felicia moved on from Pacoima Beautiful to become the parent center leader at a local middle school. She stays involved with Pacoima Beautiful by helping to recruit residents to become community inspectors. Felicia especially loves getting teenagers involved; in her own words, "all they need is an extra push and attention."

The EPA funding enabled a group of urban studies and planning students from California State University, Northridge (CSUN) to provide environmental training to the community inspectors and to develop an environmental audit of the area. At one of their meetings, the inspectors took the students out to a number of sites where there was evidence of illegal dumping. This firsthand knowledge enabled the students to draft an environmental audit that dealt with environmental problems, industrial-residential relations, enforcement, land use, and zoning. They discussed their draft with the community inspectors, made modifications based upon the group's suggestions, and developed a Spanish-language version of the survey. The students then mapped the sites of environmental pollution in Pacoima and entered the data into a Geographic Information Systems (GIS) database. The GIS is used to visually display results of the community inspector reports and forms the basis of a website containing a map locating pollution risks and hazards, which can be updated continuously and used for reporting purposes. The project was the first step toward Pacoima Beautiful's goal of developing an ongoing community monitoring system for toxic dumping, solid waste disposal, hazardous housing conditions, safety in community parks and residential areas, and environmental health and safety of residents. As a result of this initial partnership, Pacoima Beautiful has undertaken subsequent environmental justice programs for mitigating the effects of lead in homes and toxics in the community.

PROMOTING SAFER HOMES

Pacoima has some of the oldest housing stock in the San Fernando Valley; it is predominantly single-family housing, with over 80 percent of these 22,035 housing units built prior to 1980. Although lead was banned in paint in 1978, many Pacoima residents are potentially exposed because the majority of the housing units were built prior to this time. Additional concerns are the number of children living in the housing and the degraded state of the housing. Children age six and under in Pacoima have the highest probability of adverse health effects from these exposures because they are likely to ingest paint chips and dust that might contain high concentrations of lead. According to data collected by David Jacobs and his associates, about 40 percent of all housing constructed before 1980 in the United States has some lead-based paint and 25 percent has significant lead-based paint.[32] Pacoima Beautiful became interested in addressing the potential threats from lead in Pacoima when, in a February 2000 report, *A Needs Assessment Report for Primary Care Services I*, the Los Angeles County Department of Health Services (LAC DHS) estimated that there was the potential for more than 5,000 children, newborns to age six, to have high levels of lead in their blood.

Currently, an estimated 310,000 of the nation's 20 million children under the age of six have blood lead levels high enough to impair their ability to think, concentrate, and learn, according to the U.S. Centers for Disease Control and Prevention (CDC).[33] Environmental lead exposure has been linked with an increased risk for numerous conditions and diseases that are prevalent in industrialized society, such as reading problems, school failure, delinquent behavior, hearing loss, tooth decay, spontaneous abortions, renal disease, and cardiovascular disease.[34] Exposure to lead can occur from eating food or drinking water that contains lead, spending time in areas where lead-based paint is deteriorating and turning to dust, or working in a job where lead is used. Some current sources of lead, largely of foreign origin, still result in excessive exposures and sometimes intoxication. These include certain folk ceramics, lead in candy wrappers, lead-soldered juice cans, jellied fruits packed in lead-glazed ceramic pots, certain patent medicines, and some traditional home health remedies.[35] Once lead is ingested, it travels through the blood stream and deposits first in the kidneys, then in bones, teeth, and hair. Its half-life in soft tissue averages about forty days and in bones for twenty to thirty years. Most sensitive to lead is the central nervous system, and children are most affected. Children are generally more vulnerable to lead poisoning than adults and most times are exposed by eating lead-based paint chips, chewing on objects painted with lead-based paint, or swallowing house dust or soil that contains lead. The poor and children of color disproportionately suffer from high rates of lead poisoning. About 24 million homes still have a significant lead-based paint hazard. The CDC estimates that 16 percent of children living in older housing are poisoned, compared to 4.4 percent of all children. Exposure to lead is more dangerous for young and unborn children and can affect a child's mental and physical growth. Lead is thought to disrupt hormones and other chemicals in the brain. Research has shown that children exposed to lead poisoning exhibited emotional impairment characterized by impulsive behavior and short attention span. In later years, lead-poisoned children are much more likely to drop out of school, become juvenile delinquents, and engage in criminal and other antisocial behavior.

According to researcher Howard Mielke, a major concern for children's lead exposure "is whether there is a source of lead dust in the environment."[36] Lead levels in soils are usually higher in cities, near roadways, and industries that use lead, and next to homes where crumbling lead paint has fallen into the soil. Soil naturally has small amounts of lead in it, about 50 ppm (parts per million); and about 200–500 ppm of lead is commonly found in city soil. According to the EPA's hazard standard for schoolyard areas, lead levels that are equal to or above 400 ppm by weight in play areas and 1,200 ppm in bare soil in the remainder of the yard are considered hazardous for children. There are indicators that Pacoima's natural environment may exacerbate the exposure to lead dust, as the community is susceptible to high winds during parts of the year. Aerial photos show Pacoima as having the fewest number of trees and ground cover in the San Fernando Valley. Lack of ground cover is especially problematic on open spaces in the community because the dust particles scatter throughout the community. There is no vegetation along the railroad right of way or nearby Whiteman airport to buffer the community from lead dust exposure from transportation sources.

Pacoima Beautiful partnered with faculty and students from CSUN in 1999 to survey the community's knowledge about environmental hazards and health with specific questions on lead. The survey results confirmed the assumption that the community lacked knowledge about health problems associated with lead. From the survey, two efforts were initiated. The first was a coordinated research project organized by Pacoima Beautiful, between 2000 and 2002, bringing together faculty from CSUN, UCI, USC, and UCLA, to understand the potential risks to health associated with lead in two high-risk neighborhoods in Pacoima.[37] The second effort began in 2000 when LAC DHS and Valley Care Community Consortium (VCCC), a community health-planning body, invited Pacoima Beautiful to participate in a four-year grant from the Partnership for the Public's Health (PPH), established in 1999 by the nonprofit Public Health Institute and funded by The California Endowment, to identify a public health issue in the Pacoima community and to build organizational capacity to address the issue. Through the grant, Pacoima Beautiful was able to purchase urgently needed equipment and increase the capacity of existing staff members by providing trainings around environmental health issues. The research project with the universities and the efforts and capacity-building activities through the PPH grant resulted in Pacoima Beautiful starting the "Safer Homes for a Healthy Community" program. The "Safer Homes" program, which is ongoing, helps residents to create healthy homes for their families in order to reduce and prevent environmentally related health problems, including lead poisoning and asthma triggers, such as mold and moisture. In 2002, through LAC DHS, Pacoima Beautiful was invited to apply for and received funding for a pilot project through a scoping grant from the Washington-based Alliance for Healthy Homes, a national, nonprofit, public interest organization working to prevent and eliminate hazards in homes that can harm the health of children, families, and other residents. The scoping grant provided initial protocols for lead sampling in homes.

The grant from the Alliance permitted Pacoima Beautiful to hire four *Promotores*, who were mothers living in the community, to conduct sampling in 100 homes. The *Promotores* received extensive training from CSUN faculty, LAC DHS, Healthy Homes Collaborative staff, Neighborhood Legal Services, and Esperanza Community Housing Corporation. The *Promotores* learned about the importance of intravenous lead testing for children up to the age of six years. They also learned easy and simple ways to make changes in housekeeping activities to minimize lead exposures. Regarding regulation, they began to understand the legal responsibilities of landlords to maintain homes in good condition to minimize the impact of lead. They were taught the methods and criteria for securing structural lead control or reduction opportunities for their homes and the need to use "Lead Safe Work Practices." The four *Promotores* and three other Pacoima Beautiful staff were trained and became lead sampling technicians through an EPA course. Once the *Promotores* received sufficient training and had developed a comfort level with their roles, they began to reach out into the community. They visited the residents in individual and group settings and shared what was learned about lead poisoning prevention as well as asthma triggers and home health hazards. After some time, the community members learned to trust the *Promotores*. Through the Alliance for Healthy Homes pilot project, the *Promotores* met with ninety-six families, although eighty-eight families completed the entire process; thirty-four of the eighty-eight homes tested had high levels of lead. Much of the housing visited by the *Promotores* was severely overcrowded and degraded, with multiple families living in single-family residences and ancillary structures, including garages and attics of garages. However, many of the owners of rooms and garages being used as rental properties were related to their tenants, making it difficult for the residents to request changes. Most housing enforcement centers on tenants rights in apartments, not on tenants in single-family housing; and many residents were either unaware or mistrustful of the county and service organizations and the services they provide. In their discussions with parents, they learned that only about 25 percent of the children eligible for free lead testing through government assistance programs were in fact being tested for lead. Many parents did not actively seek out blood testing for lead, partly because their physicians were not recommending that they do so. Moreover, health care providers did not inform parents about lead prevention and of the need to test their children who had not exceeded national thresholds.

The *Promotores* had provided a valuable service to the community residents; however, on their own, they could not reach the numbers that needed to be reached. Therefore, Pacoima Beautiful, in partnership with VCCC and LAC DHS, actively sought ways to expand the knowledge base throughout the community. First, the Alliance for Healthy Homes, through its Community Environmental Health Resource Center, provided funding to Pacoima Beautiful to implement a rigorous dust sampling protocol, based on EPA criteria, to work with 225 families in Pacoima over a two-year period. Second, VCCC formed an Environmental Health Committee, consisting of LAC DHS, Northeast Valley Health Corporation, a local federally qualified health center, Neighborhood Legal Services, and other organizations that met regularly to discuss what was being learned about lead and lead poisoning in Pacoima. Third, the *Promotores* developed and refined their communication and presentation skills and, through the CEHRC pilot project, began outreach to groups of parents in most of the schools and parent centers in Pacoima. In 2003, PB, LAC DHS, and VCCC hosted an Environmental Health Roundtable for forty community stakeholders to share what was learned about environmental health issues. A primary focus of the roundtable was lead and lead poisoning. The roundtable produced a partnership to address lead issues in Pacoima. The first activity of the partnership was to apply for the EPA Collaborative Problem Solving (CPS) Grant. Writing the CPS grant proposal provided the partners with an opportunity to address specific issues with regard to lead and lead poisoning as well as serve as a device for sharing knowledge throughout the community. Pacoima Beautiful and partners based the project goals and strategy for the CPS grant proposal on the findings from both the work done previously by the partners and input from residents. The CPS grant focused on efforts to increase lead blood-screening rates of children ages six and under. The project sought to integrate lead hazard control with other community efforts and also to clearly identify lead hazards in high-risk neighborhoods and present workable solutions to reduce the lead burden. This would be done by analyzing and synthesizing current data, and then convening a stakeholder forum regarding lead poisoning and community development. In addition, Pacoima Beautiful and its partners would participate in efforts to effectively train the Los Angeles City Building and Safety Department to enforce lead-safe work repair practices to pre-1978 housing and to educate contractors, workers, landlords, and homeowners in lead-safe work practices and work with the city government to develop a housing registry for lead-free homes and apartments.

The work done through the EPA Environmental Justice CPS grant demonstrated a particularly high degree of success in dividing the above goals into detailed objectives that were each agreed to and achieved by one or more specific project partners or other stakeholders. In addition, these detailed objectives also were incorporated into a stepwise, detailed, comprehensive strategy for achieving each of the three project goals. The project was effective in encouraging the affected community to participate in the various activities that were presented in the project work plan. Much of this success can be attributed to the *Promotores* who provided a vital, two-way communications link between the project and community members. The project's success can also be attributed to the variety and depth of training and continuing support provided to the *Promotores* by the partners who ensured that the these lay health educators carried a high degree of knowledge about available resources for addressing a wide variety of issues in the community. In-depth knowledge of lead-related issues alone would not be sufficient to sustain the long-term mutual value and trust between the *Promotores* and the Pacoima community. This sense of trust came about by, initially, convening all of the known stakeholders as part of the grant-writing process and reaching consensus on the nature of the problem and on how to conduct the project prior to the beginning of the project. Specific community input was obtained and incorporated into the grant through nine focus groups involving 105 residents. Moreover, the *Promotores* are trusted and accepted in the community, and are trained by other stakeholders to provide the abovementioned two-way link to the needs of the community and the solutions to those needs. As stated by a key Pacoima Beautiful staff member, Leticia Rojas, the "level of trust and transparency regarding local environmental health issues is the most critical component in this process for the collaboration. Without this credibility, the other partners would have to expend considerable resources and effort to attain this level of trust."

Early identification of the issue by a community-based organization helped to engage others to address the issue and sustain the effort and make it grow. Pacoima Beautiful identified and worked closely with all stakeholders to reach a consensus on the three project goals, which allowed them to collaborate on an effective strategy that integrated the unique contributions that were available from the numerous partner organizations. Following this was the need to identify appropriate partners. Each of the partners has different constituencies so that the work done to prevent lead poisoning was spread in many different venues throughout the community: university faculty took the information gathered by the *Promotores* and the federally qualified health center and analyzed and mapped the data; the health center then provided information to its physicians and patients, specifically women, infants and children program recipients; the county health agency and a regional "healthy homes" collaborative provided technical information on lead screening tests and methods for lead exposure avoidance; the regional community health planning body provided the links to health care providers; and the regional legal services agency provided legal advice on issues such as landlord responsibilities and methods for improving enforcement of lead-free repair laws. In addition, the partners had the benefit of university-based evaluators who continued to evaluate the project during the process of planning and implementation. Once identified, considerable attention was given to the clarification of each partner's role. Pacoima Beautiful took it upon itself to communicate actively and clearly with the partners at the outset of the project to eliminate any potential misunderstandings with respect to the project goals and other data that each partner might want to collect during the project to satisfy their specific needs. During these early communications, the organization's staff maintained their role as the key decision makers with regard to project scope and direction. Throughout was the need for frequent clarifications of the issue and potential resolutions. Pacoima Beautiful served as the clearinghouse for information and data and then would pass it on to the partners. In that capacity, the organization could keep the partners informed on the current status of their main objectives as the partners worked to attain their part in the project goals. In the end, the partnership stayed together through an EPA Community Action for a Renewed Environment (CARE) program grant to identify toxics in the community, to address specific issues, such as the monitoring of all diesel sources in the community, and to extend the childhood lead-poisoning prevention and abatement work into other communities. The partnership—of public and nonprofit organizations, and of professional experts and lay advocates—is thus expanding its work beyond lead to include other toxic risks in the community, such as facilities listed in the U.S. EPA's Toxic Release Inventory (TRI), and it is poised to identify potential toxic sites through site screenings in order to develop an understanding of the impact of toxics on the health of Pacoima residents.

BUILDING A COMPETENT COMMUNITY

Pacoima Beautiful was launched in a locale where there is ongoing community organization and planning, and where regional and national educational reform groups and community-based organizations are partnering on behalf of academic and community-building efforts. These collaborative efforts have combined informal education and dialogue, following Paulo Freire's educational practice, with John Dewey's concern with experience and reflection as tools for self-awareness and "effective self-direction," beginning with the public schools where the initial exposure of children and their parents to urban professional knowledge has served as a catalyst for community building as an intergenerational process.[38] Therefore, strategies for achieving comprehensive community building have been predicated on the need to build stable and self-sustaining families as the first step to improving the quality of life in the community. The community-building initiative in Pacoima, based upon existing models of collaborative "best practices," combined the experience of schools, community-based organizations, foundations, and public agencies with local public higher education institutions' considerable expertise and resources.[39] From the beginning, the intent was to revitalize Pacoima as a "competent community," one in which all human service needs are addressed.[40] To accomplish this goal, a new form of place-focused politics is essential for re-

constructing the civic cultures of deindustrialized cities and urban neighborhoods remade by transnational migration. Once municipal leaders and residents alike view their communities or cities "as ordinary places for ordinary
people,"[41] rather than a mix of settings and social arrangements privileging
urban elites, they will be closer to establishing new forms of governance to
replace ineffective bureaucracies.

The example of Pacoima Beautiful, and its various collaborative efforts
along the way, illustrate how local-level coalitions and collaborations have allied business, government, nonprofits, and universities with neighborhood associations to partner with city governments in school reform, children's services, urban improvements, and health care. A strong tradition of voluntary
social action is an effective way of identifying and resolving a variety of
problems. In recent decades, coalitions on behalf of environmental justice,
fair housing, and equitable health care have lobbied hard for the needs of their
stakeholders. During an era of diminishing public spending on social goods,
such as infrastructure, health care, and environmental protection, coalitions
such as those discussed above have become important advocates on behalf of
their constituencies. It may be difficult, at best, to refocus single-issue advocacy groups to a broader concern for community building. Nevertheless,
those involved in community-based planning should be alert to the usefulness
of enlisting the altruism and vision of the leadership of these organizations.
Neighborhood involvement is also crucial to community-building efforts.
Members of neighborhood associations, such as neighborhood watch groups,
that become educated and informed about quality-of-life issues such as neighborhood safety, community toxics, and lead poisoning will be cognizant of
where knowledge and help might be found. As these cases indicate, the leadership and participation by residents, including youth, is important in rebuilding the community. Each of the initiatives was publicly discussed in
meetings of the various nonprofit organizations' leadership and community
advisory boards, and among neighborhood residents. Outside experts who
participated in these initiatives have had to be very sensitive to the autonomy
and leadership issues involved in the community-building model embraced
by these organizations. Such collaborative planning discloses unexplored
strategies and solutions to existing problems and allows the residents to develop sensitivities toward the early detection of problems. Community-based
planning parallels community-based research involving the collaboration of
lay community members and experts to produce new knowledge for social
change.[42] This practice carries on the work of community-development researchers so influential in creating the philosophical underpinnings for America's urban agenda since the late 1960s.[43] As "action researchers," they valued the involvement of community residents in all aspects of need and data

analysis so that when action strategies are developed, the people most affected by their consequences will have a substantial investment in the action.[44] Their approach to urban transformation also promises some assurance that community residents will continue to be participants over the long term.

NOTES

1. Leonard Pitt and Dale Pitt, *Los Angeles A to Z: An Encyclopedia of City and County* (Berkeley: University of California Press, 1997), 375.

2. Carl Johnson and Jim Morrison, *Key Issue Papers on Community Building: United Ways' Community Capacity Building Stories* (Alexandria, VA: United Way of America, 1996).

3. Lisa Villarreal and Joanne Bookmyer, *Community-School Partnerships: The Living Legacy of Healthy Start*, What Works Policy Brief (Sacramento, CA: Foundation Consortium for California's Children and Youth, 2004).

4. Matt Oppenheim, "The Critical Place of Community Development in School Transformation: The Story of the Vaughn Family Center and Pacoima Urban Village," *Teacher Education Quarterly* 26 (1999): 135–57.

5. Marsha Sharp, *Foundation Collaborations: Incubators for Change?* Research Report 14 (Los Angeles: The Center on Philanthropy and Public Policy, University of Southern California, 2002).

6. Robert J. Chaskin, *Lessons Learned from the Implementation of the Neighborhood and Family Initiative: A Summary of Findings* (Chicago: Chapin Hall Center for Children at the University of Chicago, 2001).

7. Sharon Milligan, Claudia Coulton, Peter York, and Ronald Register, "Implementing a Theory of Change Evaluation in the Cleveland Community-Building Initiative: A Case Study," in *New Approaches to Evaluating Community Initiatives: Concepts, Methods and Contexts*, edited by James P. Connell et al. (Washington, DC: Aspen Institute, 1995).

8. Arthur McCaffrey and Christine W. Letts, *Los Angeles Urban Funders*, Kennedy School of Government Case Program, CR16-03-1682.0 (Cambridge, MA: John F. Kennedy School of Government, Harvard University, 2003).

9. Philliber Research Associates, *Pacoima California: A Comparison of Data on Businesses and Residents, 2001 through 2005: The Final Report* (Accord, NY: Philliber Research Associates, 2006).

10. Prudence Brown, Robert Chaskin, Ralph Hamilton, and Harold Richmond, *Toward Greater Effectiveness in Community Change: Challenges and Responses for Philanthropy* (Chicago: Chapin Hall Center for Children at the University of Chicago, 2003).

11. Pacoima Steering Committee, *The Pacoima Model: Systems Integration and Community Change* (Los Angeles: Los Angeles Urban Funders, 2002).

12. Richard F. Roberts, *Collaboration, Change Agents, Case Management, Parent Involvement, School Reform, and Community Development in a California Healthy*

Start Collaborative, 1993–1998. Master's thesis, California State University, Los Angeles, 1998.

13. Gregory D. Squires and Charles E. Kubrin, "Privileged Places: Race, Uneven Development and the Geography of Opportunity in Urban America," *Urban Studies* 42 (2005): 47–68.

14. Tamara L. Schomber, Julie Anderson, Patricia M. Berger, Tom B. Brown, and Robert O. Zdenek, "A Place to Go: United Way as Community Builders during Crisis Response," *Community* 4 (2001): 20–25.

15. Xavier de Souza Briggs, *Bridging Networks, Social Capital, and Racial Segregation in America*, Kennedy School of Government Faculty Research Working Paper Series RWP02-011 (Cambridge, MA: John F. Kennedy School of Government, Harvard University, 2003).

16. Sonia Giordani, "War Gave Salvadoran New Home, Direction," *Los Angeles Daily News*, valley edition, July 4, 2002, sec. N.

17. Kennedy Smith, Kate Joncas, and Bill Parrish, *Revitalizing Downtown: The Professional's Guide to the Main Street Approach* (Washington, DC: National Main Street Center, National Trust for Historic Preservation, 1996).

18. Project GRAD, *Project GRAD: Working to Close the Academic Achievement Gap* (Houston, TX: Project GRAD, 2003).

19. Ford Foundation, "President's Message," in *2000 Annual Report* (New York: Ford Foundation, 2001).

20. National Center for Education Statistics, *The Nation's Report Card: Science 2000*, NCES 2003-453, by Christine Y. O'Sullivan, Mary A. Lauko, Wendy S. Grigg, Jiahe Qian, and Jinming Zhang (Washington, DC: U.S. Department of Education, Institute of Educational Sciences, 2002).

21. Michael Rutter, "Protective Factors in Children's Response to Stress and Disadvantage," in *Social Competence in Children*, edited by Martha W. Kent and Jon E. Rolf (Hanover, NH: University Press of New England, 1979), 49–74.

22. Norman Garmezy, Ann Masten, Lynn Nordstrom, and Michael Ferrarese, "The Nature of Competence in Normal and Deviant Children," in *Social Competence in Children*, edited by Martha W. Kent and Jon E. Rolf (Hanover, NH: University Press of New England, 1979), 23–43; Norman Garmezy and Ann S. Masten, "Chronic Adversities," in *Child and Adolescent Psychiatry*, 3rd ed., edited by Michael Rutter, L. Herzov, and Eric Taylor (Oxford: Blackwell Scientific, 1994), 191–208.

23. Ann S. Masten and J. Douglas Coatsworth, "The Development of Competence in Favorable and Unfavorable Environments: Lessons from Research on Successful Children," *American Psychologist* 53 (1998): 205–20.

24. Colin Ward, *The Child in the City* (New York: Pantheon, 1978); David Nasaw, *Children of the City: At Work and Play* (Garden City, NY: Doubleday, 1985); Henry L. Lennard and Suzanne H. Crowhurst Lennard, *The Forgotten Child: Cities for the Well-Being of Children* (Carmel, CA: Gondolier Press, 2001).

25. Paul Willis, *Learning to Labor: How Working Class Kids Get Working Class Jobs* (New York: Columbia University Press, 1977); Ramona Mullahey, Yve Susskind, and Barry Checkoway, *Youth Participation in Community Planning* (Chicago: American Planning Association, 1999).

26. The Field Museum, *Collaborative Research: A Practical Introduction to Participatory Action Research (PAR) for Communities and Scholars* (Chicago: Center for Cultural Understanding and Change, The Field Museum, 2006).

27. Sue Kim, Jacquelyn Haak Flaskerud, Deborah Koniak-Griffin, and Elizabeth L. Dixon, "Using Community-Partnered Participatory Research to Address Health Disparities in a Latino Community," *Journal of Professional Nursing* 21 (2005): 199–209.

28. Richard E. Sclove, "Putting Science to Work in Communities," *The Chronicle of Higher Education* 41:29 (1995): B1–B3; Richard E. Sclove, "Town Meetings on Technology," *Technology Review* 99 (1996): 24–31; Richard E. Sclove, Madeleine L. Scammell, and Breena Holland, *Community-Based Research in the United States: An Introductory Reconnaissance, Including Twelve Case Studies and Comparison with the Dutch Science Shops and the Mainstream American Research System* (Amherst, MA: The Loka Institute, 1998).

29. Jean-Francois Lyotard, *The Postmodern Condition: A Report on Knowledge* (Minneapolis: University of Minnesota Press, 1984); for an anthropological perspective, see Peter Dobkin Hall, "Blurred Boundaries, Hybrids, and Changelings: The Fortunes of Nonprofit Organizations in the Late Twentieth Century," in *Critical Anthropology Now: Unexpected Contexts, Shifting Constituencies, Changing Agendas*, edited by George E. Marcus (Santa Fe, NM: School of American Research Press, 1999), 147–202.

30. Ben Zuckerman, "The Sierra Club Immigration Debate: National Implications," *Population and Environment* 20 (1999): 401–12.

31. Daniel Faber, ed., *The Struggle for Ecological Democracy: Environmental Justice Movements in the United States* (New York: Guilford Press, 1998); Robert Gottlieb, *Environmentalism Unbound: Exploring New Pathways for Change* (Cambridge, MA: MIT Press, 2001); Robert D. Bullard, Paul Mohai, Robin Saha, and Beverly Wright, *Toxic Wastes and Race at Twenty: 1987–2007—Grassroots Struggles to Dismantle Environmental Racism in the United States* (Washington, DC: National Council of Churches of Christ, March 2007).

32. David Jacobs, Robert P. Clickner, Joey Y. Zhou, Susan M. Vlet, David A. Marker, John W. Rogers, Darryl C. Zeldin, Pamela Broene, and Warren Friedman, "The Prevalence of Lead-Based Paint Hazards in U.S. Housing," *Environmental Health Perspectives* 110 (2002): A599–A606.

33. U.S. Department of Health and Human Services, Centers for Disease Control and Prevention, Lead Poisoning Prevention Program: www.cdc.gov/nceh/lead/.

34. Bruce P. Lanphear, Richard Hornung, Jane Khoury, Kimberly Yolton, Peter Baghurst, David C. Bellinger, Richard L. Canfield, Kim N. Dietrich, Robert Bornschein, Tom Greene, Stephen J. Rothenberg, Herbert L. Needleman, Lourdes Schnaas, Gail Wasserman, Joseph Graziano, and Russell Roberts, "Low-Level Environmental Lead Exposure and Children's Intellectual Function: An International Pooled Analysis," *Environmental Health Perspectives* 113 (2005): 894–99.

35. R. T. Trotter II, "A Case of Lead Poisoning from Folk Remedies in Mexican American Communities," in *Understanding and Applying Medical Anthropology*, edited by Peter J. Brown (Mountain View, CA: Mayfield, 1998), 279–86.

36. Howard W. Mielke, "Lead in the Inner Cities," *American Scientist* 87 (1999): 62.

37. Raul P. Lejano and Jonathon E. Ericson, "Tragedy of the Temporal Commons: Soil-Bound Lead and the Anachronicity of Risk," *Journal of Environmental Planning and Management* 48 (2005): 301–20.

38. Paulo Freire, "Cultural Action and Conscientization," in *The Politics of Education: Culture, Power, and Liberation*, translated by Donaldo Macedo (South Hadley, MA: Bergin and Garvey, 1985), 66–96; Eugene Rochberg-Halton, "Inquiry and the Pragmatic Attitude," in *Meaning and Modernity: Social Theory in the Pragmatic Attitude* (Chicago: University of Chicago Press, 1986), 3–21; on the public school and the playground, see Lawrence A. Cremin, *The Transformation of the School: Progressivism in American Education, 1876–1957* (New York: Random House, 1961); Dominick Cavallo, *Muscles and Morals: Organized Playgrounds and Urban Reform, 1880–1920* (Philadelphia: University of Pennsylvania Press, 1981).

39. John P. Kreitzmann and John L. McKnight, *Building Communities from the Inside Out: A Path Toward Finding and Mobilizing a Community's Assets* (Evanston, IL: Institute for Policy Research, Northwestern University, 1993); G. Thomas Kingsley, Joseph B. McNeely, and James O. Gibson, *Community Building: Coming of Age* (Washington, DC: The Development Training Institute, Inc. and the Urban Institute, 1997); Bennett Harrison and Marcus Weiss, *Workforce Development Networks: Community-Based Organizations and Regional Alliances* (Thousand Oaks, CA: Sage, 1998); Carmen Sirianni and Lewis Friedland, *Civic Innovation in America: Community Empowerment, Public Policy, and the Movement for Civic Renewal* (Berkeley: University of California Press, 2001).

40. Ira Iscoe, "Community Psychology and the Competent Community," *American Psychologist* 29 (1974): 607–13; Ira Iscoe, "Towards a Viable Community Health Psychology: Caveats from the Experience of the Community Mental Health Movement," *American Psychologist* 37 (1982): 961–65.

41. Wallace Katz, "Make Gotham Governable," *Commonweal*, November 19, 1993, 6.

42. Danny Murphy, Madeleine Scammell, and Richard Sclove, *Doing Community-Based Research: A Reader* (Amherst, MA: Loka Institute, 1997).

43. Warren G. Bennis, Kenneth Benne, and Robert Chin, *The Planning of Change*, 4th ed. (New York: Holt, Rinehart and Winston, 1985); Roland L. Warren, "The Sociology of Knowledge and the Problems of the Inner Cities," *Social Science Quarterly* 52 (1971): 468–85.

44. Ernest T. Stringer, *Action Research*, 3rd ed. (Thousand Oaks, CA: Sage, 2007).

Chapter Eight

Common Worlds

ARENAS AS CONTEXTS FOR ACTION

The case studies in this book describe the organizational frameworks devised to resolve personal and public issues arising from contemporary crises and the roots of these organized efforts in the period between the 1890s and the 1920s, when the United States was, arguably, a "developing country."[1] These cases within contemporary "arenas" convey the varieties of decision making and strategic coping that members of local communities used in renegotiating their social worlds after a crisis. Arenas are organizational frameworks central to the resolution of issues arising from social and cultural change. They served as forums to steer work organizations through the crisis of rapid industrialization in the late nineteenth century, when the dual revolutions of technology and information processing were transforming the United States from a developing country to an industrial power. For just as the technological and economic innovations of the second industrial revolution rationalized production and distribution techniques in the material economy, the "control revolution" provided new modes of information processing and communication technology to transform the cognitive or symbolic direction of an enterprise.[2] During this transition from craft to mass production, arenas provided a social context for workers to practice strategic coping. By this I mean the task of renegotiating and reframing both their occupational techniques and their world orientations in light of dramatic technological changes.[3] However, industrial workplaces were not the only domains where arenas served to reorganize social arrangements in the midst of social crisis. Rationality and negotiation are central to action within arenas, the cultural settings crucial to maintenance of a public sphere where citizens can freely engage in political discourse and debate over common concerns.[4] Since the late nineteenth

century, numerous arenas have emerged in American communities where issues related to the quality of life, including work, housing, the environment,
and health care, are debated.[5] Within these arenas, experts as well as laypersons have engaged in public controversies to resolve disputes over competing
claims for equity and greater access to common resources. The styles of action within these arenas surround questions of identity, rights, and strategic
behavior, which are debated, negotiated, manipulated, and even coerced by
their members.[6] Within an arena, participants argue over what action to take.
These disagreements involve members of social worlds, however small, in
debates about policy. In smaller arenas, differences can usually be resolved in
a timely manner; however, arguments will often persist over generations in
larger arenas, such as the debates over civil rights, urban disorder, health care,
and the environment.

For over a century, frequently acrimonious debates over policy have taken
place within diverse public locales, from schools and union halls to municipal and voluntary agencies, and they point to a distinct style of action based
upon interaction.[7] The form of social activity emerging from ongoing negotiation of meaning within these diverse environments in part accounts for the
communitarian dimension of American culture.[8] John Dewey and his fellow
pragmatists considered such interaction within arenas as central to the construction and transformation of social "worlds."[9] The pragmatic theory of action encompasses the need for the interpretation of meaning as a process for
overcoming roadblocks, whether environmental or situational, that impede
the flow of routine activity within these worlds. Built into their scheme is the
primacy of reflection upon and discussion of alternative paths of action as interactive processes necessary for transforming the course of everyday life. By
taking time to review various options and making choices among the alternatives, a course of action could be renegotiated, thereby permitting routine action to continue, presumably until the next perturbation.[10] The definition of an
issue by experts, by laypersons, or by both in partnership, opens a domain
within the larger society where the issue continues to be argued in arenas beyond those of its founding constituencies. Organizations then form, occupy
the niche, and extend the debate across multiple constituencies for purposes
of realizing mutual benefit. Many issues, such as jobs and health care, cut
across policy arenas, as these are often linked to the human rights concerns of
new immigrants and other marginal groups, or the relationship between housing and the environment in disadvantaged neighborhoods. These networks of
civic engagement, especially the lay-founded organizations, have continuously defined the nature and quality of American public life and institutions,
most significantly during periods of civic inventiveness, such as the late nineteenth century, when new organizations formed to mediate the painful effects

of industrialization, urbanization, and immigration. Since that time, lay-oriented organizations have supported their members' active engagement in the public realm and successfully inculcated civic virtues, such as activism and citizen participation. Civic networks and other mutual help organizations, which have their basis in voluntarism, social trust, and reciprocity, are forms of social capital that facilitate cooperation and communication and are needed to resolve the myriad dilemmas of collective action.[11]

The continued growth of social capital will require broader citizen access to electronically transmitted information and interactive communication technologies to stimulate interest in local affairs and participation in national policy dialogues. Nowhere is this more apparent than in the widening gap between information elites, such as scientists and policy makers, and the lay public with respect to knowledge about and access to computing and networked communication resources. The newer information and communication technologies, such as electronic mail systems, conferencing, and data transmission, are spreading rapidly throughout the scientific research community. National and global networks of information, including the exchange of data and research findings, define the communications revolution in science. Issues surrounding privacy, confidentiality of data, security, and access are central to a scientific culture increasingly dependent upon computer-mediated communication. Advanced communication strategies presently support national and international consortia of researchers based at universities, federal agencies, and nonprofit research organizations. To keep consortia of geographically dispersed investigators functioning efficiently, research programs have pursued an information resources agenda to encourage broad communication and collaboration. As strategic resources, these information flows have become key sources of power, influence, and competitive advantage in the scientific enterprise. Large research programs that routinely use computer-mediated communication to frame and to maintain everyday interaction also settle controversies within "wired," or electronic, arenas. As technologies promoting instantaneous information and data exchange diffuse across the scientific research community, virtual arenas are emerging within research programs to debate various scientific and policy issues. Within these arenas, scientists engage in controversies and resolve disputes surrounding theoretical and research claims; they also approach pragmatic concerns about resources, funding, and, increasingly, public reactions to their work. The rapid growth in ownership of personal computers and increasing access by laypersons to networked communication technologies, including commercial e-mail and the Internet, has led to the formation of diverse lay interest groups, or "virtual communities." These are communities of frequently geographically dispersed individuals, linked together by interactive communication, who share a common concern. Similar to arenas sustained by scientific and policy elites, lay electronic networks engage and affiliate participants in spontaneous, but also considered, discussion and debate around clearly meaningful issues. Despite the substantial early apprehension of social scientists that computer-mediated communication would further isolate individuals and restrict their participation in the public sphere, alliances built electronically appear to strengthen social and civic ties, but also may blur many visually defined boundaries based on race, class, gender, and disability. Electronic alliances can potentially sustain citizen participation within an emerging federalism that increasingly requires the advice of laypersons in the development of scientific and technological policies. Culture-centered computing, which places humans at the center of computing technology and information systems, also values collaborations between professionals and the lay public on behalf of social policies linked to the course of computerization in communities worldwide.[12] The kinds of concerns that have invited affiliation and reinforced membership in electronic civic networks include improved delivery of government services, community building, access to information, political participation, and the restructuring of nonprofit and community-based organizations.[13] Locally initiated networks in Los Angeles, New York, Seattle, Boston, and San Francisco have used forms of "wired democracy" to inspire their members to share ideas, gain benefits, and solve problems. The success of these civic networks derives from the use of e-mail and other interactive features of the electronic environment to stimulate publicly oriented activity by linking individuals and directing them toward opportunities for voluntary social action.

LAY KNOWLEDGE IN A SPECIALIZED SOCIETY

Only recently have expert-run organizations begun to fully incorporate certain lay initiatives, chiefly in consultative roles, to give voice to concerns over the direction and outcome of professional interventions. This move toward pluralism was stimulated by criticism, from both professionals and laypersons, that many organizations were slow to modify their practices to reflect contemporary ethical and political concerns. To facilitate change, a few professionals set out to foster significant lay participation in governance activities and instill in their colleagues greater respect for the lay "voice." Federal agencies, such as the National Institutes of Health, require nonscientists to help set research and development priorities and community-based participatory action research agendas. Lay members on these panels often find themselves marginalized or intimidated as a result of their limited knowledge of the technical aspects of the research or social program under review. Alternatively, dual expert and lay advisory panels have been established, the latter supported by expert facilitators, to yield two sets of recommendations for policy direction.[14] A policy arena may be carved out by experts who take the initiative and advocate on behalf of a given constituency, for example planners for housing in a blighted neighborhood, labor leaders for improved conditions in an unorganized workplace, scientists for environmental action in communities on a polluted lakefront or river basin, attorneys for human rights in an immigrant enclave, or physicians for greater access to services for a chronically ill patient population. The ensuing debate may be external to the participation of representatives from the affected constituency, and partisan experts on both sides of the issue will often seek to enlist the support of community members. However, difficulties will often arise when lay citizens sit down with experts to discuss a project's social implications or technical feasibility. Lay members of a community may have already established their own arena around an issue. They usually form an alliance with experts only when members perceive an issue as a collective good that they can identify with as their own and consider worth defending against the threats from competing groups.[15] For example, planners and residents of low-income neighborhoods in a Northeastern city organized to protest urban renewal efforts in the face of the threat to their preexisting homes and neighborhoods, which were viewed as collective goods. By contrast, despite the initiatives of health care activists, low-income residents were not as eager to mobilize on behalf of the creation of health care facilities, for they viewed health care as an individual or noncollective good. Only when they perceived these facilities as potential job centers, did they organize on behalf of health care as a collective good, albeit one that carried individual incentives.[16]

Collective goods, such as health care, education, social services, public culture, city building, and public transportation, are "indivisible in that their benefits accrue to society at large."[17] However, many late-capitalist societies foster symptoms of immaturity, as with the case of "planned domestic colonization" when material goods and costly services are disproportionately utilized by certain individuals, resulting in an undersupply of "social overhead capital," or *common* resources.[18] As collective goods and services, these resources are not distributed through the market, but rather through public organizations. Because common resources are not owned by any individual, it will always require collective action to mobilize demand for greater access to them. Mature societies have recently undertaken to address inequities of both knowledge of and access to collective resources through initiatives fostering certain forms of lay involvement in the direction of publicly funded science and technology programs, including health care, information services, city building, and agriculture. The collaboration of experts and laypersons on technology assessment panels in Europe provides a model of lay participation in decision making concerning delivery of a variety of public goods. The Danish government has established citizen tribunals where ordinary citizens sit together in a consensus conference to listen to presentations by diverse experts, question them, deliberate among themselves, and produce a set of recommendations. The Danish model specifies a process of expert-layperson relations that establishes a forum to consider the voices of experts in both the technical and social dimensions of a particular technology, but also those of organized interest or stakeholder groups. However, in all cases, the final set of recommendations is left to the judgments of the informed citizens who sit on the public tribunal.[19] In the United States, consensus methods have been used by technical experts to evaluate and to solve problems in controversial areas of medicine and technology. The National Institutes of Health panels have used consensus strategies to generate state-of-the-art opinions for purposes of evaluating and setting standards of quality for certain medical and surgical procedures. In contrast to the Danish process, American consensus panels bring together representative professionals who, facilitated by objective and skilled leaders, engage in a group process that yields findings that are "clear and specific guides to action."[20]

In the area of housing and neighborhood development, federal and private funders, such as the Department of Housing and Urban Development, the Ford Foundation, and the Rockefeller Foundation, have sponsored expert lay collaborations on behalf of various community-building strategies. Over the past few decades, the community development field has been divided between two approaches to the revitalization of urban neighborhoods.[21] The first, a "place-based" strategy, centers on improving the physical infrastructure and quality of life through the building of affordable housing and business districts. The second, a "people-based" strategy, focuses on both developing residents' job skills and building networks to enhance their employability, as well as encouraging successful individuals to "escape" from disadvantaged communities. Recently, a third strategy, that of "community building," enhances both "people" and "place" by expanding the skills of individuals that link them to the regional economy, thereby building up the "social infrastructure" of a neighborhood and encouraging successful residents to remain within their community. This approach, which relies upon close working relationships between experts and lay persons, has proven successful when the partnerships forged between local government, community organizations, foundations, the business community, and the residents themselves are nurtured and sustained.

LOCAL KNOWLEDGE AND THE PUBLIC SPHERE

What appears to be "traditional" about the lay forms of civic community discussed in this book is the reliance upon a distinct type of knowledge that differs from, yet is supportive of, the universalistic assumptions of the Enlightenment. Clifford Geertz refers to this way of knowing as "local knowledge," and contends that this form of "fugitive truth" can still be derived from contemporary practices, such as politics, law, ethnography, and poetry, as all are "crafts of place" and "are alike absorbed with the artisan task of seeing broad principles in parochial facts."[22] James Scott, who, like Geertz, has studied Southeast Asian agrarian societies, observed a form of local knowledge in peasant economic, social, and moral arrangements. In the local economies of lower Burma and Vietnam, Scott found a "subsistence ethic"—or a right to a minimal guaranteed return on the harvest as a hedge against food shortages—embedded in the economic practices and social exchange relations of peasant community life.[23] Once members of these communities perceived their moral economies, based upon the right to subsistence, to have been violated by new forms of economic patronage and state-supported reforms, they mobilized into radical parties and peasant unions. In most Western societies, local knowledge has been marginalized by the dynamics of modernization, which required both a readiness for displacement, or social and technological mobility, and an acceptance of a cosmopolitan outlook. The radical transformations of modernity, including advanced transportation, communication, and information technologies, together with the demands for efficiency and speed in economic behavior, also required a new vocabulary to match the organizational frames emerging with industrialism. During this period, the discourse of local knowledge, with its roots in nineteenth-century Romanticism, was relegated to "a compensatory rhetoric" that extolled the pastoral and aesthetic pleasures of localism against the dislocations of modernity.[24] Viewing the city and the countryside as shaped by a common history, Raymond Williams cites the false dichotomy underlying so much of contemporary imagery, the "unalienated experience of an imagined rural past contrasted with the "realistic experience" projected onto an urban future.[25] In our own time, a period recently referred to as "late capitalism," "post-Fordism," and "high modernity," we have only begun to appreciate how local traditions—often inherited from our agrarian or preindustrial past—are embedded, along with modern elements, within postmodern cultural forms, much as anthropologists and others have found elements of the local in the modern civic cultures of diverse societies throughout the world.[26]

Sustainable development is an area where local knowledge has been instrumental in the reinvention of communities transformed by global processes.

The concept of sustainability holds that the social, economic, and environmental factors within human communities must be viewed interactively and systematically. The World Commission on Environment and Development defines sustainable development as meeting the needs of the present without compromising the ability of future generations to meet their own needs.[27] In 1996, an international group of practitioners and researchers met in Bellagio, Italy, to develop new ways to measure and assess progress toward sustainable development. The Bellagio Principles serve as guidelines for the whole of the assessment process, including the choice and design of indicators, their interpretation, and communication of the results.[28] Although broadly conceived, the pursuit of sustainable development is a local practice because every community has different needs and quality-of-life concerns. Despite local variation, the participation of ordinary citizens, or "deliberative democracy," remains constant across the sustainable community movement. In rural areas undergoing rapid development and urban areas transformed by planning, renewal, and clearance, new partnerships are forming on behalf of sustainable development.[29] Residents and state and nongovernmental organization experts are partnering to design indicators and to monitor land, labor, housing, health, and other quality-of-life concerns. Civic engagement by ordinary residents is essential, as local people have practical experience and bring important intuitive insights to the tasks of indicator design and monitoring, as practiced in the community-based sustainability indicator design movement.[30] For communities pursuing a sustainable path, a new way of thinking—whole systems thinking—will be necessary. This style of thinking informs bioregionalism, a concept based on ecological principles and a sense of "vernacular culture," that is voluntary and self-organizing in nature.[31] Bioregionalists envision a more equitable relationship between human and natural systems through reorganizing society around common ecosystems or bioregions and upon sustainable principles. The literature on common pool resources and common property has focused on environmental degradation and resource depletion, and scholars of the commons have offered community-based conservation as a corrective.[32] Gary Snyder has called for the "recovery of the commons" as a means of regaining "personal, local, community, and peoples' direct involvement in sharing (in *being*) the web of the wild world."[33] Wes Jackson has even suggested that a "common covenant" could result if people allied themselves by virtue of a common watershed; for in sharing a stream or a river, they would soon come to "recognize their future and that of their descendants in every square foot of that watershed."[34] Such a "place-focused politics" would become viable if local communities were rebuilt upon ecological principles, rather than upon political or economic centralization. Citing John Dewey's idea that the genesis of democracy resides in "the neighborly community," David Orr calls for a revitalized sense of citizenship "rooted in the understanding that activities that erode soils, waste resources, pollute, destroy biological diversity, and degrade the beauty and integrity of landscapes are forms of theft from the commonwealth as sure as is bank robbery."[35]

The idea of sustainability returns to the notion of the region as the ground of both reason and democracy. Regional culture provides not only a diversity of practices for its citizens to experience but also local perspectives to shape their personal identities. These experiences engender a collective identity and ecology of public symbols that help a community to define place-centered ethical and aesthetic norms. Once internalized, these norms provide individuals with the coherence that fosters more immediate and spontaneous forms of interaction. These "communities of place" would be complex and human-scaled—ones that forge connections between people, foster a sense of well-being, and ensure resilience in crises.[36] Urban planners, architects, designers, and preservationists have begun to recognize the connection between ecological principles, such as conservation, biodiversity, and restoration, and social scientific principles, such as human scale, social equity, and human development. Adherents of the "New Urbanism" design movement and other holistic planners and designers who adopt sustainable principles, are rediscovering the vision of "the regional city" as the basis of good and equitable planning and design. While much of the thinking about sustainable local communities focuses on transformations of the countryside and of suburban development, some have argued for the prospect of creating such community in the city.[37] However, potential solutions are often blurred by the cultural debate about urbanism that contrasts the anonymity and disorder of the modern city with the moral order of self-governing agrarian communities. Robert Bellah and Christopher Adams view the challenge as that of providing cities with "an appropriate moral framework, as small towns once had, while retaining urban opportunities," conceding that a collective learning process will be necessary to understand "how a city can be a community."[38] Others respond to this challenge by proposing an "ecological populism" that fuses the virtues of rural community with the benefits of urban culture. A "rurban" culture, according to Tim Luke, would redefine "the good life" as one based upon "more demanding moral codes of hard work, frugality, ecological responsibility, humility, and skill perfection," rather than on possessive individualism and the consumption ethic.[39] The new mode of life, merging "the commerce, art, society, letters" that define city life with "rural crafts, culture, community, customs," could potentially diminish urban anonymity and rural isolation. Luke views "rurban" institutions as a stimulus to decentralized governance and a way to foster community based upon mutual aid, cooperative forms of association, and an ethos of craftsmanship "by situating people in nature and by reintroducing nature's needs to society."[40]

A move toward stimulating urban ecological consciousness has been underway at the Cathedral of St. John the Divine, the world's largest Gothic cathedral, on Manhattan's Upper West Side at the edge of Harlem, with a vision of creating "an oasis and a dynamic urban village that contributes to the neighborhood." This twenty-first-century version of a medieval cathedral has developed into a metropolitan town common, providing a public forum for diverse political and religious views and a center for intellectual dialogue.[41] Often called the "Green Cathedral," St. John the Divine, under the direction of James Parks Morton, who served as dean for twenty-five years, from 1972 (just after the first Earth Day Celebration in Manhattan's Union Square on April 22, 1970) to 1997, organized a consortium of diverse environmental programs, ranging from an ecological think tank and conferences that bring together environmentalists, theologians, and scientists to envision a sustainable future, to an annual St. Francis Day celebration that includes music, dance, the Blessing of the Animals, and daylong workshops on sacred ecology and Franciscan spirituality. Beyond these intellectual and ceremonial ventures in "green spirituality," under Morton's leadership the Cathedral staff engaged its congregation and neighbors in grassroots activities, such as efforts to restore urban wetlands, the operation of the Upper West Side Recycling Center, the first recycling center on the West Side of Manhattan, and the Cathedral Stoneworks Project, a stone masonry apprenticeship program that trained neighborhood youth in traditional stonecutting and carving, who then worked under the supervision of European masters to complete the building of this unfinished cathedral.[42] Although the apprenticeship program, begun in the 1980s, did not survive the economic downturn of the mid-1990s, many of the young cathedral masons remained in the trade.

A powerful argument for civic reconstruction is that a public realm reemerges through collective action on behalf of ecological responsibility and the quality of life in major cities. In Boston's Roxbury district, the Dudley Street Neighborhood Initiative (DSNI) has worked since the mid-1980s to organize local residents, mostly African Americans, Latin Americans, and Cape Verdeans, from islands off the coast of West Africa.[43] Neighbors focused initially on a "Don't Dump on Us" campaign to rid the area of the dumps that had sprung up in the vacant lots that made up a fifth of the Dudley Street area, and the wrecked cars that had been abandoned on the streets. After the illegal garbage was removed, DSNI began to plan for ways to purchase the empty land and to build affordable housing. About 150 residents initially worked in planning meetings to set goals and then launched projects such as an annual neighborhood cleanup, community gardens, a multicultural festival, a child care network, and youth activities. DSNI has grown to over 3,000 residents, and the nonprofit community-based planning organization with a thirty-four-seat board of directors has rehabilitated over 400 housing units. Launched by such groups as Habitat for Humanity, Community Builders of Boston, New York City Housing Partnership, San Francisco Bay Area's BRIDGE Housing Corporation, and Concerned Citizens of South Central Los Angeles, the community-based housing movement has helped promote civic engagement by involving residents of the nation's most disadvantaged communities in the planning and building of livable neighborhoods.[44] In May 2007, Los Angeles Mayor Antonio Villaraigosa spearheaded "GREEN LA—An Action Plan to Lead the Nation in Fighting Global Warming." The ambitious initiative to transform Los Angeles into the nation's greenest big city has a goal of reducing the city's greenhouse gas emissions 35 percent below 1990s levels by 2030, beyond the targets set in the Kyoto Protocol, with citywide campaigns on behalf of recycling, tree planting, and sustainable, or "green," buildings.

Critics of mass society have lamented the diminishment of the public realm, especially in densely populated cities where people engage daily in numerous anonymous interactions. City dwellers not only experience an "eclipse of distance" brought about by the foreshortening of time and space due to advances in transportation and the instantaneous nature of electronic communication, but also a "loss of insulating space," or an eclipse of social, aesthetic, and psychic distance from events because of the widespread dependence upon mass media.[45] Hannah Arendt argues for an increase in common space in mass societies that would provide room for people to freely voice their concerns in various public arenas but also would allow them to reestablish a sense of social and psychic distance:

> The public realm, as a common world, gathers us together and yet prevents our falling over each other, so to speak. What makes mass society so difficult to bear is not the number of people involved, or at least not primarily, but the fact that the world between them has lost its power to gather them together, to relate and to separate them.[46]

The public realm, or public sphere, is where individuals move beyond their self-interests, express themselves, and reach a set of common understandings about public problems, including quality-of-life concerns such as the environment, housing, work, and health. It is through the establishment of arenas for discussion and debate about these concerns—among ordinary citizens, engaged scientists, and public officials—that public trust, an essential form of social capital, is built. Only when people establish a sense of social trust will they ever engage in joint action on behalf of a common purpose such as urban sustainability. As the various institutions that address urban quality-of-life matters begin to take into account their constituents' concerns freely expressed in public forums, or arenas, their policies will come to connect more closely to the needs and interests of a common world.

NOTES

1. Martin J. Sklar, *The United States as a Developing Country: Studies in U.S. History in the Progressive Era and the 1920s* (New York: Cambridge University Press, 1992); see also Robert Wiebe, *The Search for Order, 1877–1920* (New York: Hill and Wang, 1967); Jackson Lears, *No Place of Grace: Antimodernism and the Transformation of American Culture, 1880–1920* (New York: Pantheon, 1981); Warren I. Susman, *Culture as History: The Transformation of American Society in the Twentieth Century* (New York: Pantheon, 1984); Thomas P. Hughes, *American Genesis: A Century of Invention and Technological Enthusiasm* (New York: Viking, 1989).

2. James R. Beniger, *The Control Revolution: Technological and Economic Origins of the Information Society* (Cambridge, MA: Harvard University Press, 1986).

3. Joseph Bensman and Robert Lilienfeld, *Craft and Consciousness: Occupational Technique and the Development of World Images*, 2nd ed. (Hawthorne, NY: Aldine De Gruyter, 1991).

4. Jürgen Habermas, *The Structural Transformation of the Public Sphere*, translated by Thomas Burger (Cambridge, MA: MIT Press, 1989).

5. Christopher Lasch, *The New Radicalism in America, 1889–1963* (New York: Random House, 1965); James T. Kloppenberg, *Uncertain Victory: Social Democracy and Progressivism in European and American Thought, 1870–1920* (New York: Oxford University Press, 1986); Alan Dawley, *Struggles for Justice: Social Responsibility and the Liberal State* (Cambridge, MA: Harvard University Press, 1991); Elizabeth S. Clemens, *The People's Lobby: Organizational Innovation and the Rise of Interest Group Politics in the United States, 1890–1925* (Chicago: University of Chicago Press, 1997); Kevin Mattson, *Creating a Democratic Public: The Struggle for Urban Participatory Democracy During the Progressive Era* (University Park: Pennsylvania State University Press, 1998); Daniel T. Rodgers, *Atlantic Crossings: Social Politics in a Progressive Age* (Cambridge: Harvard University Press, 1998); Elizabeth Sanders, *Roots of Reform: Farmers, Workers, and the American State, 1877–1917* (Chicago: University of Chicago Press, 1999).

6. Anselm L. Strauss, *Continual Permutations of Action* (Hawthorne, NY: Aldine de Gruyter, 1993), 226.

7. Many of the case examples derive from a "symbolic interactionist" perspective, which holds that symbolic processes mediate human interaction in the context of situations. Within this framework, action is organized by "mutual interpretations of perspectives" held by persons in these situations. Symbolic interaction theory views the self as an actor and the object of action. An individual is capable of self-constitution,

and reconstitution after crisis, through processes of communication and interpreting meaning, that is, through conscious action. Group action is the articulation of individual lines of action on the basis of "mutuality of perspectives." Shared meanings emerge from previous interactions and define modes of action in immediate situations. See Herbert Blumer, *Symbolic Interactionism: Perspective and Method* (Englewood Cliffs, NJ: Prentice-Hall, 1969).

8. John P. Hewitt, *Dilemmas of the American Self* (Philadelphia: Temple University Press, 1989), 231–32.

9. Richard J. Bernstein, *Praxis and Action: Contemporary Philosophers of Human Activity* (Philadelphia: University of Pennsylvania Press, 1971); John J. McDermott, *The Culture of Experience* (New York: New York University Press, 1976); Eugene Rochberg-Halton, *Meaning and Modernity: Social Theory in the Pragmatic Attitude* (Chicago: University of Chicago Press, 1986); John Patrick Diggins, *The Promise of Pragmatism: Modernism and the Crisis of Knowledge and Authority* (Chicago: University of Chicago Press, 1994); James Livingston, *Pragmatism and the Political Economy of Cultural Revolution, 1850–1940* (Chapel Hill: University of North Carolina Press, 1994); Martin Jay, *Songs of Experience: Modern American and European Variations on a Universal Theme* (Berkeley: University of California Press, 2005); Joan Richardson, *A Natural History of Pragmatism: The Fact of Feeling from Jonathan Edwards to Gertrude Stein* (New York: Cambridge University Press, 2007).

10. Strauss, *Continual Permutations of Action*, 225.

11. Robert D. Putnam, "Bowling Alone: America's Declining Social Capital," *Journal of Democracy* 6 (1995): 67.

12. David Hakken, "Culture-Centered Computing: Social Policy and Development of New Information Technology in England and the United States," *Human Organization* 50 (1991): 406–23.

13. Hazel Ashton and David C. Thorns, "The Role of Information Communications Technology in Retrieving Local Community," *City and Community* 6 (2007): 211–29); see also Maria C. Papadakis, *Computer-Mediated Communities: A Bibliography on Information, Communication, and Computational Technologies and Communities of Place* (Arlington, VA: SRI International, May 2004).

14. Richard E. Sclove, *Democracy and Technology* (New York: Guilford Press, 1995), 211; Phil Brown, "Popular Epidemiology and Toxic Waste Contamination: Lay and Professional Ways of Knowing," *Journal of Health and Social Behavior* 33 (1992): 267–81.

15. Mancur Olson Jr., *The Logic of Collective Action: Public Goods and the Theory of Groups* (Cambridge, MA: Harvard University Press, 1968), 14.

16. Lily M. Hoffman, *The Politics of Knowledge: Activist Movements in Medicine and Planning* (Albany: State University of New York Press, 1989), 181–82.

17. Adolph Lowe, *Has Freedom a Future?* (New York: Praeger, 1987), 93.

18. Lowe, *Has Freedom a Future?*, 92.

19. Sclove, *Democracy and Technology*, 217–18.

20. Arlene Fink, Jacqueline Kosecoff, Mark Chassin, and Robert H. Brook, "Consensus Methods: Characteristics and Guidelines for Use," *American Journal of Public Health* 74 (1984): 982.

21. Manuel Pastor Jr., "Post-Riot Recovery Cannot Happen Overnight," *Los Angeles Times*, April 27, 1997, sec. D.

22. Clifford Geertz, "Local Knowledge: Fact and Law in Comparative Perspective," in *Local Knowledge* (New York: Basic Books, 1983), 167.

23. James C. Scott, *The Moral Economy of the Peasant: Rebellion and Subsistence in Southeast Asia* (New Haven, CT: Yale University Press, 1976), 6–7.

24. David Simpson, *The Academic Postmodern and the Rule of Literature* (Chicago: University of Chicago Press, 1995), 143–44, 158–59.

25. Raymond Williams, *The Country and the City* (New York: Oxford University Press, 1973), 291.

26. David Harvey, *The Condition of Postmodernity: An Enquiry into the Origins of Cultural Change* (Oxford: Blackwell, 1989).

27. World Commission on Environment and Development, *Our Common Future* (Oxford: Oxford University Press, 1987).

28. International Institute for Sustainable Development, *Bellagio Principles: Guidelines for the Practical Assessment of Progress Towards Sustainable Development* (Winnipeg, Manitoba, Canada: International Institute for Sustainable Development, 1997).

29. Lamont C. Hempel, *Sustainable Communities: From Vision to Action* (Claremont, CA: Claremont Graduate University, 1998).

30. Maureen Hart, *Guide to Sustainable Community Indicators*, 2nd ed. (North Andover, MA: Hart Environmental Data, 1999).

31. Ivan Illich, *Shadow Work* (Boston: M Boyars, 1981).

32. Arun Agrawal, "Sustainable Governance of Common-Pool Resources: Context, Methods, Politics," *Annual Review of Anthropology* 32 (2003): 243–62.

33. Gary Snyder, "The Place, the Region, and the Commons," in *The Practice of the Wild* (San Francisco: North Point Press, 1990), 36.

34. Wes Jackson, "Toward a Common Covenant," in *Altars of Unhewn Stone: Science and the Earth* (San Francisco: North Point Press, 1987), 155.

35. David W. Orr, *Earth in Mind: On Education, Environment and the Human Prospect* (Washington DC: Island Press, 1994), 168.

36. Peter Calthorpe and William Fulton, *The Regional City: Planning for the End of Sprawl* (Washington, DC: Island Press, 2001); Andres Duany, Elizabeth Plater-Zyberk, and Jeff Speck, *Suburban Nation: The Rise of Sprawl and the Decline of the American Dream* (New York: North Point Press, 2000); Michael Mendez, "Latino New Urbanism: Building on Cultural Preferences," *Opolis* 1 (2005): 33–48.

37. Jennifer Wolch, "Green Urban Worlds," *Annals of the Association of American Geographers* 97 (2007): 373–84.

38. Robert N. Bellah and Christopher Freeman Adams, "Strong Institutions, Good City," *The Christian Century* June 15–22, 1994, 606.

39. Tim Luke, "Community and Ecology," *Telos* 88 (1991): 78–79.

40. Tim Luke, "Searching for Alternatives: Postmodern Populism and Ecology," *Telos* 103 (1995): 108–9.

41. Douglas Martin, "An Era Ends as Innovative Dean Plans to Leave St. John the Divine," *New York Times*, February 27, 1996, national edition, sec. 1.

42. William Bryant Logan, ed., *The Green Cathedral* (New York: Cathedral of St. John the Divine, 1992), 2.

43. Peter Medoff and Holly Sklar, *Streets of Hope: The Fall and Rise of an Urban Neighborhood* (Boston: South End Press, 1994); Jay Walljasper, "When Activists Win: The Renaissance of Dudley Street," *The Nation* 264 (1997): 11–17.

44. Alexander von Hoffman, "Urban Affairs—Good News: From Boston to San Francisco the Community-Based Housing Movement Is Transforming Bad Neighborhoods," *Atlantic Monthly*, January 1997, 31–35; Neal Richman and Allan David Heskin, "The California Mutual Housing Association: Organizational Innovation for Resident-Controlled Affordable Housing," in *Affordable Housing and Urban Development in the United States*, edited by Willem Van Vliet (Thousand Oaks, CA: Sage, 1997), 210–28.

45. Daniel Bell, "The Adequacy of our Concepts," in *A Great Society*, edited by Bertram M. Gross (New York: Basic Books, 1968), 138–39.

46. Hannah Arendt, *The Human Condition* (Chicago: University of Chicago Press, 1958), 52–53.

Index

acquired immuno-deficiency syndrome (AIDS): activists for, 81–82; FDA and, 81–82

ADA. *See* Americans with Disabilities Act

adaptive learning: environmental, 17–18; external, 17; human survival and, 17; internal, 17

Addams, Jane, 99

advertising: industrialism and, 36

aerospace workers: postwar, 44

African Americans: art/music culture of, 97; city life of, 96–97; Civil War and, 98; cultural styles of, 96; equality struggle of, 98–100; family life of, 98; high blood pressure education for, 108–9; hypertension in, 101–2; low-income, health care for, 123–26; in Pacoima, 188–89; in Progressive Era, 96–98; reform efforts for, 97; in South Central Los Angeles, 100–101; in Southern United States, 99

agriculture: evolution and, 18; in Southern United States, 96

AIDS. *See* acquired immuno-deficiency syndrome

airplanes: development of, 33–34

alcohol problems: support programs for, 54

Alliance for Healthy Homes, 222–23

allied health, 72

All Quiet on the Western Front, 164

Altadena: fire in, 173–76

America 1880–1930: immigration in, 133–37

America 1920s: automobile suburbs in, 36–39; recession in, 41–43

America, Victorian: in World War I, 163–64

American cities, modern, xiv, 1–2

American civic culture, postwar, 12

American Dream, 215

American homes: electricity in, 35; in Pacoima, 220; promoting safety in, 220–26; radio in, 35; telephone in, 35

American labor, 39–43

American Medical Association, 67–68

American Midwest, 7

American Red Cross, 166–67, 171; in disaster times, 176; in earthquake, 178

Americans with Disabilities Act (ADA), 80–81

anthropology: ecological, 19; holism in, 18

Apollo Theatre, 97
architecture: after Chicago fire, 2–3
arenas: after crisis, 233–36; in
  nineteenth century, 233–34; research
  on, 235; technology and, 235–36
art: by African Americans, 97
Asia: global economy challenges from,
  43; Pacific immigrants from, health
  care, 147
assembly line, 35
Atlantic Monthly, 135–36
attachment theory: personal identity in,
  15; studies in, 14–17
automobile: development of, 33–34;
  increased use of, 37; industry,
  postwar, 42, 45; motorization and
  modernity, 34–36; suburbs, in 1920s
  America, 36–39; workers, layoffs to,
  60

Baker, Ella, 100
Baldwin Hills: fire in, 171–76
Beck Depression Scale, 173–74
behavior: disasters and, 169–70;
  environmental adaptive, 17–18;
  environment and, 169
Bell Foundry, 46
Bellagio Principles, 240
benefits: for community, xi; HMO,
  139–42; from Sears, 52; from unions,
  54
Berkeley: fire in, 182
Bethlehem Steel Corporation, 59–60
Bethnal Green, 13–14
bioregionalists, 240
Black National Anthem, 106
body image: in CAPD, 86
Bourne, Randolph, 135–36
Bradley, Tom, 101
Broadous-Humphrey Park project,
  204–5
bureaucracy: health, 68–69
bureaucratic control: technical control
  v., 69

Burgess, Ernest, 7
Burke, Kenneth, 21
Burnham, Daniel, 2–3

California: fire, of 1985, 171–72; fire,
  of 1993, 162, 172–73; HMO benefits
  for, 139–42; immigrants, health care
  barriers for, 138–39; job placement
  in, 46–47
California State Department of Mental
  Health, 57
CAPD. *See* continuous ambulatory
  peritoneal dialysis
CASE. *See* Children are Saving the
  Environment
Cathedral of St. John the Divine, 242
CDC. *See* Centers for Disease Control
  and Prevention
Center for Independent Living (CIL),
  80
Centers for Disease Control and
  Prevention (CDC), 221
Central Americans: health/health care
  of, 143–47
CETA. *See* Comprehensive Employee
  Training Act
Chandler, Harry, 39
Chavez, Cesar, 42
Chicago: architecture after fire, 2–3;
  early mapping of, 7; neighborhood
  life in, 8–9; school sociologists, 8; as
  social laboratory, 7
Chicago's Great Fire of 1871: damage
  from, 2; rebuilding after, 3
children: in community service, 211–17;
  handicapped, self-help for, 79–80; of
  immigrants, 215–16; lead exposure
  in, 221–23; mentoring experience
  for, 215; in science activities,
  211–17; underprivileged, community
  opportunities for, 208–17
Children are Saving the Environment
  (CASE), 204
Chinese immigrants, 149

chronic illness: coping with, 78; family
life and, 77–78; hospital care for, 77;
psychological attributes for, 78–79;
stigma and, 65–66
chronic renal failure, 83
Chrysler Corporation, 43
Citizens' Industrial Association, 40
CIL. *See* Center for Independent Living
CIO. *See* Congress of Industrial
Organizations
city: civil rights organizations in, 97;
division of labor structured, 10;
economical expanse of, 3; economic
transformations, 19–20; extended,
1–2; infrastructure systems of, 3–4;
modern American, 1–2; networked,
2–5; nineteenth-century New York,
4–5; postwar, 162–63; vertical, 1–2;
waste removal in, 2; workforces, 20.
See also specific city, e.g., Los
Angeles
city development: ecological crises
from, 5; feeling loss from, 15–16;
technological advances in, 5
city life: adjustment to, 10; of African
Americans, 96–97; marriage and,
12–13; personal relationships in,
12–13; psychological attributes of,
16–17; qualitative/quantitative
approaches to, 12; regional
associations impact on, 11–12; social
roles in, 10; after World War II, 10–11
civic community: characteristics of,
22–23; traditional, 239
civic engagement, 240
civic professionalism, 4
civic solitude, 4
civil rights organizations: beginning of,
98–99; in cities, 97; in northern
United States, 99–100
Civil War, 4; African Americans and,
98; hospitals after, 66–67
class: urban space and, 4–5; working,
13. *See also* middle class

Collaborative Problem Solving (CPS),
224
College Institute, 212–17
common resources, 237
communitas, 21
community: benefits for, xi; change,
systems integration and, 192–94;
civic, 22–23, 239; components of,
14–15; crisis, disasters as, 170–71,
176–80; engagement survey, 198;
folk, 9; gardens, 196–200; low-
income, health care in, 95; in
neighborhood, 6; "New Negro," 37;
opportunities, for underprivileged
children, 208–17; organizations
within, xi–xv; recovery, after
disaster, 181–83; redevelopment of,
206–11; scale crisis, 161–62;
support, dilemma of, 59–61; virtual,
235–36
community building: after disasters,
187; involving residents, 194–96;
models for, 226–28; strategies for,
238–39
community health educators:
hypertension education by, 110–11
Community Redevelopment Agency
(CRA), 206–7
community service: children in, 211–17
commuter zone, 7–8
Comprehensive Employee Training Act
(CETA), 103–4
Compton High School Chorus, 106
Congress of Industrial Organizations
(CIO), 41
continuous ambulatory peritoneal
dialysis (CAPD): body image issues
in, 86; characteristics of, 83–84; self-
care in, 85–86; sexuality issues in,
86; support in, 85–86
cooperatives, 22
coping: in chronic illness, 78; examples
of, 112–17; models of, 117; with
strangers, 10; stress management,

117; style, 16; traumatic stress
  studies and, 17
cortisone: for lupus, 87
cosmopolitan culture, 12
CPS. *See* Collaborative Problem
  Solving
CRA. *See* Community Redevelopment
  Agency
Craiglockhart War Hospital, 167
crisis: in American life, xi; arenas after,
  233–36; community, disasters as,
  170–71, 176–80; community scale,
  161–62; Los Angeles response to,
  xii, xiv; response, in schools, 180;
  tools for, xii
cultures of solidarity, xii

Danish model, 238
Darwinism, 99, 134
Department of Housing and Urban
  Development, 238
depression: in displaced workers,
  60–61; Great, 41; after South Gate,
  50; with systemic lupus
  erythematosus, 88
Dewey, John, 99, 234
dialysis unit, 84–85
disability rights movement, 79–82
disasters: behavior and, 169–70;
  community building after, 187; as
  community crises, 170–71, 176–80;
  community recovery after, 181–83;
  family life after, 171–72; health after,
  170–71; modern images of, 162–65;
  PTSD after, 174; Red Cross in, 176;
  resources after, 181–83; studies after,
  174–76. *See also* natural disasters
disciplinary professionalism, 4
disease-specific organizations, 80
displaced workers: community support
  for, 59–61; depression in, 60–61;
  family life of, 61; psychological
  aspects of, 60; stress of, 61
division of labor: city structured by, 10
Douglas, McDonnell, 44

drug problems: support programs for, 54
DSNI. *See* Dudley Street Neighborhood
  Initiative
Dudley Street Neighborhood Initiative
  (DSNI), 242–43
Dymally, Mervyn, 106–7

earthquake, Northridge: of 1994,
  176–80, 191
East Yorkers, 14
ecological crises: from city
  development, 5
economic globalization, 20
economy: expanse of, 3; global,
  postwar, 41–43; immigration and,
  132; transformations of, 19–20
Education for all Handicapped Act of
  1974, 80
electricity: in American homes, 35
Emancipation Proclamation, 98–99
Employment Development Department,
  57
end-stage renal disease (ESRD), 82–83
engine: development of, 33
environment: behavior and, 169;
  projects, of Pacoima Beautiful,
  204–11; World Commission for, 240
environmental adaptive learning, 17–18
Environmental Protection Agency
  (EPA), 224
EPA. *See* Environmental Protection
  Agency
ESRD. *See* end-stage renal disease
Europe: in World War I, 163–65
evolution: agriculture and, 18; global
  system and, 18; industry and, 18
extended city, 1–2

family life: chronic illness impact on,
  77–78; of displaced workers, 61;
  after disasters, 171–72; first-
  generation, 5–6; at Ford Motor
  Company, 41; HD, 84; hypertension
  and, 106–7; of Latino Americans,
  118–21; lost work, 51–54; of

Progressive Era African Americans, 98; after South Gate, 51

FDA. *See* Food and Drug Administration

Federal Emergency Management Agency (FEMA): aid by, 170–71; models of, 195

Federation for American Immigration Reform, 131

FEMA. *See* Federal Emergency Management Agency

fictive kinship, 124

field theory, 14

fires: in Altadena, 173–76; in Baldwin Hills, 171–76; in Berkeley, 182; California 1985, 171–72; California 1993, 162, 172–73; Chicago 1871, 2–3; destruction after, 173–76; Los Angeles 1985, 171–72; studies after, 174–76

Firestone Tire and Rubber Company, 46

first-generation immigrants in America, 5–6

floods, 189

folk community, 9

Food and Drug Administration (FDA): AIDS drugs and, 81–82; introduction of, 79

Ford Foundation, 238

Ford, Henry, 164; "peace ship," 164

Ford Motor Company, 34–35; families working for, 41; Model T, 35

Fordism, 35; American labor and, 39–43; labor relations and, 39–40; layoffs after, 45–47; postwar, 42

"forward psychiatry," 168

Freidson, Eliot, 76

Fried, Mark, 15

"fugitive truth," 239

Gallup Organization, 132

gardens: community, 196–200; in Pacoima, 196–98; in Pacoima Urban Village, 196–97

Geertz, Clifford, 239

General Motors: layoffs at, 47–48; relocation of, 49–50; retraining workers for, 50; at South Gate, 46–47; support at, 59

Geographic Information Systems (GIS), 220

GIS. *See* Geographic Information Systems

global economy: Asian challenges to, 43; control in, 18–19; postwar, 41–42; transformations in, 19–20

Gluckman, Max, 10

Great Depression, 41

Great War. *See* World War I

Greenwich Village, 37

handicapped children: self-help for, 79–80

Harlem Renaissance, 97

Harrington, Michael, 98–99

Hassam, Childe, 163

HD. *See* hemodialysis

health: allied, 72; bureaucracies, 68–69; center, in Pacoima, 225–26; after disasters, 170–71; of immigrants, 143–47

health care: for Asian Pacific immigrants, 147; barriers, to California immigrants, 138–39; for Central American immigrants, 143–47; early development of, 7; for immigrants, 138–42, 155–56; for low-income African Americans, 123–26; in low-income communities, 95; in South Central Los Angeles, 123–26. *See also* hospitals; self-care

health insurance organization (HMO): for California residents, 139–42; for immigrants, 139

hemodialysis (HD), 83–84; family life and, 84

high blood pressure: education, for African Americans, 108–9;

foundation for, 106; treatment of, 108–9. *See also* hypertension

Highland Park plant, of Ford Motor Company, 34

HMO. *See* health insurance organization

Holistic Disaster Recovery, 183

Hollywood: in 1920s, 39

hospitals: bureaucracy in, 68–69; chronic illness in, 77; after Civil War, 66–67; Craiglockhart War, 167; depersonalized care in, 74; in Gilded Age, 68; hypertension education in, 105–7; ideology of, 69–74; interactions in, 69–74; Latino Americans in, 119–23; modern, 65; patient needs in, 71; personnel in, 68–69, 75; in Progressive Era, 67–68; social interests of, 74–75; in therapeutic revolution, 66–69; treatment styles in, 72–73

Hospital Social Services, 111

Huntington, Henry E., 39

Huntington's Red Cars, 38

hypertension: in African Americans, 101–2; education, in hospitals, 105–7; education, leaders in, 109–10; education, workers in, 110–11; family life and, 106–7; support for, 103–4; treatment compliance for, 108–11; treatment of, 102–3

Hypertension Control Project, 103–4; counseling program in, 108; leaders of, 106–7

Hypertension Workshop, 105–7

identity: in attachment theory, 15; place and, 10; spatial, 15

Ignatieff, Michael, 9

Il Mezzogiorno, 148

ILGWU. *See* International Ladies' Garment Workers' Union

illness careers, 74–79; physicians and, 76

illness, chronic: coping with, 78; family life and, 77–78; hospital care for, 77;

psychological attributes for, 78–79; stigma and, 65–66

illness, somatic, 70

immigrant(s): Asian Pacific, 147; California, health care barriers for, 138–39; Central American, 143–47; children of, 215–16; Chinese, 149; concerns for, 154–56; economy/jobs of, 132; food of, 149; ghetto, 5–6; health care for, 138–42, 143–47, 155–56; health of, 143–47; HMOs and, 139; Japanese, 149; kinship of, 150–54; MAAs for, 149–50; racism toward, 134–35; social formations of, 147–50; stress of, 129; Tzintzuntzan, 153–54; in urban America 1880–1930, 133–37

Immigration Act of 1917, 136

Immigration and Naturalization Service, 131–32

Immigration Reform and Control Act (IRCA): development of, 131; legislations of, 137–38

Impact of Event Scale, 174

Industrial Revolution: advertising and, 36; first, 18; second, 33

Industrial Workers of the World (IWW), 40

information highway, 2

International Ladies' Garment Workers' Union (ILGWU), 40

IRCA. *See* Immigration Reform and Control Act

Italy: civic traditions in, 22–23; Renaissance, 4

IWW. *See* Industrial Workers of the World

Jackson, Jesse, 106

Jackson, Kenneth T., 37

Japanese immigrants, 149

job: early middle class, 6–7; loss, organized support for, 54–59; placement, in California, 46–47

Johnson-Reed Act of 1924, 136

King, Martin Luther, 99–100
kinship: fictive, 124; of immigrants, 150–54

labor relations: Fordism impact on, 39–40
LAEP. *See* Los Angeles Educational Partnership
land fills, 189–90
landscape: war, media and, 164–65; war, unfamiliarity in, 168–69
Latino Americans: in hospitals, 119–23; in Los Angeles, 100–1, 118–21; neighborhoods of, 154; school districts and, 118–19; social support for, 119–20
LAUF. *See* Los Angeles Urban Funders
layoffs: to automobile plant workers, 60; at General Motors, 47–48; hardships after, 57; at Sears, 53–54; at South Gate, 45–47; support after, 56. *See also* displaced workers
lay-oriented organizations, 234–36
lead: exposure in children, 221–23; safe work practices, 223
Lewin, Kurt, 168
life politics, 22
Lifton, Robert Jay, 21
living systems theory, 17–18
local culture, 12; internal control in, 19; positive feedback system in, 20–21
local power, 19
Long Beach Freeway, 46
Los Angeles: in 1920s, 38; crisis response of, xii, xiv; development of, xiv–xv; fire, in 1985, 171–72; Latino Americans in, 100–101, 118–21; migration to, 38–39; movie colony of, 37; as social laboratory, xii. *See also* South Central Los Angeles
Los Angeles Educational Partnership (LAEP), 190
Los Angeles Urban Funders (LAUF), 192–93
lost work families, 51–54

low-income community: of African Americans, 123–26; health care in, 95
Lupus Foundation of America, 88–89. *See also* systemic lupus erythematosus
Lusitania, 164–65
lynchings, 40
Lynwood High School, 106

MAA. *See* Mutual Aid Associations
management: FEMA, 170–71, 195; Frederick Taylor, 34; of stress, 112–17; training for, 34
Manchester School, 10–11
marriage: city life and, 12–13
Martínez, Rubén, 142
Mayer, Philip, 11
mazeway, 20
McKenzie, Roderick, 7
media: war landscape and, 164–65
Medicaid, 69
medical profession: assumptions about, 74; labels in, 76; personnel in, 75; social interests of, 71; transformations in, 67–68
medical science: advancements in, 68
medical socialization, 71–72
medical technology: labels and, 76
mentoring experience: for children, 215
Merton, Robert, 12
metropolitan life: history of, 1; nervousness in, 2
Mexico City, 9
middle class: early jobs of, 6–7; new, 3; postwar London, 13; steel mill workers, 60; suburban, 36–38
Mielke, Howard, 221
modernity: motorization and, 34–36
moral arbiter: physician as, 76–77
motorization: modernity and, 34–36
municipal services, 37
municipal water systems, 2
music: by African Americans, 97
Mutual Aid Associations (MAA): for immigrants, 149–50
mutual aid organizations, 22

NAACP. *See* National Association for the Advancement of Colored People

NAM. *See* National Association of Manufacturers

NAMI. *See* National Alliance for the Mentally Ill

National Alliance for the Mentally Ill (NAMI), 81

National Association for the Advancement of Colored People (NAACP), 97

National Association of Manufacturers (NAM), 40

National Civic Federation, 40

National Counsel of Independent Living Centers (NCILC), 80–81

National Institutes of Health (NIH), 236

National Labor Relations Board, 41

natural disasters: as community-scale crisis, 161–62; earthquake, 1994, 176–80, 191; floods, 189; survivors of, 162. *See also* fires

nature: man and, 241–42

NCILC. *See* National Counsel of Independent Living Centers

neighborhood: Chicago, 8–9; community in, 6; Latino, 154; Pacoima, 190–92; strategies for, 238–39

networked city: types of, 2–5

"New Negro" communities, 37

"new populism," 82

"New Urbanism," 241

"New Women," 37

New York: nineteenth-century, 4–5

NIH. *See* National Institutes of Health

northern United States: civil rights in, 99–100; Progressive Era in, 99

Northridge earthquake of 1994, 176–80, 191

Occupational Safety and Health Administration (OSHA), 79

Oklahoma City plant, of General Motors, 49

OSHA. *See* Occupational Safety and Health Administration

Pacoima: African Americans in, 188–89; community building, involving residents, 194–96; establishment of, 188; gardens in, 196–98; health center in, 225–26; homes in, 220; neighborhoods of, 190–92; promoting safety in, 220–26; schools programs in, 200–204

Pacoima Beautiful: building models of, 226–28; environmental projects of, 204–11; garden projects of, 196–98; pollution monitoring projects by, 217–20; school projects of, 200–204

Pacoima Beautiful Youth Environmentalists (PB YES), 208–11

Pacoima Model, 192–94

Pacoima Partners, 206

Pacoima Urban Village: foundation of, 191–92; garden projects in, 196–97

Park, Robert, 7

Parks, Rosa, 99

patients: demands of, 75–76; hospitalized, 65; needs of, 71; physician's interactions with, 73–74, 75; rules of, 70; stigmatized, 66

PB YES. *See* Pacoima Beautiful Youth Environmentalists

physicians: demands on, 73; in general hospitals, 68; illness career and, 76; in modern hospitals, 65; as moral arbiters, 76–77; patient interactions with, 73–74, 75; roles of, 72–73; rules of, 70; self-regulation of, 74; sick role and, 71

planned domestic colonization, 237

policemen: joining unions, 41

politics, life, 22

pollution: monitoring of, 217–20

population: 1870 to 1920 increase in, 5–6

posttraumatic stress disorder (PTSD): after disasters, 174; symptoms of, 16

postwar: aerospace workers, 44; American civic culture, 12; American labor, 42; arms race, 43–44; automobile industry, 42, 45; city, 162–63; Fordism, 42; global economy, 41–42; middle class London, 13; recession, 45–46; Sears distribution, 45–46; unions, 41–42; West Coast production, 44

Progressive Era: African Americans in, 96–98; family life in, 98; hospitals in, 67–68; in Northern United States, 99

Project GRAD, 211; Project GRAD LA, 211–13

Promotores, 222–25

"protean self," 21

Proteus, 21

psychiatry: new, 168

psychological attributes: in chronic illness, 78–79; of city life, 16–17; of displaced workers, 60

PTSD. *See* posttraumatic stress disorder

public realm, 243–44

Putnam, Robert, 22

Pynoos, Robert, 178

race: postwar arms, 43–44; riots, 40; urban space and, 4–5

racism: toward immigrants, 134–35

radio: in American homes, 35

recession: in 1920s, 41–43; postwar, 45–46

Red Cross. *See* American Red Cross

Redfield, Robert, 9

renal disease, 82–83

research: on arenas, 235; on attachment theory, 14–17; on disasters, 174–76; history of, xii–xiii; Rockefeller Institute for, 67–68; Schomburg

Center for, 97; on self-help, 91; in social phenomenology, 14–17; on traumatic stress, 14, 17

resettlement: stress with, 129

resources: common, 237; after disasters, 181–83

Rieff, Philip, 69

Riordan, Richard, 206

ritualization: scientific views of, 21

Rivers, W. H. R., 167–68

Rockefeller Foundation, 238

Rockefeller Institute for Medical Research, 67–68

Rockefeller, John D., 67–68

Romains, Jules, 8

Roosevelt, Theodore, 135, 164

Root, John, 2–3

rural-urban transition, 11

Safety: in homes, 220–26; in workplace, 79

Salmon, T. W., 168

Salvadoran immigrants: health/health care of, 143–47

San Fernando Valley, 188–89

Sante Fe: artist colonies of, 37

Schomburg Center for Research in Black Culture, 97

schools: Chicago sociologists for, 8; Compton High School Chorus, 106; crisis-response system in, 180; Latino Americans in, 118–19; Lynwood High School, 106; Manchester School, 10–11; during Northridge earthquake, 178–80; Pacoima programs for, 200–204; sustainable, 200–204

Schorske, Carl, xiii

science: activities, children involved in, 211–17; medical advancements in, 68

scientific management, 34

SCLC. *See* Southern Christian Leadership Movement

Scott, James, 239
Sears: benefits from, 52; closing of, 51–54; layoffs at, 53–54; life after, 53; postwar distribution for, 45–46; warehouse workers for, 53
self-care: in CAPD, 85–86; within self-help movement, 79, 85–86; support groups and, 91; in systemic lupus erythematosus, 90–91; in women's movement, 79
self-concept development, 15
self-dialysis, 85
self-help movement, 79–82; cases within, 82–91; disease-specific organizations and, 79–80; NAMI, 81; national coalitions within, 80–81; self-care within, 79, 85–86; studies about, 91; systemic lupus erythematosus and, 90; women's movement and, 79
sexuality: in CAPD, 86
"sick role," 70–71
Simmel, Georg, 6, 9, 25–26
"Sisters in Black," 106
SNCC. *See* Student Nonviolent Coordinating Committee
social dramas, 21
social-life world: components of, 14–15
social margin, 76–77
social model programs, 82
social movements: of late twentieth century, 82; self-help/disability rights as, 79–82; women's, 79
social phenomenology: studies in, 14–17
social workers: hypertension education by, 110–11
Societa Calabria, 148
"society of organizations," 5
somatic illness, 70
South Africa, 11
South Central Los Angeles, 100–101; health care in, 123–26; transformations in, 118–23

Southern Christian Leadership Movement, 99, 100
southern United States: African Americans in, 99; agriculture in, 96
South Gate: counseling workers after, 49–50; depression after, 50; family life after, 51; General Motors at, 46–47; layoffs at, 45–47; move to, 46; shutdown at, 46–51; unions after, 48
Soviet Union: postwar arms race with, 43–44
steel mill workers: at Bethlehem Steel Corporation of, 59–60; United Steel Workers, 41–42
St. Francis Day, 242
stigma: characteristics of, 65–66; chronic illness and, 65–66; of patients, 66
strangers: coping with, 10; theories about, 6
stress: of displaced workers, 61; with immigration/resettlement, 129; management of, 112–17; PTSD, 16, 174; traumatic studies of, 14, 17
Student Nonviolent Coordinating Committee (SNCC), 99
suburbs: automobile, in twenties America, 36–39; development of, 36–37; middle-class in, 36–38
Sullivan, Louis, 2–3
support programs: for alcoholics, 54; for CAPD, 85–86; community, 59–61; for displaced workers, 59–61; for drug problems, 54; at General Motors, 59; for hypertension, 103–4; for job loss, 54–59; for Latino Americans, 119–20; after layoff, 56; for lupus, 89; for self-care, 91; in unions, 58
survival, human: adaptive learning and, 17
sustainable development, 19, 240–41, 244
sustainable schools, 200–204
"symbolic interactionist," 244n7

systemic lupus erythematosus:
characteristics of, 86; cortisone for, 87;
depression with, 88; diagnosis of,
86–87; foundation for, 88–89;
prognosis of, 87–88; self-care in,
90–91; self-help organization
participation and, 90; support for, 89;
symptoms of, 87
systems integration: community change
and, 192–94

Targeted Neighborhood Initiative (TNI),
206–8
Taylor, Frederick, 34
technical control: bureaucratic control v.,
69
technology: arenas and, 235–36; in city
development, 5; medical, 76
telephone: in American homes, 35
Tepoztlan, 9
theme interference, 57–58
therapeutic revolution: hospitals in, 66–69
three-pronged investment strategy, 34
Titanic, 165
TNI. *See* Targeted Neighborhood
Initiative
transnationalism, 129–32; impact of,
154–56
traumas: PTSD, 16, 174; of war,
165–68
traumatic stress studies: coping and, 17;
importance of, 14
"treatment family," 85
tree planting, 209–10
tribes: values of, 11
"two-way trade," xiv
Tzintzuntzan immigrants, 153–54

UAW. *See* United Auto Workers
Underserved Geographic Areas Project,
190
unemployment unions, 58
unions: benefit packages from, 54;
development of, 41; leaders of, 54–55;
mass-production, 42; organized

support in, 58; policemen in, 41;
postwar, 41–42; after South Gate, 48;
theme interference in, 57–58;
unemployment, 58; during World War
II, 41
United Auto Workers (UAW), 42
United Farm Workers, 42
United High Blood Pressure
Foundation, 106
United Mine Workers, 40
United States: northern, 99–100;
southern, 96, 99
United Steel Workers, 41
urban space: racial/class boundaries
and, 4–5
urban villages, 5–6
U.S. Bureau of Labor Statistics, 41
U.S. Gypsum, 46

Valley Community Clinic, 179–80
Van Nuys Boulevard, 205, 208–9
Van Nuys facility, of General Motors,
49
Vaughn Family Center, 190–91
Vernon Avenue–Central Avenue
corridor, 39
vertical city, 1–2
Victorian: America in World War I,
163–64; domestic arrangement, 38;
moralist, 7
virtual community, 235–36
voluntary associations, 22

Wagner Act of 1933, 41
war: Civil, 4, 66–67, 98; landscapes,
media and, 164–65; landscapes,
unfamiliarity in, 168–69; traumas
of, 165–68; World I, 135, 154,
162–65; World II, 10–11, 41
waste removal: in city, 2
water systems: municipal, 2
Wellman, Barry, 14
West Coast production: postwar, 44
West End, Boston, 15
wildcat strikes, 42–43

Wirth, Louis, 8
Wiseman, Jacqueline, 76–77
Wolf, Eric, xii
women's movement: self-care in, 79
Women's Overseas Service League, 167
workers. *See specific type*, e.g.,
    displaced workers
Workforce Development Initiative, 194
working class: postwar London, 13
Works Progress Administration (WPA),
    100
World Commission on Environment and
    Development, 240
World War I, 135; as divine
    retribution, 154; Europe in, 163–65;

modern disaster images and,
    162–65; Victorian America in,
    163–64
World War II, 10; city life after,
    10–11; unions during, 41
WPA. *See* Works Progress
    Administration
writers: African American, 97

Xhosa peasants, 11; "Red" Xhosa,
    11

Yucatan peninsula, 9

zone of transition, 7–8

About the Author

Carl Maida is professor of public health at UCLA, where he teaches medica[l] anthropology and scientific research ethics in the Graduate Program in Ora[l] Biology. His research focuses on how community-scale crises, including nat[-]ural hazards, community toxics, and disease epidemics, impact urban popu[-]lations. At UCLA Geffen School of Medicine, he conducts studies of the im[-]pact of natural disaster on children, adolescents, and their families as [a] member of the National Center for Child Traumatic Stress, and as a membe[r] of the UCLA AIDS Institute, among persons living with HIV. At UCLA In[-]stitute of the Environment, he conducts action research in urban sustainabil[-]ity. He has conducted community-based research funded by the National Sci[-]ence Foundation, National Institute of Mental Health, Robert Wood Johnso[n] Foundation, Ford Foundation, Howard Hughes Medical Institute, and Th[e] California Endowment, and currently consults to the Terrorism and Disaste[r] Center at the University of Oklahoma Health Sciences Center and to th[e] Miller Children's Abuse and Violence Intervention Center at Miller Chil[-]dren's Hospital in Long Beach, California, which are both organizationa[l] members of the National Child Traumatic Stress Network. He is a partner i[n] a community-based participatory research project, Community Action for [a] Renewed Environment (CARE) Program–Reducing Toxic Risks, funded b[y] the U.S. Environmental Protection Agency. His recent book, *Sustainabilit[y] and Communities of Place* (2007) explores sustainable development as a lo[-]cal practice, worldwide. He is a member of the UCLA Campus Sustainabilit[y] Committee, and chairs its Academic Subcommittee. He is a Fellow of th[e] American Association for the Advancement of Science, the American An[-]thropological Association, and the Society for Applied Anthropology.